Iraqi Migrants in Syria

Contemporary Issues in the Middle East
Mehran Kamrava and Carol Fadda-Conrey, *Series Advisers*

Select titles in Contemporary Issues in the Middle East

Colonial Jerusalem: The Spatial Construction of Identity and Difference in a City of Myth, 1948–2012
  Thomas Philip Abowd

Improbable Women: Five Who Explored the Middle East
  William Woods Cotterman

In the Wake of the Poetic: Palestinian Artists after Darwish
  Najat Rahman

Law of Desire: Temporary Marriage in Shi'i Iran, revised edition
  Shahla Haeri

The Mizrahi Era of Rebellion: Israel's Forgotten Civil Rights Struggle, 1948–1966
  Bryan K. Roby

Preserving the Old City of Damascus
  Faedah M. Totah

Reading Arabia: British Orientalism in the Age of Mass Publication, 1880–1930
  Andrew C. Long

Shahaama: Five Egyptian Men Tell Their Stories
  Nayra Atiya

Iraqi Migrants in Syria

The Crisis before the Storm

SOPHIA HOFFMANN

Syracuse University Press

First Edition 2016

16 17 18 19 20 21 6 5 4 3 2 1

∞ The paper used in this publication meets the minimum requirements of the American National Standard for Information Sciences—Permanence of Paper for Printed Library Materials, ANSI Z39.48-1992.

For a listing of books published and distributed by Syracuse University Press, visit www.SyracuseUniversityPress.syr.edu.

ISBN: 978-0-8156-3485-0 (hardcover)
978-0-8156-3471-3 (paperback)
978-0-8156-5383-7 (e-book)

Library of Congress Cataloging-in-Publication Data

Names: Hoffmann, Sophia, author
Title: Iraqi migrants in Syria : the crisis before the storm / Sophia Hoffmann.
Other titles: Contemporary issues in the Middle East.
Description: Syracuse, New York ; Syracuse University Press, 2016. | Series: Contemporary issues in the Middle East | Includes bibliographical references and index.
Identifiers: LCCN 2016028819 (print) | LCCN 2016040067 (ebook) | ISBN 9780815634850 (hardcover : alk. paper) | ISBN 9780815634713 (pbk. : alk. paper) | ISBN 9780815653837 (e-book)
Subjects: LCSH: Iraqis—Syria. | Iraq—Emigration and immigration. | Syria—Emigration and immigration. | Refugees—Iraq. | Refugees—Syria. | Iraq War, 2003–2011—Refugees.
Classification: LCC DS70.8.S95 H64 2016 (print) | LCC DS70.8.S95 (ebook) | DDC 305.892/756705691—dc23
LC record available at https://lccn.loc.gov/2016028819

Manufactured in the United States of America

To Anna-Maria Wiessner

** December 30, 1925, Hoffnungstal, Romania*

† March 28, 2015, Hude, Germany

Contents

Acknowledgments

This book emerged via the generosity of many people and countless lucky coincidences. Those I wish to thank are many, I write about them here in no particular order. First, the woman to whom I dedicate this book: my maternal grandmother Anna-Maria Wiessner, nee Halt. I remember her incredible warmth and the steadiness of her love that enveloped me my entire life. Recalling her clear moral compass, her belief in honesty, her experience of tedious and hard work, of loss and survival, as well as her silly humor and her giggles helped me persist during fieldwork when paranoia and exhaustion threatened to overwhelm me. Anna-Maria's retelling of her experiences of displacement also taught me that *Heimat* is something changeable, and that, as dear and wonderful as possessions and places may be for our roots, losing them means nothing compared to human relationships, which are always the most important. Her stories made me puzzle about how and why political structures may intrude on individual lives, and thus provided the basis for my studies and this book.

Second, I remember the intelligence burning in the eyes of my PhD supervisor, Professor Laleh Khalili, when I first walked into her office, after finding her via an Internet search. This was one of the lucky coincidences. Laleh is a perfect blend of Snow White and Maleficent, and the most charismatic woman I know. Her exceptional responsiveness, intellectual and practical guidance, and astonishing belief in my potential helped me persevere ever since that first meeting. Role models are important. Thank you, Laleh, for taking on that mantle. My second supervisor, Professor Charles Tripp, provided important advice at crucial moments, and, like Laleh, answered to a seemingly never-ending stream of requests for reference letters. Thank you.

The Syrians and Iraqis who welcomed me into their homes in Damascus, who provided the core information on which this book builds, did so in the environment of a police state in which such actions could have had dire and unpleasant circumstances. Their generosity and courage humbles me, and I thank all of them greatly for being my most important teachers. Nearly all of them have now left Syria and are scattered around the globe. Their names are withheld or changed throughout the book, and I will preserve their anonymity here. According to good ethnographic practice and mindful of the particular risks of recording research results in Syria, I always revealed my identity as a researcher and the purpose of my work to all of my research participants and interview partners. At the beginning of interviews and observations, I obtained oral permission to use quotes and field notes as long as the identities of speakers would be anonymous or occasionally presented under pseudonyms.

The directors of the Iraqi Student Project took me on as a volunteer teacher and supported my research. Numerous employees of the UN refugee agency UNHCR and international NGOs agreed to talk to me—when others did not—and although I cannot name them here, I am grateful for their openness. I particularly thank Firas Majeed, of Native without a Nation, for all his help during my time in Syria, as well as Bisan al-Bunni and her family.

The research in Syria was funded by the Council for British Research in the Levant and the Central London Research Fund, and I thank Alex Bellem, then director of the CBRL's Syria project, for her support, in particular during a difficult moment on the Jordanian-Syrian border, which I will never forget.

Parts of chapters 1, 4, and 6 appeared previously as "International Humanitarian Agencies and Iraqi Migration in Preconflict Syria," *International Journal of Middle East Studies*, 48 (2016), and, in very different fashion, in "The National Body in Israel and Syria: Comparing Processes of Unity and Fragmentation," *Middle East Critique* 25 (2016). Parts of chapter 4 appeared previously as "The Humanitarian Regime of Sovereignty: INGOs and Iraqi Migration to Syria," *Refuge: Canada's Journal on Refugees*

28, no. 1 (2009). I kindly thank the editors and publishers of the journals for allowing the reproduction of these passages.

Many colleagues commented on parts of this book at different stages or invited me to participate in their events. For their help I thank in particular, and again in no special order, Geraldine Chatelard, Ali Ali, Tahir Zaman, Daniel Neep, Mohamed Kamel Dorai, Diane Duclos, Riccardo Bocco, Elian Weizman, Katherine Natanel, Nadje al-Ali, André Bank, Susanne Schmelter, Katharina Lenner, Erik Mohns, Janine Budich, Urs Fruehauf, Hanan Toukan, Benjamin White, Gianluca Parolin, and the fellow PhD students at the School of African and Oriental Studies, London, who commented on early versions of the project.

I thank Deanna McCay, a former editor at Syracuse University Press, for her initial interest in the manuscript, and I thank Suzanne Guiod, Syracuse's editor-in-chief, for her support and the care she took to see the manuscript through the editing and publishing process, as well as the rest of the supportive and enthusiastic team at Syracuse. Mary Petrusewicz was a meticulous and encouraging copy editor; thank you.

The Iraqi painter Salam Atta Sabri generously gave permission to use his beautiful artwork on the book sleeve, and the curators of Belgium's SMAK museum reacted quickly to my last-minute request for high-resolution photographs of the drawings.

I am eternally grateful to my parents, Reimer Hoffmann and Heidrun Wiessner-Hoffmann, my paternal grandmother, Heide Hoffmann, and my brother Lorenz Hoffmann for their unwavering support and love.

During the process of producing this book I married and had a child. For accompanying me on this journey, and for being willing to give and receive so much love, my deepest thanks go to Theo Murphy and Leander.

Iraqi Migrants in Syria

Introduction

Two displacement crises have hit Syria in the past decade. The first began in 2005, as thousands of Iraqis started crossing Syria's borders to flee the violence engulfing their country in the aftermath of the 2003 invasion by the United States and its allies. Since 2012, it is Syrians themselves who are departing their homes en masse, as conflict has overwhelmed Syria, which only shortly before had provided a safe haven to hundreds of thousands of Iraqis.

These two migrations overlapped in time and express important political and social continuities shaping Syria and its neighboring states. The most obvious of these continuities is the seemingly unstoppable growth of extreme violence against civilian populations and infrastructure. This violence is accompanied by other transformations to the social and political landscape that will continue to shape states and societies after any conflict has subsided. Today's violence is an "axis of social reordering," as Mark Duffield observed about the post–Cold War conflicts of the 1990s, and a "powerful mechanism for the globalisation of economic, political and scientific relations" in and around Syria.[1]

This book analyzes aspects of this "reordering" as they began to develop in the context of Iraqi migration to Syria. Based on ten months of field research, which I carried out while living in an Iraqi-dominated suburb of Damascus in 2010, and several previous long-term visits to Syria since 2005, the book documents some of the political, social, and spatial changes that the Iraqi refugee crisis brought to Syria shortly before the outbreak of revolutionary demonstrations and subsequent war. Even the use of the phrase "Iraqi refugee crisis" implies one such reordering: the identification of Iraqi immigration to Syria as a humanitarian emergency of universal concern, and the subsequent heavy involvement of foreign actors in its management. In hindsight, foreign actors' work on the Iraqi refugee crisis was a learning phase in which these actors became familiar with Syria and its neighbors and adapted their standard operating procedures and categories to function there. It proved a learning phase because, when the Iraqi crisis subsided and the Syrian crisis began, these procedures and categories could be rolled as a seemingly coherent response to the newly arriving displaced Syrians. The Iraqi refugee crisis served as the incubator for the massive, international aid sector that has since 2007 become entrenched in the Middle East.

Most visible among this sector are the numerous aid organizations. Before Iraqi migration was identified as a crisis, most of these organizations had never worked in the Middle East. Syria in particular, with its controlling government, suspicious of all foreign presence, was a new and difficult country for foreign-aid operations. In fact, before the Syrian government took the step to permit large-scale aid operations in Damascus from 2008 onward, the country had been closed off from international humanitarian discourse. The aid sector's expansion in Syria presented a watershed for the country and the region, exposing the Syrian government's interest to increasingly outsource the caring for poor populations to international providers. Aid organizations, which arrived with a mandate to care only for Iraqi refugees, soon extended programs to poor Syrians. Since then, owing to the escalation of violence, these organizations have become a key resource through which Syria's "war-affected" (an aid-jargon term) population is provided with the basic means of survival. In 2012, after strong lobbying, the Syrian Arab Red Crescent, a quasi-government organization through which all foreign aid to government-controlled areas must flow, allowed aid to be extended to internally displaced Syrians, though still under very close government control and not in all areas. Thus many of the humanitarian categories and categorizations that this book describes as being applied to *Iraqis* living in Syria are today being applied to *Syrians* living in Syria and in neighboring states. The Middle East is today witnessing an expansion of humanitarian governance carried out via a growing international aid sector, which this book documents during the moments of its beginning.

Humanitarian governance in the Middle East is expanding not only in geographical space but also in intensity of effect. The growing practice of marking the Iraqi migrant population in Syria as fundamentally different on the basis of their different nationality, which this book describes as an effect of the expanding aid sector, has, for example, today significantly escalated in Jordan's new encampment policies aimed at the Syrian refugee population. Whereas no camps were built for Iraqi refugees, poor Syrians in Jordan are increasingly forced to reside in either Zaatari or Azraq camp, opened in 2012 and 2014, respectively, and run jointly by aid organizations and Jordanian security forces. A tightening of visa and immigration laws and a growth of the government-led practice to insulate and differentiate refugees from the national population have accompanied the expansion of the international refugee aid sector in the Levant. This book covers, in richly observed detail, how and why the ideas, concepts, programs, and projects of international refugee aid are a reason for isolating refugees, a practice that stands in marked contrast to regional refugee politics of the past. Previously, refugees often rapidly integrated and/or were considered as symbols of political wrongs that needed to be corrected.

UNHCR has played a lead role in the international management of the Iraqi and Syrian displacement crises. During the course of my regular visits to Syria between 2005 and 2011, I witnessed UNHCR's rapid rise from a humble, small office in downtown Damascus with an annual budget of less than USD 2 million, to a formidable regional player wielding budgets of several billion dollars. Considering UNHCR's strongly proclaimed commitment to human rights and indeed democracy, the agency's success story in the Middle East continues to astound, especially the ease with which UNHCR managers have formed warm partnerships with oppressive authorities in Syria, and as of this writing with others in the region. UNHCR's beginnings in Syria proved to be only the groundwork for a widening and deepening of its programmatic footprint in the Levant, and of its relations to state authorities in Syria, Jordan, Lebanon, and Iraq. In Syria, UNHCR's close cooperation with authorities, which indeed provided a solid foundation to deliver aid to the Iraqi migrant population in the past, has at the time of this writing turned into something more sinister and tragic. UNHCR continues to comply with the Syrian government's wishes that no relief aid should reach civilian populations living in areas controlled by opposition groups. In mid-2016, UNHCR continues to deliver over 90 percent of its aid in government-held areas. Many of its multimillion dollar projects aimed at supporting civilian infrastructure in Syria are implemented in partnership with Syrian ministries and government agencies, through which much of the money is channeled. Whatever UNHCR's public defense of this practice and stand toward the Syrian government may be—and UNHCR has remained silent on this topic—it indicates a disturbing bias, which has led to a growing distrust and even open hostility toward the agency by other aid providers. The Syrian government's ability to control and manipulate aid providers has gained force since the early days of the Iraqi refugee emergency. At the same time, aid providers also cling to and implement in their programs their own political vision and interests, as well as those of donor governments that continue to pay for the multibillion-dollar aid effort.

Of these donor states, the United States is the biggest by far, providing more of UNHCR's budget than the next biggest five donors, which include the European Union and Japan, combined. This fact presents a further important continuity between the Iraqi and Syrian crises: although the overall amount of aid money pouring into the Levant has grown, the relative distribution of where it comes from has remained constant. In this book, I document and analyze the politics of two important donor states, the United States and Germany, toward the Iraqi crisis. Considering the situation five years later in 2016, the contradictory mix of domestic and international interests found to be guiding donor politics toward Iraqi displacement has remained the same with regard to the Syrian crisis.

One of the effects of Western donor states' lack of strategy—and indeed genuine political interest regarding violence and displacement in the Middle East—has been the surprising rise and fall of the Syrian government's international standing in the past several years. One of the things that most surprised me during field research was the comet-like rise of Bashar al-Asad, and his government, from 2008 onward, to the position of generous and genuine protectors of Iraqi refugees. A steady stream of praise from aid workers and diplomats at the time contributed to this. Although the Syrian government sharpened its crackdown of even the mildest form of public political dissent and rearrested a number of high-profile prodemocracy activists, gone were the recently prominent attacks by international human-rights watchdogs and the internationally voiced disappointment about Bashar's lack of reform, and gone was Syria's place on the axis of evil. Instead, humanitarians, diplomats, and journalists formed a steady chorus of applause to celebrate Syria's provision of "protection space" (another term from aid-sector jargon) to Iraqi refugees. Syrian ministers were invited to publicly collect acclaim for this "openness" at UN conferences and interviews, and Syria's foreign minister and the head of the Syrian Arab Red Crescent were invited to write articles for magazines such as *Forced Migration Review* and others.[2]

Since then, of course, the Syrian government's international reputation has taken another U-turn. Symbolic of this reversal is the crash-and-burn career of Syria's First Lady, Asma al-Asad, the wife of President Bashar al-Asad. In 2010, to great fanfare, Asma opened Syria's first conference on international development to a packed house in Damascus's most elegant hotel, The Four Seasons (where, incidentally, the international aid workers still left in Damascus in 2016 reside). Since the early 2000s Asma, with the help of numerous international consultants, had shaped an active role for herself as the reformer of Syria's pro-poor development programs, helping to boost Syria's international image. Whereas experienced insiders whispered about her organization's lack of focus and effect, the post-2007 newly arrived aid crowd eagerly imbibed Asma's charisma and fluent rhetoric, seemingly oblivious to the hollowness of its phrases, at a time when inequality, poverty, and oppression were reaching new heights in Syria. But Asma's star was ill-fated. Only one year later (and only weeks after a puff portrait in *Vogue* that exalted her apparent love of democracy), the international crowd turned its back on Asma, now decrying her as the cynical wife of a brutal dictator who was happy to conduct PR events while snipers attacked unarmed demonstrators.

The boom-and-bust cycle of the al-Asads' palatability to Western political tastes speaks to something that Bente Scheller recently termed "the wisdom of Syria's waiting game."[3] Western public diplomacy toward Syria is driven by endlessly changing, short-term considerations, which sometimes require shunning the Syrian state and sometimes require flattering it. Although in this book I document a highly instructive incident of the latter, my overall argument is that this international boom-and-bust cycle to Syria's standing in the West is a structural feature in itself, which maintains the precariousness of Syria's postmandate statehood and its overall international weakness. As of 2016 this weakness seems to be at an apex, as even the territorial integrity of the Syrian states is very much in question. Yet it may soon turn again, if the perception of Bashar al-Asad as a bulwark against "Islamic" terrorism gains traction and a compromise can be found in which the rebuilding of Syrian cities can happen in partnership with Western-sponsored aid agencies and contractors.

This introduction is naturally colored by the terrible violence that the Syrian government has unleashed on hundreds of thousands of unarmed civilians since late 2012. But at the time of researching and writing this book, it was, ironically, the *greater freedoms* that Syrian politics offered Iraqi refugees that led to the most interesting political insights and analyses. Compared with the increasingly draconian and brutal restrictions placed on refugees in the supposedly liberal states of Europe and North America, the Syrian government's laissez-faire attitude toward hundreds of thousands of Iraqis appeared contradictory. More important, for a student of the international relations of the Middle East and of Syria in particular, it raised questions about why a rigorous differentiation of its own national population was apparently not important for the maintenance of the Syrian state. The drawing of boundaries around territory and population, and the "inclusive exclusion" of strangers (introduced as a concept by Giorgio Agamben, and since then widely followed as well as critiqued), had after all been in the past decades understood to be a crucial hallmark of modern statehood.[4] Following Iraqi migrants around who were rebuilding their lives in Damascus eventually revealed what the Syrian government's liberal treatment of foreigners told about Syrian *statehood*, and why the "open door" to Iraqis could only be understood as exceptional or strange from a viewpoint that fundamentally misunderstood Syria's statehood and the state-society relations that underpinned it.

This book explains aspects of Syrian statehood at a time of domestic, regional, and international upheaval, which began in 2003 and continues unabated in 2016. Since at least 2007, when it was identified as a hub of Iraqi displacement, Syria has been at the epicenter of this upheaval. And although Syria's about-face from a safe haven for Iraqi refugees to a site of violent exodus is extreme, the continuities in its domestic and international relations are also remarkable, as this book demonstrates. What changed is the behavior of millions of Syrians, who decided, in an utterly stunning moment, to throw fear to the wind and risk all to change a situation that had become unbearably stifling and hopeless. Tragically, the government did not follow the signs of the time, but, literally, stuck to its guns: the elimination of open opposition at all costs, even if this opposition now included vast parts of the population.

Today, the continuity of the very basics of Syrian statehood—its territory, its population, and its government—are decidedly in question. What is certain, however, is that its future will be shaped by the politics of international humanitarian emergency aid and the donor states that fund it. These politics are already making unprecedented headway in Syria and its neighbor states. Awareness of the new partnerships, materials, communications, categories, and bureaucracies the aid sector is transporting is key to understand emerging state-society relations in the Middle East in this uncertain context. This book documents the beginnings of Syria's role as a center of humanitarian emergency, and the effects that this development had on the daily life of those caught mostly in the middle of it: Iraqi migrants and refugees. Their shifting place in the Syrian body politic, affecting bodies, minds, economies, opportunities, and locations, was the observable manifestation that state-society relations in Syria were understood and mobilized differently by domestic and international actors, and that this difference was having an effect on everyday politics. With the intensification of forced displacement in the Middle East and its growing international management, the developments discussed in this book continue to expand and deepen.

1

The Politics of Iraqi Migration to Syria

In early 2010, one short year before the start of a popular uprising that quickly deteriorated into a spectacularly cruel war, Syria provided a safe haven for hundreds of thousands of Iraqi migrants who had fled Iraq's violent chaos. Most of these had settled in Syria's capital city of Damascus, where signs of a vibrant Iraqi community abounded, especially in a handful of neighborhoods that had become "little Baghdads" or "little Fallujas." There, Iraqi bakeries sold thickly crusted Iraqi Samun bread, Iraqi restaurants offered bean stew with rice, travel agencies advertised daily trips to all major Iraqi cities, and the Iraqi dialect was heard everywhere. Around the well-known Shi'a shrine of Saida Zainab in southern Damascus, a market for the sect's funereal religious décor had sprung up, displaying goods imported from Iraq: blankets and wall hangings depicting the martyrs Ali and Hussein, little amulets, small decorative self-flailing devices, and religious books. In another southern suburb called Jaramana, a cosmopolitan mix of mostly middle-class urban Iraqis from all religions and backgrounds crowded the streets, and their presence had given rise to small Iraqi cultural societies and mutual-aid organizations. The wide diversity of Iraqi society, used as excuse for so much violence in Iraq, was on lively and harmonious display in Damascus.

While some Iraqi families had invested heavily in Syria, opening thriving businesses and clearly planning for the long term, others were more worried: "Fii Suria, ma kuu mustammara" (In Syria, there is no stability), was a phrase I often heard during field research and interviews, uttered by Iraqis for whom Syria's lack of legal clarity, lack of economic and educational opportunities, and lack of political and social freedom created a too-unstable environment for them to imagine a happy future in the country. How prescient this mistrust turned out to be. Ten short months later Syria began to implode as fear of government repression dissolved. By early 2012, Syria was producing its own flow of mass migration as hundreds of thousands of Syrians crossed borders to escape violent chaos, many thousands living in dismal camps or other temporary shelter in Lebanon and Jordan. "Seeking stability in Syria," as one report on Iraqi refugees was titled, was over.[1]

In this book, I make an argument about the kind of stability that Iraqis found in Syria. To do so, I tell two stories: one empirical, the other theoretical. The empirical story recounts the social and political changes that Iraqi migration brought to Syria and the international politics surrounding the Iraqi refugee crisis. Special attention is given to the expansion of international aid to Syria, which was an unprecedented development.

The theoretical story argues that international aid organizations introduced a different concept of "state-citizen relations" and a different concept of "statehood" to Syria. The roots of this development lie in the importance that liberal states give to stringently distinguishing between citizens and foreigners. To maintain their boundaries and sovereignty, liberal states require a constant differentiation between those who belong to the nation and those who do not. Refugee-aid organizations follow this concept of statehood. But in Syria, and the politics of the Bashar al-Asad government, marking foreigners as different was by far not as important. This explains why Iraqi migrants encountered much greater "freedoms" in Syria than those usually allocated to migrants in Western states. My aim is to interweave the empirical and the theoretical story into a comprehensive narrative so that the more abstract arguments become illuminated by numerous examples from fieldwork and interviews. Necessarily, this narrative contains several subthemes, but together they argue that the domestic and international politics surrounding Iraqi migration resulted in a transformation of statehood in Syria, if on a small scale.

I undertook seven months of intensive ethnographic research in 2009 and 2010 while living in the then Iraqi-dominated suburb Jaramana, in the south of Damascus. I had visited Syria regularly since 2005 for study and research. I conducted interviews with dozens of Iraqis, Syrians working with aid organizations and expat aid managers. My entire group of research participants consisted of around eighty persons. Two field sites were of particular importance. First, the operations of a small international NGO, based largely on volunteer work, that provided Iraqi students with educational projects. At this NGO, I worked as a volunteer teacher for several months, forming a close bond with several of the students and getting to know closely the NGO's directors, other volunteer teachers, and students' families. The second field site was also a small international NGO, which offered leisure and sports activities for Iraqis and Palestinians from Iraq. At this NGO I occasionally participated as a volunteer but mostly spent time observing how their operations grew via a growing interaction with large international institutions such as the United Nations Children's Emergency Fund (UNICEF) and the United Nations High Commissioner for Refugees (UNHCR). Frequent home visits to Iraqi acquaintances were a further important source of information. Adopting a "fly on the wall" approach allowed me to understand how domestic and international institutions influenced Iraqi migrant life and how Iraqis considered their options vis-à-vis these organizations and judged their behavior. I interviewed Iraqi migrants of all ages and genders. Several UNHCR managers provided detailed insights into the institutions' operations in Syria and I also interviewed international and Syrian employees of international aid organizations.

My research found that Iraqis' lives had become an arena for interventions by Syrian and foreign actors. These interventions played out political disagreements subtly, in a way that avoided open conflict, because the stated focus of all actors was the well-being of Iraqis. But beyond this superficial mutual goal lay different interests: on the one hand the Syrian government's interest to maximize the financial and reputational potential of hosting the international-aid elite, and on the other hand aid organizations' and donor states' interest to push their technical standards and immigration regimes. Each actor projected a distinct vision of Iraqis' role in Syrian and international politics, and of how they should behave as guests or refugees in Syria. Domestic and international interventions into Iraqi migrant lives were based on opposing ideas about the shape and content of the Syrian state and on the kind of political relations that state sovereignty should be based on more generally.

Also, my research produced insights about state-society relations in Syria, both on the domestic level and in the more abstract international realm of humanitarianism and diplomacy. By analyzing small details of Iraqis' lives, as well as those of Syrians and international aid workers, through the prism of an always-ongoing construction of statehood, I hope to contribute to the rich discussion about the content and form of politics in the Middle East. Following the trail blazed by Timothy Mitchell and Lisa Wedeen, which has been widened by scholars such as Salwa Ismail, Reinoud Leenders, Steven Heydemann, Oliver Schlumberger, Raymond Hinnebusch, and others, my analysis employs methodology from anthropology and sociology to explain a highly dynamic moment of state transformation in Syria.[2] With this interdisciplinary approach, I hope to contribute to the ongoing effort to counter simplistic understandings of Middle Eastern states and societies, for example, by problematizing the authoritarian-democratic or liberal-illiberal binary, and by painting a more nuanced picture of freedom and oppression in the region.

Syria and Iraqi Migration

Historically, Syria has welcomed strangers. Throughout the nineteenth and twentieth century, Syria offered safe haven to various groups of forced migrants. These included Chechens fleeing from wars in the Caucasus, as well as Armenians, Assyrians, Kurds, and Turks forced out of Turkey and Iraq in the 1910s and 1920s. This reception culminated in the generous shelter given to tens of thousands of Palestinians displaced by Israeli forces in 1948 and 1967.

Several groups of Iraqi exiles, escaping different phases of oppression, received asylum in Syria throughout the twentieth century. Iraq's second prime minister after the fall of Saddam Hussein, Nouri al-Maliki, was sheltered by Damascus for years in the 1990s after being condemned to death in Iraq for his political activities. As highlighted by Hanna Batatu in his 1981 article "Some Observations on the Social Roots of Syria's Ruling Military Group and the Causes for Its Dominance" and by Volker Perthes in his 1995 book *The Political Economy of Syria under Asad*, the Syrian state's growing oppression of political pluralism after the arrival of the Ba'th Party to power in 1963, did not stand in contradiction to social, ethnic, and indeed national pluralism.[3] A 2013 article by Kheder Kaddour and Kevin Mazur, "The Struggle for Syria's Regions," brilliantly updates this argument to contemporary Syria.[4] By the late twentieth and early twenty-first century Syria's "illiberal" state afforded greater freedom to migrants than the "liberal" states of Europe and North America, with their increasingly draconian and deadly regimes of migration control.[5]

This tolerance toward immigration appears at first sight as a stark contrast to Syria's history of governmental oppression. Since the early years of its state formation under French colonial power, harsh violence has been a core feature of governance in Syria, as Daniel Neep has shown in his reworking of Syria's mandate history, *Occupying Syria under the French Mandate*.[6] For most of its existence as a modern independent state, which began with the withdrawal of French forces in 1946, a ruthless security apparatus has dominated Syria, applying extreme violence to enforce acquiescence to the personality cult of its leaders.

On paper, Syria possesses all the institutions of a parliamentary republic, including a constitution guaranteeing equal citizenship rights to all persons of Syrian nationality. Yet a number of formal and informal changes to the structure of the state since the 1960s mean that most of these institutions have been defunct for decades, in the sense that they have little power over the regulation of everyday politics and over the way the state appears in people's everyday lives. Formal changes include the 1964 constitutional anchoring of the Ba'th Party as the "leading party in society and the state," which weakened the notion of free electoral competition (this elevation of the Ba'th was formally abandoned in 2011 as a belated reaction to unfolding popular protests). Informal changes include the vast expansion of internal intelligence agencies and their use of state instruments to violently suppress any form of opposition, which ensured the repeated reelection of the al-Asad presidents, father and son, and of loyalist parliamentarians in apparently free elections.[7]

The al-Asad family has occupied the presidency since 1970 via personal power relationships and deft manipulation of institutions, as has been documented by a relative extensive literature on Syrian authoritarianism, central to which are the writings of Steven Heydemann, Raymond Hinnebusch, Oliver Schlumberger, and Volker Perthes.[8] This has ensured that in Syria, the person occupying the presidency—formally an element of the governmental structure determined via suffrage—enjoys extraordinary personal power and, crucially, does not change through any form of significant popular choice.

The imposition of emergency law in Syria between 1963 and 2011 can be regarded as the culmination of the al-Asads' strategy to manipulate state instruments for presidential power. Emergency law undermined the constitution, and was officially justified by Syria's continued state of war with Israel. In practice it provided a veneer of legitimacy to the oppression of any form of opposition to al-Asad. Stripping state institutions of their intended meaning and steering them toward becoming vacuous shells served to entrench in Syria a politics of "as if," a key term coined by Lisa Wedeen in her 1999 influential book on governance in Syria, *Ambiguities of Domination*. Through a politics in which both government and subjects participate in performances of "as if," the outward shape of a harmonious national state is constructed through lip service and fantasy, while the actually lived body politic does not cohere around national unity but primarily around (pretend and actual) loyalty to the al-Asad rulers.[9]

So how does this history of violent control square with Syria's open borders and tolerance toward foreigners? Throughout this book, I argue that it is precisely the absence of liberal politics that explains the relative freedom that Iraqis, and other migrants, enjoyed in Syria. Syria's government did not rely on forming a special bond with an imagined national community of citizens. Thus, although the government did not extend special protection to Syrians, it also did not discriminate against other nationalities living on its territory. Creating a national population, and an assumed special bond between this population and the government, was not the way that the Syrian government created its shaky domestic legitimacy. For migrants, this meant that as long as they accepted the limitations of life in Syria, they were welcome and would not face any particular hurdles to integration.

Iraqi mass migration was the first such event in Syria to become recognized as an international humanitarian emergency. For a few years, the

"Iraqi refugee crisis" dominated headlines from the Middle East. As a consequence, it was also the first instance of mass migration to Syria that attracted the attention and involvement of powerful international actors. First and foremost, UNHCR, behind which stand its donors, primarily the United States and the European Union. In UNHCR's wake, dozens of international NGOs arrived in Syria with standardized refugee-aid projects. Both UNHCR and its partner NGOs rely on a political rationale, according to which states rigorously separate refugees from the national population. The longer the international humanitarian approach to migration management penetrated in Syria, the more it began to interact with the existing governmental approach: while international actors rapidly acquiesced to Syrian authorities' growing demand for control, Syrian actors rapidly began to copy the rhetoric and, to a lesser degree, practice of marking Iraqis as foreign and problematic.

At the beginning of the Iraqi migration crisis Syrian government officials rarely used the Arabic word "refugee" (*lāji'*) to refer to Iraqis. Instead, in public appearances, Syrian officials spoke about Iraqis as "brothers" or "guests." But despite this couching of Iraqi migration in terms of Arab solidarity, the more internationalized the Iraqi refugee crisis became, the more the Syrian government also portrayed Iraqi migrants as a financial liability and a threat to social peace and prosperity. The sudden arrival of thousands of migrants in urban areas had indeed increased the consumption of state-subsidized goods such as heating oil and flour. Iraqis placed pressure on already rising real estate prices, which, by 2010, had reached astronomical heights in Damascus. The cost of vegetables and other daily goods doubled within two years. But was Iraqi immigration truly the main cause of inflation? The absence of reliable economic data left even the most well-placed analysts, such as a team of IMF observers, unclear about Iraqi migrants' economic impact.[10] The sharp cuts to diesel-oil subsidies, which the government implemented at the same time, together with a growing influx of hard currency from the tourism boom, placed enormous upward pressure on inflation, which the government failed to manage or control. Thriving new Iraqi businesses, evident signs of an increased consumables trade between Syria and Iraq, and not least, the burgeoning rental market, showed that Iraqis had also brought with them significant amounts of cash and investments, and that much of this money was going to the pockets of Syrian businesses and landlords. And whereas there were no evident signs that the Syrian state had been forced to build new infrastructure specifically for Iraqis, aid money for the regeneration of health and education facilities was flowing into the country by the hundreds of millions.[11]

Despite the publicly voiced concerns about the economic effects of Iraqi migration, the mobilization of Syrian state institutions to control Iraqis' access to Syrian territory and labor market remained very weak. Until late 2007, travel from Iraq to Syria did not require a visa, and setting up shop in one of Syria's urban centers was straightforward, as long as Iraqis had enough funds to rent a property and ensure daily expenses. From this perspective, it was mostly what the Syrian government did *not* do in regard to Iraqi migrants that was of greatest interest. Unlike the assumptions of policy and academic expertise about states and migration, once Iraqis arrived in Syria, the state bureaucracy did *not* clearly categorize Iraqis as migrants and did *not* slot them into defined bureaucratic procedures that would process them stringently as foreign citizens, as "outside" of the Syrian state. Iraqis' position vis-à-vis Syria was treated as a political rather than a technical relationship. And the particular situation of an Iraqi individual depended more on his or her specific network and assets than on the color of the passport.

The most important elements determining an Iraqi's success or failure in Syria were the same that determined the success or failure of Syrians. They included having money and property, the presence or absence of connections to powerful individuals, to a lesser degree skills and business acumen, and, most important, loyalty to the Bashar al-Asad presidency. Iraqis' experience with Syrian officialdom clearly showed that in Syria, the ability to reside and integrate depended on whether a person or community respected the government's authority and not whether they respected official rules and laws. Nationality and citizenship mattered little for whether a person's presence would be tolerated on Syrian territory. No specific regulatory regime existed through which Iraqis could obtain a resident permit (or fail to do so). Many rumors circulated about how to obtain such a permit (*iqama*), which could be arranged via multiple methods, depending on varying documents, personal situations, and luck with the immigration clerk one dealt with.

In Syria, the reasons justifying a permit were never known, either by petitioners or clerks, and there were no public places where they could be ascertained. New reasons could always appear, while previously good reasons might not work anymore. This situation highlighted a key difference between the way the Syrian government mobilized its state apparatus and the way it is mobilized by liberal-democratic states: in Syria, unpredictability signified constant instability, including the constant opportunity to turn the state in one's favor or against one. For Iraqi migrants this meant that while the possibility of a disastrous intervention by state forces was constant, so was the opportunity for integration and success in spite of official rules. Syrian state sovereignty—the elevation of the Syrian state as the most powerful actor on Syrian territory—was confirmed not via a Weberian "iron cage" of bureaucracy but via muddling through. State power appeared and disappeared at unexpected turns in the way. Perhaps one particular clerk within the chaotic public administration was unclear about the correct procedure and requested a different action than did his colleague. Perhaps another clerk would feel benevolent, or take pity, or, owing to his personal relationship with a minister, hold powers far beyond his official status and could process an application faster. Perhaps the petitioner was especially wealthy or was himself a friend of the powerful, which would speed up his request. Or perhaps a new government decision from "higher up" had suddenly occurred, knowledge of which had not yet spread to the public. Rarely were such decisions announced, and the public could find out what the rules of the day were only through experiencing them and spreading them by word of mouth.

Degrees of obscurity exist in every state bureaucracy. Yet in Syria obscurity became a tool of governance in itself. The absence of knowable laws gives the government systematic leeway to apply, drop, or change rules without giving citizens the possibility to complain. Similarly, the existence of some laws, the digression of which was widely tolerated, gave authorities the possibility to suddenly swoop down on and condemn those in violation of it. Such instability of regulation created a situation in which the outward appearance of the Syrian state as an independent entity could be maintained, whereas in fact governmental and personal power completely dominated the state apparatus.

The Iraqi Migrant Population in Syria

The Iraqis who arrived in Syria after 2003 included people from all walks of life, excluding only those too poor to afford the start-up costs for a life abroad. The breakdown of order in Iraq, the communal violence, kidnappings, roadblocks, targeted killings, and the continuing house searches, arrests, and attacks by American soldiers affected Iraqis across the board, rather than any particular faction. As a result, Iraqis living in Syria after 2003 included the more or less pious, the more or less wealthy, the more or less educated, and those close to the previous Iraqi government as well as those that had been oppressed.[12] All religious groups were represented. The only group conspicuous by its absence were Iraqi Kurds, owing to their preference to seek refuge in the quasi-autonomous Kurdish region in northern Iraq, which was more stable than the southern provinces. Fears that Iraqis would import sectarian violence to Syria, as some Western observers feared, proved unfounded.[13]

Iraqi migration to Syria resulted from major upheaval in Iraq, but at the same time, neighboring states also experienced violent conflicts that produced their own refugee flows. A general sense of uncertainty pervaded the region. The occupation of Iraq left future alliances and political directions unclear as the inability to form a functioning national government became more and more evident. Coordinated bomb attacks in Amman, Jordan, in 2005 raised fears of a regional contagion of sectarian violence and resulted in severe restrictions to hitherto tolerated Iraqi immigration to Jordan. Only a year later, in the summer of 2006, Israel's bombardment of southern Lebanon created a wave of short-term displacement of thousands of Lebanese into southern Syria. Finally, Israel's brutal assault on the Gaza Strip in December 2008, which proved to be only the first of several to follow, served as a reminder of the growing radicalization of the rightwing Israeli government and the remoteness of a solution to the Palestinian-Israeli conflict.

In addition to this regional uncertainty, Iraqis arrived in Syria at a time of significant domestic change. Still in a phase of consolidation since the death of Hafiz al-Asad in 2000, who had ruled for twenty-nine years, Syrian politics was adjusting to the rule of Hafiz's son Bashar, who had been installed as his successor. Bashar's refusal to support the invasion of Iraq had confirmed Syria's place in the US "axis of evil," and for a short while in 2003, there appeared the real possibility of US troops marching onto Damascus. Once that danger had passed, Bashar, in 2005, announced a new effort at economic deregulation. He appointed a cohort of economic reformers to lead the cutting of subsidies, reduction of trade barriers, and expansion of the private sector. But as the fruits of deregulation remained within a small network of regime-affiliated business people, as documented in Bassam Haddad's 2011 book *Business Networks in Syria*, visibly growing inequality and poverty were the immediate result of these reforms.[14]

Also in 2005, the assassination of Lebanon's prime minister, Rafik Hariri, forced the Syrian military to withdraw from Lebanon, where it had held a dominant position since 1990. The withdrawal from Lebanon was a political earthquake in Syria, accompanied by the staged "suicide" of a senior regime figure and widespread insecurity about what else it might bring. In the midst of all these major changes, Iraqi migration, and the international attention it garnered, would in many ways bring to the fore many of the tensions occurring in Syria in this first decade of the new millennium.

Iraqi research participants frequently compared Syria's open-door policy favorably with the restrictive entry policies of Jordan or Lebanon. Many expressed gratitude to the Syrian government for granting them at least temporary residency. At the same time, many Iraqis were highly aware of their political role as a potential bargaining chip to various powers and often expressed fear that the winds of regional or global politics could change in their disfavor. Veterans of violent and unpredictable rule, many understood very well, and much better than most of the aid workers who had rushed to their assistance, the limits and opportunities extended to them by the al-Asad government and the Syrian population. Careful to toe the important red lines they could discern, but keen to push their opportunities where possible, Iraqis tended to integrate foreign aid as an additional livelihood and future strategy rather than rely on aid workers to "protect" them.

Iraqi Refugees in the International Community

By 2009, Iraqi flight had become firmly established as an internationally discussed and highly visible humanitarian crisis, and consequently, had become a site of intervention for a wide range of international actors. Public reports regularly referred to 2 million Iraqi refugees in the region. The Syrian government claimed up to 1.5 million Iraqis had arrived. Although analysts soon considered these figures inflated, they continued to dominate the discussion.[15] And as the plight of Iraqi refugees became a talking point in US domestic politics, it also became an embarrassing reminder of the US' failure to stabilize Iraq. The US government began injecting large funds into UNHCR and announced its intention to receive thousands of Iraqi refugees through UNHCR's resettlement programs. A number of other governments followed suit and UNHCR expanded rapidly in the Middle East, developing a regional response across Syria, Jordan, and Lebanon, setting up offices, reception centers, food distribution points, and other humanitarian programs. As host to the largest Iraqi refugee population, Syria became the focus of a new range of interests and agencies: journalists, aid workers, immigration clerks in Europe and the United States, UN officials and academics suddenly had Syria and its Iraqi migrants within their sights. Dozens of reports about Iraqi migration were issued by think tanks and advocacy organizations, researchers were hired to look into the topic, radio and magazine reports were commissioned, and conferences organized.

The fact that internationally Iraqis were consistently referred to as "refugees" is relevant. A refugee enjoys particular rights, which do not apply to other migrants. To qualify as a refugee, a person must have left their country of origin out of fear of being persecuted because of their politics or their identity. Poverty and loss of livelihood are not considered valid justifications. Thus, speaking about an "Iraqi migration crisis" instead of an "Iraqi refugee crisis" would have not implied the same level of international responsibility and urgency.

UNHCR and Western governments place much emphasis on differentiating between refugees and migrants, seeking to single out and reject non-refugees. Human-rights activists have long denounced this practice, pointing out, inter alia, that all humans should have the right to improve their situation by migrating. In the Middle East, on the other hand, the term "refugee" is closely linked to the tragic fate of the Palestinians displaced from historic Palestine. To avoid the pitfalls of the refugee versus migrant discourse, Polly Pallister-Wilkins has suggested using the term "life-seeker" for people crossing international borders in search of a better future.[16] In this book, I mostly refer to Iraqis in Syria as "migrants," in the general sense of the term as someone who has crossed an international border. I do this first because the Iraqis I encountered included both refugees in the legalistic sense as well as regular migrants, and second, because I, at this stage, am not interested in this particular debate about terms.

Thus, along with a differently accented Arabic, new foodstuffs, and significant investment and trade, Iraqi mass migration also transported a hitherto unknown actor into the Syrian domestic political arena: international aid organizations. From 2007 onward a humanitarian sector wielding hundreds of millions of dollars arrived. This development was significant by any measure. It exposed the Syrian government's awareness that state provision of welfare was failing across large sectors of Syrian society and its interest in fostering a controlled expansion of private or nongovernmental aid providers to fill the gap.[17] This approach, in which basic services are moved out of the state sector to third parties, has been observed in other Middle Eastern countries, notably in Egypt by Salwa Ismail in her 2006 book *Political Life in Cairo's New Quarters*.[18] Echelons of the Syrian government, in their push to privatize the economy and reduce subsidies, believed that international aid money and expertise should play an important role in the Syrian social market economy announced by Bashar al-Asad in 2005. This move to economic deregulation led to rare public rifts among Syrian government figures, such as the unusual public criticism voiced in 2009 by Syria's economic planning commission head Tayssir Raddawi against the plans of the newly installed former World Bank technocrat Abdullah Dardari.[19] Raddawi was subsequently fired from his post by presidential degree, a clear indication that the government, at that time, believed the price for liberalizing the economy was worth paying.

The high-profile involvement of Bashar's wife Asma al-Asad as leader of the country's internal development organizations indicated high-level support for developmentalism and "ngo-ization." A year before her stunning fall from grace via the Syrian revolution, Asma served as the figurehead for Syria's first NGO conference. The event was titled "The Emerging Role of Civil Society in Development" and was held at Damascus's most elegant and expensive hotel in January 2010. The conference was so oversubscribed that people had to be turned away, and it was filled with the international aid crowd, very recently arrived on the back of the Iraqi refugee crisis, ready to pay their respects to the First Lady's apparent attempts to revitalize Syria's nongovernmental sector. Only a surprisingly small number seemed to understand the deeply deceptive nature of the government's outward concern for the well-being of its population. Instead, most attendees appeared to regard Syria as the latest humanitarian emergency, a promising aid market with a host of internal problems crying out for humanitarian and development intervention.

The arrival of international aid organizations challenged Syrian government agencies with new rhetoric and processes. Distributing welfare according to individual needs, complying with internal accounting and banking rules, and handling the international donor community were new to Syrian politics. The categorizations and concepts according to which aid organizations divided the Iraqi population differed starkly from those used by the Syrian state, especially when regarded from the bottom up, that is, by observing Iraqis' daily encounters with each actor. Humanitarian agencies and Syrian state institutions required distinctive forms of behavior from Iraqis in exchange for their services, while presenting similarly life-changing opportunities and threats to which Iraqis had to react: with the arrival of the aid sector, it became necessary for Iraqis to develop strategies to integrate aid organizations into their daily lives and future planning. Trying to summarize the confusing inconsistencies between Syrian and humanitarian migration regimes to an Iraqi migrant, a UNHCR clerk explained: "With us, you are a refugee, but outside with Syrian authorities, out there, you are a tourist." By creating a parallel system of refugee management, which was based on a deeply different idea of politics, humanitarian agencies became a second sovereign power for Iraqis living on Syrian territory, which not only shaped Iraqis' material conditions but also the prevailing meaning of their refugee situation and position within the Syrian state.

This overlapping or, to borrow a phrase from the anthropologist Aihwa Ong, "graduated" sovereignty between Syrian and international actors became more and more observable after the layers of money and decision making surrounding Iraqi migration were peeled away through research and inquiry. Behind the international aid effort stood the sovereign power of donor states. UNHCR receives its funding as voluntary contributions from UN member states, which makes it particularly dependent on constant lobbying and fund-raising. The chief contributor by far is the United States, whose donation is more than that of the next five donors combined. Despite the evident bias of UNHCR's donor base, the direct power of donor states on the agency's policies has been documented only rarely (as in Helga Baitenmann's stunning 1991 *NGOs and the Afghan War: The Politicisation of Humanitarian Aid*). What did the different states involved in the aid effort promise and provide to Iraqis in Syria? Observed thus, the Iraqi migration experience became a prism through which the politics of domestic and international statehood were filtered and became unbundled into distinct layers and relationships of power.

Aid organizations strove to establish an intensely information-heavy regime of standardized categories into which Iraqis were slotted. One of aid organizations' central concerns was the paucity of knowledge available about the Iraqi population in Syria.[20] Indeed, the most basic fact, namely, how many Iraqis actually lived in Syria, was unknown and disputed. In 2009 it became clear that the very large figures announced by the Syrian government, which had quickly been adopted by NGOs and the United Nations, were inflated.[21] As the government strictly forbade any independent research, UNHCR was able to compile basic statistics only on Iraqis who had registered with the organization, which reached around 250,000 at their peak. Information about the rest, which, as UNHCR claimed, far exceeded the number of registrations, remained out of reach. The fact that Iraqis were "urban refugees" distributed across Damascus and not concentrated in camps made it much harder for humanitarian actors to assess the extent of the crisis.[22] But for the Syrian government, the absence of independently verified data was a means to create a monopoly of knowledge through which funders and NGOs could be influenced.

The collection, examination, and ordering of Iraqi testimonies of suffering was a key element through which UNHCR and its partner organizations managed Iraqis. This took place through the collection of bio data, the recording of detailed interviews, the examination and selection of files, and by fitting Iraqis with one of several preconceived social identities, such as "female-headed household," "widow," "older refugee," or "minor." To become deserving of the various benefits offered by aid organizations, Iraqis had to prove in great detail the foundations of their fear of persecution, their lack of political activity, and their poverty and suffering. In long interviews, which often took several hours and sometimes stretched over days, Iraqis had to narrate their distress to clerks charged with determining the specific nature of Iraqis' fear, their relationship to the Iraqi government, and any remaining opportunity for survival.

International aid organizations considered Iraqis through the lens of a harmonious people-territory-government trinity, which, in this abstract vision, presents an idealized version of liberal statehood. Here, states and their citizens are bound by a relationship of mutual representation via the government. Refugees and other undesired migrants present a significant disturbance to this harmonious trinity. Consequently, liberal ideas about refugees proceed from the assumption that they are perpetual outsiders to the state-citizen bond. From this perspective, Iraqis had been expelled from a situation of governmental protection and were now floating outside of any stable relationship with a sovereign-state protector to guarantee their rights. The more vulnerable and lacking governmental protection a person was considered to be according to UNHCR criteria, the more likely aid would be forthcoming. In accordance with this particular version of statehood that structured humanitarian thinking, the more Iraqis lacked any of the characteristics of a liberal type of citizen, the more likely they would be regarded as true refugees and therefore in need of UNHCR's help.

Syrian domestic politics only weakly reflected such ideas about citizens, governmental protection, and the nation. Still, aid organizations elevated the national/non-national distinction as the key reason why Iraqis were different and disadvantaged in Syria. Aid agencies presented Iraqis, owing to their status as foreigners, as a systematic problem for Syria. Rather than recognizing the regional history of Iraqi migration and integration, aid agencies constantly positioned Iraqis as alien to, and outside of, Syrian society. The continued portrayal of Iraqis as unmanageable for the Syrian state and society served as a key justification for the presence of the international aid sector. Ironically, it was precisely the actions of this sector that, through its constant portrayal of Iraqis as difficult outsiders, tended to confirm the natural right of the Syrian state to exclude them on the basis of their citizenship. By marking Iraqi migrants in Syria as refugees cast outside of politics, and by emphasizing their suffering, dependency, and exclusion, aid agencies promoted an ideal of nation-based state sovereignty for which the exclusion of strangers is a political necessity.

A look at Iraqi existence in Syria showed that they were integrated remarkably well into the Syrian body politic and that the Syrian state did not mark them systematically as strangers. Nevertheless, such Iraqi activities in Syria, which plainly contradicted the humanitarian vision of their situation and placed into questions the notions of "legality," "citizenship," and "nationality" on which it was so heavily based, were absent from the perception of the aid sector. Despite the continuing troubles in Iraq and their often horrible recent past, Iraqis in Damascus were also thriving: through their own strength and a political, social, and cultural context that did not project them as hopeless, nonsovereign outsiders. But in humanitarian texts and projects, the natural and ideal location for Iraqis was the territory of Iraq and the sovereign space of the Iraqi state, and it was only highly exceptional circumstances that had undone this natural and baseline situation. Through an extremely selective presentation of Iraqi existence in Syria, humanitarian agencies strengthened the idea that the exclusion and illegal status of international migrants was a necessary, natural, and correct element of political community and state sovereignty.

1. This sign, photographed in an Iraqi-owned restaurant, states: "I am Iraqi, I have Iraqi citizenship and do not want any other. Only al-Asad and the Syrian people opened their doors to Iraqis, the rest of the Arabs ask for an official visa." Photo by author.

This Book's Framework and Organization

My analysis of the reconfiguration of Syrian statehood in the context of the Iraqi refugee crisis engages a rich literature on Syrian politics past and present, as well as the literature on statehood in the Middle East more widely. Further, I build on a growing number of interdisciplinary works about how large-scale political structures are reproduced through quotidian social interactions and should be understood as embedded in society rather than external to it.

In 1991, Timothy Mitchell wrote that state-society boundaries are "distinctions erected internally, as an aspect of more complex power relations."[23] My analysis extends Mitchell's observation from the domestic realm to the international to show how foreign states spread their state-society relations onto Syrian territory as a result of the construction of Iraqi flight as an international emergency. Not only are the boundaries between state and society found to be blurred, but the separation between different state-society complexes are also shown to be flexible, with little relation to their official, territorial demarcations. The interventions of foreign states on Syrian territory may appear as a weakening of Syrian state sovereignty, but careful analysis of the interactions between Syrian authorities, the international aid apparatus, and the Iraqi migrant population showed that this was not the case: state power was found not to be a zero-sum game in which one state loses as others gain. Rather, the Iraqi refugee crisis created new international interactions and spaces in which Syrian government officials received an elevated platform and significant diplomatic praise for their handling of Iraqi migrants. As a result, Syria's international recognition and sovereignty received a boost, at the same time as foreign diplomats and aid workers increasingly built a parallel migration and welfare regime in the country.

Mitchell also draws attention to the importance played by technologies and technological innovation for the continuous adaptation and tenacity of the state and its relation to society. This insight has since been mobilized in different ways by Middle East scholars to understand transformations to state and society. For example, Ilana Feldman's 2008 book *Governing Gaza* takes this approach to demonstrate the centrality of bureaucratic technologies, such as surveillance, recordings, and filings of population behavior, to produce authority in a context in which governmental legitimacy is lacking. In "the absence of an organic connection between government and population," writes Feldman, "people were not requested to believe that it [bureaucracy] stood for something else, rather they were asked to believe [and participate in it] for its own sake."[24] Since both the relationship between Syrian authorities and the Iraqi migrant population, as well as that between aid providers and Iraqi migrants, lacked an "organic connection," bureaucracy indeed played an important role in the construction of domestic Syrian and international aid agencies' authority over Iraqi migrants. Yet the form, content, and intensity of bureaucratic mobilization differed starkly between the two, revealing, as this book argues throughout, vastly different beliefs about the material and immaterial structures on which state sovereignty and legitimacy should be based.

The Iraqi refugee crisis in Syria revealed another state-society boundary, whose shape shifted as the crisis unfolded. This was the boundary between Syria's own domestic and international state. Syria's domestic state has received significant academic attention, in particular with regard to the continuity of its governments and style of rule. Seminal works such as Hanna Batatu's 1981 article "Some Observations on the Social Roots of Syria's Ruling Military Group and the Causes for Its Dominance," Volker Perthes's 1995 book *The Political Economy of Syria under Asad*, or Raymond Hinnebusch's 2001 book *Syria: Revolution from Above* and Lisa Wedeen's 1999 book *Ambiguities of Domination* have long highlighted the social complexity of Syria's government through the decades, as well as the nuanced usage of consent and coercion, through which it has ruled. Together with recent books, such as Thomas Pierret's *Religion and State in Syria*, Daniel Neep's *Occupying Syria under the French Mandate*, Bassam Haddad's *Business Networks in Syria*, as well as Raphael Lefevre's *Ashes of Hama*, this literature, which combines rich empirical details of everyday life in Syria with a political-economic framework of analysis, dispels any simplistic notion of the Syrian state as a realm of static, monochrome authoritarianism (as it has, alas, often been misunderstood).

Syria's foreign relations have received equally significant academic attention. Here, a number of recent studies by Radwan Ziadeh, Bente Scheller, Raymond Hinnebusch have added to the seminal classics of Patrick Seale and Volker Perthes.[25] But what has received little to no explicit attention are the different manners in which Syrian statehood is exercised on the international scene and within the domestic sphere. Zeroing in on this distinction highlights international, hegemonic standards of statehood, according to which a state has to perform on the international stage. Internationally, Syrian officials performed and were received *as if* Syria was ruled via a system of liberal national representation, however, domestically, no pretense to this fiction was made. The gulf between the Syrian international and domestic state became particularly obvious in the course of the Iraqi refugee crisis, as, toward the humanitarian sector and other foreign actors, the Syrian government behaved *as if* the humanitarian approach to refugees, and its assumptions about the government-territory-population unity, was a tangible reality in Syria. In speeches and reports aimed at the international community, government officials paid lip service to the humanitarian vision, eventually even using the term "refugee" to describe Iraqis, moving away from the formerly accepted terms "guests" or "brothers." In conversation with international organizations, Syrian officials would adopt the internationally hegemonic rhetoric about Iraqi life in Syria as precarious, temporary, and problematic, rather than, for example, pointing out examples of successful Iraqi integration or the resources Iraqis were adding to the Syrian economy.

In a curious inversion of this performance, the aid community consistently heaped praise on the Syrian government for its tolerance and acceptance of Iraqis. Gone were the accusations of human rights violations, the accusations of torture, the highlighting of political prisoners and arrests that usually confronted Syrian officials. Instead, senior UN managers commended the Syrian government's provision of "humanitarian space" for Iraqis, actively sought partnerships with Syrian government institutions, provided investment into public infrastructure, and regularly lauded Syrian cooperation and help with humanitarian efforts. In countless media reports, the Syrian government's image as a generous provider of safety and refuge was polished and favorably compared with other, less generous regional hosts of Iraqi migrants such as Jordan or Lebanon. Yet during this period, the Syrian government did not at all alleviate its brutal treatment of political activists, its intensive surveillance, and its harsh punishments for even minor forms of government criticism and social organizations. Adding yet another layer of awkward and odd *as if* behavior to Syrian politics, the overriding concern to expand humanitarian services in Syria and to open the field for more international NGOs had swept any other human rights concerns of aid workers under the carpet.

This book also draws on ethnographic accounts of how state sovereignty becomes constructed through everyday practices. Works by anthropologists such as Brenda Chalfin (*Working the Border: Constructing Sovereignty in the Context of Liberalization*), geographers such as Alison Mountz ("Where Asylum-Seekers Wait: Feminist Counter-Topographies of Sites between States"), and indeed political scientists such as Wendy Brown (*Walled States, Waning Sovereignty*) have led the way in showing how the contradictions created by the domestic-international binary are naturalized in everyday life.

Mark Duffield has aptly described the post–Cold War situation as a "slow political struggle" between liberal and illiberal regimes over how to integrate rapidly deregulating economies at the global and domestic level. Since the arrival of Bashar al-Asad as president, in Syria this struggle has played out within the innermost circles of government, as numerous steps to privatize and deregulate the economy in the past decade demonstrated. But corruption, ineffective bureaucracies, and promotion according to political rather than merit-based considerations entrenched existing forms of inequality and exploitation. This book shows that the tension between globally hegemonic norms of liberalism and national representation (according to which Syria's international statehood was performed) and the material reality of Syria's domestic sphere reached unprecedented heights in the course of the Iraqi refugee crisis and the arrival of the international aid sector. For apart from shaping Iraqi life materially, international aid and Syrian government programs revealed different understandings of where Iraqis should be located in relation to Syrian territory and as an element of the population. These differences exposed two distinct visions of how the sudden arrival of a large group of migrants could be brought into harmony with the political demands of nation-based statehood. Ironically, the liberal, national politics of statehood contained in the humanitarian approach did not promote a politics of integration. Rather, humanitarian rhetoric and practice constantly emphasized Iraqis' inability to integrate into Syrian society in the long-term and consistently confirmed the right of states to exclude foreigners. By marking Iraqis as refugees cast outside politics, and by emphasizing their suffering, dependency, and exclusion, aid providers in Syria promoted a form of national politics for which the casting out of strangers was a political necessity, as the natural basis for state sovereignty. This was doubly ironic, as the unpredictable but tolerant Syrian approach to migration precisely did not cast out Iraqis in this manner.

Chapter Structure

The book is organized according to different actors involved in managing Iraqi migrants in Syria between 2003 and 2011. The second chapter focuses on the Syrian state, and the al-Asad government, in order to provide an overview of Syria's domestic political situation at the time. The chapter argues that the government extended its existing mixture of laissez-faire politics and the permanent possibility of a violent crackdown to the Iraqi population, resulting in a situation in which Iraqis and Syrians were ruled in a remarkably similar manner. Chapters 3, 4, and 5 focus on the key actors making up the foreign aid community: UNHCR, international NGOs, and the donor states providing the financing to both. The three chapters argue that these actors' approach to Iraqi migration starkly contradicted the way in which the Syrian government managed foreigners. Chapter 6 focuses on the Iraqi population itself to demonstrate, via portraits of several research participants and detailed observations from field work, its diversity and the varied strategies of accommodation and resistance individuals engaged in to counter the overwhelming local and international forces governing their lives. The daily life of Iraqis in Syria, and the opportunity for intervention that Iraqi existence in Syria provided to numerous actors, here provides a starting point for a detailed explanation of how the many absurdities and contradictions of a state-centric politics become logical under its peculiar political imaginary.

2

The Syrian State and Iraqi Migration

Uneven Sovereignty

To understand how the Syrian state shapes people's daily lives it is necessary to grasp its essential ambiguity.[1] Syrian state institutions consistently act in an unpredictable fashion, creating an atmosphere of insecurity that prevails across society. Just how overwhelming and stifling this insecurity was, previous to the 2011 uprising, is difficult to convey in writing, especially as it was simultaneously subtle, in the way of a constantly droning background noise.

The paradox of "predictable unpredictability" was reflected in the way government violence was exercised before 2011. Up until then, Syrian towns and villages were safe and appeared peaceful. The intense cruelty of the subsequent conflict appears as a shocking reversal of fortunes. Before 2011, protests, public violence, street crime, burglaries, or robberies were exceedingly rare, and even after dark, walking home alone in Damascus or getting into a cab was normal. In villages, being invited into a stranger's home late in the evening was a welcome opportunity for exchange and not a moment of worry. Incidences of violence against foreigners were so uncommon that any exception instantly became a talking point. A single episode of violence against two American students in Damascus in 2010 caused a sensation and prompted the American Embassy to issue unprecedented warnings to its staff, such was the exceptionality of the issue.

But this was the situation in public. In private conversations, I learned about the ubiquity of violence in hidden spaces, which blurred any notion of "private" and "public" (this separation being itself a result of liberal politics, in which the state's power to intrude is curtailed). In police stations, prisons, torture cells, and interrogation rooms, Syrian security officers had meted out random oppression and violence for decades, not just against political opponents but also, if one was unlucky, for minor transgressions. No one was protected against a security apparatus that stood above and beyond the law.

An Opening Anecdote

One evening in early 2010, a Syrian friend of mine, Faris, arrived at my house for dinner and to give an interview about Iraqi migration. Faris was in his midtwenties, living a cosmopolitan and successful life in Damascus. Fluent in English, he had traveled abroad several times and had begun his career in one of the recently opened foreign private banks. Now he had been hired by the United Nations and was working on a number of social issues, including Iraqi migrants. Faris did not hail from a wealthy family and his success resulted from the Syrian government's long-standing provision of free public services such as free schooling and university education. Also, he had benefited from the government's more recent decision to open the economy to foreign investment.

To my surprise, when we sat down for the interview, Faris opened our conversation by asking whether I ever discussed "critical issues" with Syrians. It was obvious that he was referring to Syrian politics. At this time, just hearing a person say the president's name in public turned heads. Politics, if discussed at all, was talked about in private homes among close friends and relatives. Although I trusted Faris, I answered his question vaguely. Faris responded that he too was now watchful. This was because his previous openness had resulted in a government interrogation, during which he discovered that the government maintained a file on him and "knew everything, you know, *everything.*"

The interrogation happened after security agents stormed a meeting of a small group of young people trying to organize some environmental-awareness activities. Environmental campaigns, such as garbage pick-ups, at the time were popular among the small number of Syrian social activists, as they were considered relatively uncontroversial. But the official ban on gatherings of more than five people always opened the opportunity for a sudden swoop. The agents took phone numbers and requested individual meetings at the headquarters of air force intelligence, which was feared as the most ruthless branch of the intelligence apparatus. Faris believed that one of the friend's neighbors must have heard their meeting and passed on information.

Several days later, Faris was led down three staircases, ending up in a narrow cell far underground that had a single table and lamp. Describing a scene "just like in the movies," Faris recalled his fear when he heard the screams of people being beaten in adjacent rooms. An officer brought a green file, and to Faris's shock, not only knew about his previous landlords and addresses but also read out reports on Faris's activities, attitudes, and intentions. After several hours of detailed questioning and bullying, he was relieved to be released without having had to endure a beating. He had heard that they "usually beat the guys, but not the girls." Since this incident, Faris had become much more careful about his public persona and had ceased any form of social activism. He was also urgently looking for a way to leave Syria to begin a life abroad. His experience of the violent side of Syrian state power had led to his complete loss of faith that Syria would ever offer him the kind of life he hoped for.

In this chapter, I hope to convey an understanding of how the Syrian government ruled and what kind of state-citizen relations emerged from this rule. This groundwork lays the foundation for my argument that international aid organizations and their donors introduced a new understanding of such relations to Syria. Space, and the shaping of space into domestic and international realms, into the local and the foreign, is important for my analysis. For this reason, the following section begins with a description of Damascus's social topography and of the role that migrant neighborhoods—in this case a Palestinian and an Iraqi neighborhood—played for the production of domestic and international statehood in Syria. I then move into an analysis of how the Syrian government managed Iraqi migrants and show how the Iraqi refugee crisis influenced Syrian statehood, domestically and internationally.

The Urban Space and Public Sphere of Damascus

According to the Syrian government's Central Bureau of Statistics, central Damascus and its suburbs, which form an administratively separate area called the "Damascus Countryside" (*dimashq rīf*), were, in 2009, home to around 4.3 million people.[2] The bureaucratic distinction between the two areas stemmed from a time when Damascus was a compact city surrounded by fields and farms. Today, sprawling suburbs are linked to the center by motorways, which are themselves lined with low-rise, often illegally constructed habitats, forming the most downtrodden residential areas.[3] Damascus's rapid population growth in the past decades was not accompanied by political or bureaucratic reforms, which, by the end of the 2000s, was apparent from the city's overloaded infrastructure and failing public services.

The administrative separation between center and suburbs, which privileged central Damascus in terms of government attention and investment, is reflected in the city's design and architecture. Whereas central Damascus exhibits careful urban planning, such as tree-lined boulevards, homogeneous groups of apartment buildings, and decorated city squares, suburbs are characterized by much rougher infrastructure: unfinished roads and buildings interspersed with undeveloped land and narrow, potholed lanes.[4] This uneven reach of governmental control over urban space was a physical expression of the uneven control the Syrian state maintained over its population. Central urban areas enjoyed a much better availability of services, such as garbage collection, water and electricity supply, education, health and leisure facilities, and public transport. Whereas central streets were swept daily by government employees pushing large metal trolleys, suburban areas were much less well maintained, to the degree that in some areas garbage festered in unofficial dumps between buildings and fresh water had to be bought from private vendors. Central Damascus was home to French, German, and Spanish cultural centers offering language classes, exhibitions, and cinema programs, private art galleries and public museums, a number of high-end hotels, and it hosted governmental buildings and embassies. Although some of the wealthier suburbs were served by upscale restaurants, and many private schools and universities were also located in new developments out of town, in the poorest suburbs all of these services were absent.

Whereas the center of town, where wealthy elites resided in French-style modern apartment blocks, gave the appearance of a space heavily shaped and ordered by efficient and caring state institutions, this was not the impression gained from visiting poor and middle-class suburbs. There, the lack of planning and care for public spaces indicated a population abandoned by the state, at least in terms of welfare, concern for the quality of life, and essential services. This stark discrepancy had grown rapidly since 2005 when economic liberalization had received a further push. In the last six years before the Syrian uprising began in 2011, central Damascus had become ever more chic, hosting an increasing number of eye-wateringly expensive international coffee chains and upscale fashion shops. At the same time, the cutting of subsidies and the astronomical inflation of real estate prices were pushing the last remnants of the middle class into poverty and the poor into an increasingly desperate and hopeless situation.

Poor and rich neighborhoods shared at least one aspect of daily life in Syria: ubiquitous visual reminders of presidential and Ba'th Party power. Portraits of the current president Bashar al-Asad adorned walls, government buildings, billboards, murals, shop walls, and car windows across the city. Mostly, they showed a portrait of the president from the chest upward, but the style of the portray varied: sometimes he was shown simply wearing a brown suit and tie, sometimes he was in full military gear including aviator sunglasses and cap, sometimes his religiosity was emphasized, over a background of Arabic calligraphy, which lent a pious air to the image. The latest development in Syrian propaganda art consisted of modern hard-plastic billboards that showed the president strolling toward the viewer, waving, accompanied by slogans such as "we are all with you" or "we love you."[5]

Painted images or photographs of Bashar al-Asad's late father, Syria's former president Hafiz al-Asad, and Bashar's late older brother Basil al-Asad also appeared frequently; Hafiz al-Asad was occasionally presented in the form of a statue or bust. Frequently, Hafiz and his two sons were shown together as a trinity, wearing military caps and looking stern.

2a. and 2b. Two extremes—a central and a suburban square. *Top*, public space in central Damascus; *bottom*, public space in Jaramana, a suburb of Damascus. Photos by author.

Occasionally, joint portraits of Bashar and Hassan Nasrallah, the leader of Hizbullah, were seen; these adorned cars and smaller posters. Another rarer image showed Bashar as a family man surrounded by wife and children.

Propaganda served as a constant reminder of the dominance of government institutions over Damascus's public space. Youth clubs, unions, women's organizations, and business chambers had long been integrated into the Ba'th Party and lost all independence. Their buildings, covered in slogans and photos of the al-Asads, were everywhere, creating a monotone background crowding out all other signs of political, cultural, or social activity. Lisa Wedeen has argued that in Syria, the visual expression of the al-Asad personality cult "cluttered" the imagination, filling every nook and cranny and leaving no physical or mental space for other representations of society, and, despite some steps toward pluralism, this was still valid in Syria in 2009 and 2010.[6]

Damascus's physical topography, created by the government's uneven application of state power, intertwined with the city's social topography. Researching the impact of global, regional, and domestic events on the city showed how the city space interacted with everyday life. The arrival of Iraqis was the most recent such event, but many of Damascus's neighborhoods spoke of previous changes that had shaped the city. Two neighborhoods were particularly interesting for such an analysis, as they housed two groups of immigrants to which the Syrian government applied a very different form of population management: first the suburb Yarmuk, home to tens of thousands of Palestinians, and second the suburb Jaramana, where, since 2005, thousands of Iraqis had arrived. The appearance of immigrant identities in these two suburbs gave insights into how the Syrian government mobilized its state apparatus to manage these two very different population groups as elements of the Syrian body politic.

The Palestinian Neighborhood Yarmuk

Yarmuk, a densely populated suburb, lies around 8 kilometers to the south of the city center. Yarmuk was built in the 1940s as an unofficial camp for Palestinian refugees. Since 2012, Yarmuk has made international headlines as one of the first neighborhoods subjected to a government siege that cut off most public services, including the supply of essential goods. Most of Yarmuk's infrastructure was destroyed by shelling in 2014, and the camp has come under the control of various fanatical groups. But in 2010, Yarmuk was still known as a lively neighborhood that had gained some popularity among foreign students and artists, offering many amenities in a relatively central location.

Depending on traffic, a bus trip from the city center to Yarmuk took around 30 minutes. Throughout Yarmuk, Palestinian national and political identity was expressed in a highly visible, established, and explicitly political manner. Streets were dotted with posters celebrating Palestinian martyrs and the liberation struggle for Palestine. Offices of Palestinian institutions such as the Palestinian Liberation Army on Yarmuk's high street were highly conspicuous, and the Palestinian Hospital was a central landmark in the area. The official name of the main thoroughfare was Palestine Street, and side streets were named after Palestinian villages. Many shops and offices in Yarmuk had explicitly Palestinian names, such as "al-Quds" (the Arabic name of Jerusalem). The Palestinian colors appeared everywhere as an important element of Yarmuk's public space, frequently displayed on posters hung onto the walls of buildings along the sideway. Yarmuk had a politicized feel to it with regard to the continuing struggle for the liberation of Palestine and the role that Palestinian refugees and Syria as their host played in it. In this manner, Yarmuk's public spaces served as a link to refugees' Palestinian homeland and shaped the way second-, third-, and fourth-generation Palestinians, born in Syria, experienced Palestine, its heritage and politics.[7]

Yet this vivid expression of Palestinian life functioned *also* as a manifestation of Syrian domestic state sovereignty and the al-Asad government's dominance. None of Yarmuk's Palestinian activism would have been possible without government sanction, and only such activism was tolerated that matched the government line. Public support for the Palestinian cause was a pillar of official Syrian policy, even if it was only lip service. The government's self-portrayal as a staunch defender of the historically most central "Arab" cause was crucial to its image as a regional leader and enemy of Israel. Many observers believed that this image also served an important role for the government's domestic legitimacy. Yet the politically active Syrians and Palestinians I met during my research were all too knowledgeable of the government's duplicity in this regard and correctly believed that Palestinians would quickly be "sold down the road" if they no longer served a purpose. The particularly brutal crackdown on Yarmuk after the camp joined the uprising (though waiting several months to do so) showed this, as did the situation of Palestinian refugees from Iraq, who became marooned in No Man's Land in 2009 after the Syrian government failed to allow them entry.

But in 2010, allowing for the expression of a particular Palestinian identity in Yarmuk was still in line with the government's tactical preferences. No other political statements, let alone any that may have been critical of the government, appeared in Yarmuk, even though many residents had reason to be dissatisfied, and in private conversations expressed this. But Yarmuk was not a sudden oasis of freedom of expression in Damascus's urban landscape otherwise fully cluttered by Ba'th Party propaganda and presidential power. Instead, the way that Palestinian identity appeared in Yarmuk indicated how Syrian state sovereignty was confirmed, justified, and enforced in relation to the Palestinian issue. Through portraying itself as a protector of "Palestine," the Syrian government created boundaries—between Syria and Palestine as distinct spheres of control, between the Syrian and Palestinian population, between Syria and Israel, and between Syria and the international community—wherein the question of Palestine occupies a wide range of diplomatic activities, and in which Syrian state figures could yet again perform Syrian sovereignty.

One evening, I met with a Palestinian friend, a man who had worked with various Palestinian organizations and was experienced in dealing with Syrian state agents. I remarked to him that I had noticed that more young Palestinians appeared to be interested in politics than their Syrian counterparts. Yazan explained that because of the Syrian government's support for the Palestinian liberation struggle, Palestinians, in certain areas, had more freedom to discuss and get involved with politics than Syrians. For example, he told me with an ironic smile, if his organization was interested in running a workshop on human rights, the government would not allow it. However, if the workshop were framed as support for the human rights of Palestinians, they would have a much better chance in going ahead. It was in this light that the expression of Palestinian politics in Yarmuk could be explained, not as a contradiction to other urban areas where no political statements other than loyalty to the president and Syrian patriotism were tolerated, but as a confirmation of the same approach.

The situation of Palestinian refugees from Iraq, who began to arrive in Syria from 2003 onward, highlighted the government's duplicity toward Palestinian liberation. From around 2008 onward, the government began refusing entry to Palestinians arriving from Iraq, where they were experiencing particular violence for being perceived as winners of Saddam's policies.[8] Unable to return to Iraq, several thousand Palestinians became stranded in the small strip of desert known as "No Man's Land" between the Iraqi and Syrian border posts, in two dismal camps meagerly serviced by the UN. According to UN employees, the Syrian government's justification for this policy was that these Palestinians should be allowed to travel to their original homes in Palestine, and that allowing them into Syria undermined the Palestinian right to return. Of course, these Palestinians had no chance of traveling to or entering Israel. To prove its rhetorical point, the Syrian government was willing to allow Palestinians from Iraq suffer unbearable conditions and even curtailed humanitarian assistance. The two border camps reminded Palestinians and Syrians alike of how precarious Palestinians' existence in Syria was, and that they were at the mercy of the government's generosity. Here, once again, Palestinian bodies and spaces served as a mechanism to reaffirm Syrian statehood, albeit in a shifting and typically ambiguous way.

The Iraqi Neighborhood Jaramana

Like Yarmuk, the suburb Jaramana, where I lived during field research, also lay to the south of central Damascus. A bus journey from central Damascus to Jaramana took around 20 minutes. Until the early 2000s Jaramana had been sparsely populated, retaining its fields, small farms, and rural character, and had a mixed population of mostly Christian and Druze residents. Since the upsurge in Iraqi migration in 2006, Jaramana became known as a neighborhood dominated by Iraqis. The influx of people had contributed to an ongoing building boom that destroyed most of Jaramana's remaining fields. In 2010, around half of Jaramana's apartment blocks were newly built, including many unfinished, concrete shells that were nevertheless inhabited owing to demographic pressure. Typical for the rapid and unplanned development of many Syrian suburbs, parts of Jaramana's previous rural infrastructure, such as an old water tower, small gardens, and the occasional farm shed, were simply left standing as they were overtaken by urban growth, now obsolete and lacking any apparent ownership or stewardship. The lack of urban planning and state interest in it, emphasized by the absence of paved roads between brand-new five-story apartment blocks and the sudden appearance of parcels of farmland or open, sandy squares between rapidly developed residencies, gave Jaramana an atmosphere of change.

Unlike the official and government-sanctioned expression of Palestinian identity in Yarmuk, in Jaramana Iraqi identity was made visible exclusively through the private activity of the inhabitants. Iraqi presence showed, for example, in the Iraqi names of many restaurants and shops that had sprung up, as well as in the sale of specifically Iraqi goods, such as Iraqi flags, key rings with Iraqi images, and Iraqi food. Restaurant signs reading "Mosul" or "Baghdad" were the most easily recognizable, but insiders also recognized outlets of major Baghdadi restaurant chains and shops. A large number of travel companies advertising journeys to Iraqi cities were further signs marking the Iraqi character of Jaramana. More indirectly, the large number of real estate agents pointed to the existence of a transient population seeking rented accommodations. Jaramana was also the only place in Damascus where I saw secondhand clothing shops. These shops were unique to Iraqi areas of Damascus and catered to those Iraqis who, once selected for resettlement or immigration, were keen to sell those belongings they could not transport. On an earlier visit to Jaramana in 2007, I had noticed that many explicitly Iraqi shop and restaurant signs had been destroyed or covered up with tin foil. Residents had explained that Syrian security forces had demanded that Iraqi shop owners display their nationality less visibly. Three years later, the authorities' position on this matter clearly had changed, as Iraqi names were now displayed frequently. Iraqis had moved from being seen as a threat to social stability to being considered an emerging social field in which the government could confirm Syrian sovereignty in a greater variety of ways than simple prohibition.

Still, in stark contrast to Yarmuk, no signs of expressed political activity were visible in Jaramana. Nothing indicated any official support for Iraqi refugees or any position toward the highly politicized issue of postwar Iraq. Instead, Jaramana was covered in standard Syrian government propaganda; one of Jaramana's main squares was called President's Square (Saḥat al-Raīs) and had a bust of Hafiz al-Asad. While roads and sewage and water pipes sat unfinished, several of the new billboards with Bashar al-Asad's image already dotted the main thoroughfare. But there were no posters stating any particular opinion on the American-led invasion of Iraq, or on the current political situation in Iraq, or any other element of Iraqi politics.

This suddenly changed in February 2010. Iraqi parliamentary elections were scheduled for early March, and as in the first post-Saddam elections in 2005, Iraqis abroad were allowed to participate. To widespread amazement, the Syrian government not only permitted the establishment of voting locales, which it had already done in 2005, but also tolerated a blizzard of electoral campaigning in the Iraqi-dominated neighborhoods of Jaramana and Saida Zainab. Overnight, banners and posters advertising dozens of different candidates and their parties appeared all over the areas. The normally prominent images of Asad were erased from view by the sheer amount and variety of male and female headshots scattered across the streets. My Iraqi friends reported having campaigners at their doorstep without interference by Syrian intelligence or security agents. On the day of the elections, ballots were cast peacefully, and when Ayad Allawi, a secular and nonsectarian candidate, was announced as the winner on Iraqi television, Jaramana erupted in a street party that lasted the whole night.

Seeing such vivid and spontaneous expressions of political participation in Syria was extraordinary. During the election period, Iraqi migration created a true space of exception in Syria's otherwise strictly controlled political sphere. Why the government decided to allow this freedom remained mysterious. Some observers speculated that the government's preference for Allawi, and an awareness that most Iraqis in exile would vote for him, prompted the casual approach to the elections. Perhaps the government believed that the pictures of celebrating and voting Iraqis would go around the world and improve Syria's image. Iraqi migration had created a space of intervention, or rather nonintervention, for the Syrian government, in which Syrian statehood was enforced and constructed. And as in Yarmuk, the ambiguous integration of Iraqis into Syrian society, where they were denied long-term legal residency but on the other hand freedoms akin to those of the resident population, made this construction of Syrian statehood possible.

Syrian Policies toward Iraqi Migration

By 2009 Iraqi migration had become a field of activity that brought Syrian authorities not only into direct contact with a new migrant population but also required interaction with a range of foreign institutions: UN agencies, international NGOs, donor states, and the media. These new interactions shaped Syrian statehood on different levels: domestically, as the presence of a new group of people residing on Syrian territory was negotiated, and internationally, as Iraqi refugees had become a matter of international concern, which influenced how the Syrian state and government were viewed on the international stage.

Iraqi Migration and the Syrian State's Domestic Sphere

Upon entry into Syria, Iraqis' passports received a stamp stating that the passport owner was not allowed to work in Syria.[9] Given the frequency with which Iraqis had to show their passports to different authorities, this declaration served as a constant visual reminder of the exceptional status of Iraqis living on Syrian territory. Foreign observers often mentioned the employment ban as a central element of the Syrian government's approach to Iraqis, and a reason why Iraqis were excluded from Syrian society. Many of my Iraqi interlocutors, notably those with a middle-class or academic background, also referred to it often. Yet puzzlingly, the more observations and conversations I conducted, the more contradictions to this apparently clear prohibition on Iraqi labor emerged, showing a much more nuanced way through which employment and investment by Iraqis was linked to state practices.

In certain areas of Damascus, signs of Iraqi employment and investment abounded. The majority of my male Iraqi acquaintances were either employed or self-employed. When asked about their jobs, Iraqis mentioned the ban rather as an additional hurdle on the difficult Syrian labor market, for example, because it prohibited working in higher-level jobs as a doctor or lawyer, and it banned Iraqis from working for the public sector. The employment ban was often mentioned together with the broader discrimination against Iraqi jobseekers, or the fact that Syrian unemployment was already high, or that cooperation and bribery of Syrian local authorities complicated the setting up of businesses. But I soon found out that in some areas Iraqis were indeed working as doctors or professors, and Iraqi investors had created a number of substantial new businesses. I concluded that Iraqis faced very similar conditions on the labor market as did Syrians, and that skills, money, and connections were far more important than nationality for success in the Syrian economy. This point was astutely summarized in an insightful research study on Iraqi employment conducted on behalf of UNHCR, for which twenty-one working Iraqis were interviewed. The study states:

> All the participants had a stamp on their residency card saying they were not allowed to work. They knew what the stamp meant, but this did not stop some from being puzzled at the idea of needing a permit to work. Many assumed that their working would be tolerated as they had seen other Iraqis doing so, and assumed that they also had the stamp forbidding them to work. "N" thought that permits were only needed for setting up businesses. "E" and "O" did not understand what a work permit was. "Z" left Iraq specifically to work and send remittances to his family in Iraq. He was not aware of any permit requirements and is working in a hotel without one.
>
> "G" was aware that she was not supposed to work. Her husband, a Chinese chef in Iraq, had applied to work in a Chinese restaurant in Dūmar. They said they would hire him if he went to get a work permit from the "National Leadership". Experience had taught "G" that work permits were not an issue in the Saīda Zaīnab neighbourhood. She believed that the Syrian government tolerated Iraqis working there, and

> setting up businesses too. She mentioned that there were Iraqis working as professionals in the medical clinics associated with the Haūzas (the Shia religious seminaries).[10]

These observations showed that the employment ban was not effectively upheld. The directive (or possibly habit) of border clerks to stamp Iraqi passports with a "no work" visa did not match the activities of municipal officials in charge of monitoring businesses, or even those of local security agents controlling neighborhoods. One Iraqi interlocutor, specifically asked about his experience setting up a small billiard salon, explained his interactions with the local municipality, his landlord, and local security. The fact that he and his business partner were Iraqis was not a problem, he stated. What eventually led to the abandonment of the project, despite its popularity with local young men, was that all profits were eaten up by bribes and quasi-bribes, which made the salon unviable.

Iraqis did not encounter the Syrian state as a single power with a united purpose, but rather very much as a construction in multiple locations, through multiple agencies and people. This "assemblage of technologies," as Aihwa Ong has described the complex arenas of behavior that together constitute statehood, produced an order, but this order could only be defined and understood in moments of time and place, as it could change in unpredictable ways.[11] State sovereignty clearly appeared as an agreed-on belief, constantly reinforced through instances of bureaucracy, violence, and propaganda. The micro techniques and everyday activities through which individuals and institutions mobilized Syrian state sovereignty to govern and to maintain their power was not agreed on and was in constant flux.

The effect of this grassroots tolerance of Iraqi work was that Iraqis developed into a dynamic, sustained, and visible population in Damascus, enhancing and changing consumption and business patterns in certain neighborhoods. Far from the humanitarian trope of refugees as helpless human beings in camps, Syrian state and government policies and politics allowed those Iraqis who had the means to build sustainable and occasionally thriving existences on Syrian territory. When questioned about this tolerance of Iraqi work, Iraqis and Syrians explained it with reference to the Syrian government. The brother of my Syrian landlady, who ran a small shoe factory and had employed Iraqis, explained that the government "closed both eyes" on the matter, as it knew that Iraqis had to make a living somehow. Iraqis referred to the fact that they were allowed to take only low-skilled jobs anyway (not fully correct), which was considered to take the threat out of their activity, and some Iraqis also directly stated that they believed the Syrian government wanted to help them.

Interestingly, even those Syrians critical of Iraqi immigration, who believed that Iraqis were taking over low-skilled jobs and pushing down wages, never referred to the possibility of enforcing the employment ban. Overall it appeared that in the political imagination of my interlocutors, whereas preventing Iraqis from entering or remaining on Syrian territory was an option available to the authorities, the stringent enforcement of an employment ban did not figure. In the Syrian and Iraqi context, it appeared fully logical and natural that an Iraqi restaurant owner would turn first to relatives and then to nearer or farther Iraqi acquaintances for staff. Such personal ties and power relations, often running across state borders, coexisted and criss-crossed state-related power structures, and their power was an accepted element of the sovereign order on Syrian territory.[12] The interactions between Iraqis and various representations of the Syrian state thus showed how, in the daily lives of Iraqis, the space around them was transformed into the domestic, sovereign sphere of the Syrian state via this infinite and constantly changing collection of human relationships. The physical and permanent elements of the state—borders, ministerial offices, and local municipalities—provided a constant reminder of the existence of a separate Syrian territory, making Syrian sovereignty visible and tangible, and representing it both domestically and internationally. But as an order of governance that implemented the abstract notions of "state," "government," "nation," and "foreignness," Syrian state sovereignty was always a constantly transforming set of power relations.

Among the frequent topics of conversations among my research participants, the matter of residency permits ranked at the top. The issuing and obtaining of such permits formed the chief encounter and relationship between Iraqis and the Syrian state, and a key element in the construction of Syrian domestic, sovereign space vis-à-vis Iraqi migration. The puzzling aspect of the permit question was that I never encountered an Iraqi who had actually been deported owing to the absence of a residency permit, although rumors of such deportations circulated. In general, both Iraqis and international aid workers expected deportations to occur when an Iraqi was involved in serious "wrongdoings," and in that case deportation would happen regardless of whether the person possessed a permit. Neither did it appear that Iraqis frequently experienced random passport checks for up-to-date residency permits. The importance allocated to the permit came rather from the fact that it was the one clearly defined, state-related bureaucratic routine that allowed Iraqis to systematically demonstrate their allegiance to the Syrian state, to show their willingness to conform to official requirements, and to obtain some form of justification, legality, and protection for their stay.

Residency permits were issued through the Office of Immigration and Passports and consisted of either a stamp in the passport or a separate ID card. They were mostly obtained and renewed through a personal visit to the office. Most foreigners living in Syria for longer than one month experienced this office. The main branch was located in the busy Baramka area and consisted of a four- or five-storied, run-down, dirty, concrete office block where clerks behind glass windows tended to queues of harangued people trying to figure out how to meet the needs of Syria's labyrinthine bureaucracy.[13] Iraqis could obtain residency permits for a range of reasons, although this range was not easily understood and not fixed. The most frequently encountered justification was having a child registered in school (which afforded a one-year permit for the whole family), but seeking medical services, membership in a professional union, membership in the Ba'th Party, or a UNHCR protection paper could work as well if the seeker paid bribes and had personal connections.

Depending on the type of permit received, Iraqis had to renew their papers every year or every three months; other variations also existed. Once a permit had expired and an Iraqi had spent some time without a permit, it was still possible to regularize the situation; however, there did not appear to be a standard procedure for this. The lack of clarity and varied information meant that news about how to obtain permits was eagerly exchanged among Iraqis. Whether because of deliberate opacity, bad rulemaking in the ministries, or badly trained clerks, the effect of this inconsistency regarding rules was to insert Syrian state sovereignty into daily-life considerations. Through the residency permit issue, the Syrian state became present in Iraqi consciousness as something to consider regularly, as something that required tending and physical and financial effort. Whether Iraqis considered obtaining the permit a matter of easy routine or as a significant worry (this strongly depended on an individual's situation), all were aware of the matter and had gone through inquiries and efforts to obtain a permit. The following interview extract serves as a typical example.

> RESEARCHER: At the moment, what kind of residency permit do you have?
>
> PARTICIPANT: We received a permit on the basis of the education of my youngest daughter. Before that, also because of Sally [the older daughter]. But I told you that Sally finished secondary school last year and now we depend on Sarti [name of youngest daughter], so now [*laughs*] she threatens us, if you don't give me something I will [*laughs*]. . . .
>
> RESEARCHER: How often do you go to the immigration office?
>
> PARTICIPANT: When we have to renew the permit each year, and they told us each time . . . you have to return back after one month, and then after . . . it depends on their rules. (Wife adds: Every three months!)
>
> RESEARCHER: So sometimes they give you one month, sometimes three months?
>
> PARTICIPANT: It depends on the rules! In the first year it was not like last year. Something changes all the time, you know. It depends on something, it belongs to the government.[14]

The residency issue transported the domestic Syrian state into the daily routines and even family relations of Iraqi migrants. The uncertainty of the regulations is highlighted, as is the acceptance of random changes, which were explained with reference to the government and served as a catchall explanation for matters beyond control and explanation: for those belonging to the government.

My interviews and observations among Iraqis only rarely touched on the matter of Syria's well-known and feared intelligence agencies. Apart from one case, referred to below, none of my research participants complained about surveillance or intimidation by security agents.[15] When queried about their fears regarding Syrian police or intelligence officers, most Iraqis pointed out that, as their papers were in order, they had nothing to worry about. A small number of acquaintances, notably those who had had difficulties obtaining a residency permit or were in an otherwise precarious situation, expressed concern about the possibility of random harassment or questioning. In general, participants characterized Syria as a place of safety and calm, comparing it with the disastrously dangerous situation in Iraq. Two interlocutors reported home visits by intelligence officers, but considered them normal security measures related to obtaining a residency permit.

However, one Iraqi woman I interviewed in November 2009 was an exception. As a feminist activist who regularly worked as an assistant to foreign journalists, maintained a network of international friends, and had traveled abroad to international conferences on women's rights, she had moved onto the radar of security officers. Maya had moved from Baghdad to Syria in 2005 to escape communal violence. Two years after her arrival, she was called in for unpleasant questioning by intelligence officers who, she discovered, had created an elaborate file on her life and activities since her arrival in Syria. More seriously, she subsequently discovered that she was subject to a travel ban and had to apply for permission every time she wanted to leave Syria.[16]

The Syrian government frequently deployed travel bans against Syrian intellectuals or political activists as a measure of harassment, intimidation, and oppression. Several of my Syrian acquaintances were subject to such a ban, but I was surprised to see it used against an Iraqi citizen. Deploying a travel ban against a foreign citizen was paradoxical from the perspective of modern state sovereignty. According to its logic, incarceration, deportation, or withdrawal of the residency permit would have been in keeping with the policy to exclude strangers from the national population. Instead, to control this Iraqi activist, Syrian intelligence services made use of their standard toolkit usually applied to Syrian activists. This indicated that Iraqis per se were not subject to increased controls from the security apparatus. Maya's situation highlighted that an individual's relationship to the Syrian state, and their ability to reside peacefully on its territory, depended much more on individual behavior than on systematic exclusion based on nationality. Iraqis were not singled out categorically or constructed as exceptional foreigners through consistent measures. Fear, red lines, and random government violence were as present in Iraqi life as elsewhere in Syria and functioned as a general device of control not specifically aimed at migrants.

Iraqi Migration and the Syrian State's International Sphere

Managing Iraqi migration did not just entail dealing with a new migrant population. It also required government strategies toward aid organizations, diplomats, and foreign media. To this so-called international community, which was in fact dominated by a handful of donor states, Syrian officials spoke about Iraqis according to the concepts of international refugee aid. In speeches and articles, they portrayed Iraqis as a destitute community that was draining Syrian public funds. The Syrian government's reasons for allowing Iraqis access to public resources were pity and kindness.[17] At the time, Syria had an international status as a pariah state, and Syrian officials seized on the legitimizing potential of Iraqi immigration to improve Syria's acceptance.[18] Ironically, Syria's weak application of the expectation that a state should close its borders to a mass influx of migrants allowed Syrian officials to point out Syrian generosity; in this way they portrayed the Syrian state's management of migration not as "unsovereign" but as a generous exception to the rule that Iraqi migrants should, if sovereignty were properly applied, be systematically excluded (even if this rule had never existed or applied to Iraqis in Syria).

At a UNHCR conference held in Geneva in April 2007, the official Syrian presentation included the following abstract:

> In the spring of 2003 the region witnessed the biggest exodus from Iraq to its neighbouring countries. The Syrian Arab Republic was one of the first countries targeted by this exodus. The Syrian government and people moved to offer a safe haven for the Iraqi brothers and sisters from different spectrums and social affiliations including children, women and elderly, who fled the destruction and dangers inflicted on them. Syria

> offered and is still offering those refugees all possible help and assistance necessitated by the ties of brotherhood and neighborliness, despite the scarcity of material and financial potentials. . . . It is noteworthy that regulations in Syria do not require an entry visa for Arabs.[19]

The quote demonstrates some of the contradictions in the construction of Syrian international statehood. On the one hand Syria is presented as a separate sovereign terrain through reference to its borders, government, and people, on the other hand emphasis is placed on the fact that "Arabs"—a vague identity—enjoyed visa-free access to Syrian territory. The image that emerges from this quote is that of a caring sovereign, and of a government and people that move in unison, happy to allow those living in the dangerous outside access to their secure and orderly inside territory: classic rhetorical, sovereignty-producing strategies.[20] The Syrian government officials who wrote the speech were demonstrably aware of the values and idealized social relations required from a good, liberal sovereign on the international stage, even if the political reality within Syria did not correspond to these.

Despite strong UNHCR lobbying, Syria had not joined the Geneva Refugee Convention, and the Syrian state's relationship with UNHCR was governed by surprisingly ad hoc arrangements, given the extent of the agency's operations in the country.[21] Until summer 2010, when UNHCR signed a cooperation agreement with the Syrian Ministry of Foreign Affairs, the agency operated on the basis of informal partnership agreements with specific ministries, such as the Ministry of Health or the Ministry of Education.[22] Also in 2010, UNHCR signed a memorandum of understanding with the Syrian Ministry of Social Affairs, which regulated UNHCR's cooperation with local associations, as well as a partnership agreement with the Syrian Women's Union, a quasi-government organization.[23] The absence of systematic arrangements with even such a powerful actor as UNHCR emphasized the extent to which unpredictability and instability served as an element of governance in Syria, and how this instability blurred the boundaries between state, government, and personal power. By denying UNHCR an independent legal standing, Syrian state agents asserted not just Syrian state sovereignty vis-à-vis the organization, but also the influence of particular ministers and their staff. At the same time, these piecemeal arrangements weakened the notion of the Syrian state being a unified institution with a legal existence independent of the sum of its parts. Rather than affirming the existence of an independent state, as an overall agreement with the Syrian Arab Republic would have done, these ad hoc agreements confirmed the existence of a multitude of entities, each drawing power from an assumed attachment with the state, ultimately backed up by the implicit understanding and threat that support for UNHCR's operations could be at any time withdrawn. In Syrian-UNHCR relations, Syrian state sovereignty appeared as a web of social relations and implicit understandings that contained certain beliefs about the power of Syrian state institutions, which, though not regularly tested openly, were signaled to UNHCR employees through the harassment of low-level UNHCR associates and NGOs by state security agents.[24]

The flexible arrangements that Syrian institutions struck with UNHCR gave the agency room to maneuver on Syrian territory, supposedly exclusively controlled by the Syrian state. Through this maneuvering, UNHCR's actions dominated areas of governance usually understood to be the exclusive realm of the state. One interesting example of how UNHCR's activities undermined Syrian sovereignty concerned the treatment of gay Iraqi migrants. Even though homosexual acts were prohibited by Syrian law and state agents regularly cracked down on gay people, UNHCR could extend special protection to gay Iraqis experiencing persecution due to their sexual orientation and prioritize their resettlement to the United States.[25] Not only was Syrian state law concerning the public order reversed by UNHCR but, more important, the conduct of persons on Syrian territory was also determined on a very basic and strongly normative level, given the religious and cultural controversy surrounding homosexuality, by UNHCR. Further, given that UNHCR had a mandate only for intervening in Iraqi lives and could not extend protection to persecuted Syrian gays or other vulnerable Syrians, UNHCR's activities had an impact on the ordering of the population living on Syrian territory and the shape of the body politic. UNHCR's activities led to an imagined disentangling of Syrian passport holders, considered the legitimate residents on Syrian territory, and the alien Iraqis, who needed to be managed through international intervention until their sovereignty-disturbing presence would be somehow neutralized. A similar argument could be made about UNHCR's significant welfare provisions to Iraqis, which continued at a time when the Syrian state did not provide such services to poor Syrians, even those in greater desperation, and to other areas.

It appears surprising that the Syrian government allowed UNHCR such scope of intervention. I argue that UNHCR's areas of intervention were simply not relevant to the government's strategies of power, and were therefore tolerated and perhaps not even highly perceived. The fact that a gay Iraqi's particular situation, out of coincidental reasons, included access to UNHCR protection, which facilitated a positive resolution of his problem with the Syrian state, was not an affront to Syrian sovereignty, even though UNHCR favored this person in direct contradiction to Syrian state law. Other persons on Syrian territory committing illegal acts may circumvent the law because of their wealth or their personal relationship to someone who could manipulate state institutions. Such an analysis of the maintenance of Syrian state sovereignty within Syrian territory makes it possible to understand how sovereignty is truly created via relationships and human activity, especially in Syria, where the legal codifications of the state were weak.

The increased presence of foreign humanitarian nongovernmental organizations in Syria was one of the most remarkable aspects of Iraqi immigration. Prior to 2008, foreign NGOs were largely absent from Syria, and the Iraqi issue acted as a catalyst for their entry. Since 2005, the Syrian government's economic-policy statements had pointed toward increased participation of NGOs in the country's economic development.[26] The activities of the president's wife, Asma al-Asad demonstrated an increasing interest to build a development sector in Syria focusing strictly on economic and social welfare issues rather than political empowerment or human rights. This approach, in which basic services are moved out of the state sector to third parties, is an established element of neoliberal economic development and has been observed in other Middle Eastern countries, notably Egypt.[27] The move toward economic deregulation led to open disagreements among Syrian government figures, pitching more traditional Ba'thists, concerned about the effect on poverty and Syrian industry, against the modernizers favored by the president.[28] The Iraqi issue may have served as a convenient opportunity for the modernizers to allow the registrations of foreign NGOs. Initially, foreign NGOs were to provide services only to Iraqis; toward the end of 2009, it was becoming clear that services were also increasingly provided to Syrians, if on a very small scale. With around a dozen medium-sized NGOs active, overall NGO activity in Syria remained relatively low in 2009 and 2010.[29]

Unlike the relations between the Syrian state and UNHCR, NGO relations with the state were codified and formal. For a foreign NGO to become active in Syria, it needed to obtain formal approval from the Syrian Ministry of Foreign Affairs. After this, a memorandum of understanding had to be signed with the Syrian Arab Red Crescent, a quasi-governmental organization associated with the Ministry of Health. This memorandum was the key document authorizing an NGO's activities. The registration process for foreign NGOs was notoriously difficult and lengthy. NGOs had to wait for at least one year to obtain the required paperwork.[30] Further, once operations had begun, NGOs were subjected to regular and intensive controls by security agents and ministry staff. Rumors about the extent of state harassment circulated among foreign-aid workers, often mentioned with hushed excitement, as the "dangers" of working in Syria lent NGO work importance and a degree of adventure.[31] In fact, such harassment generally targeted Syrian staff with direct and regular contact with Iraqi aid recipients. Foreigners were rarely targeted, instead agents relied on Syrian colleagues to relay any messages to their foreign managers.[32] Open surveillance of senior aid staff was avoided, given the likelihood that this would have weakened Syria's international image. Harassing those whose plight would not engage international interest strengthened Syrian state sovereignty, as the induced fear served to uphold internal acquiescence and the impression that the people living on Syrian territory were happy with the representation provided by the Syrian government, all necessary attributes of a truly sovereign state.[33] In the case of NGOs, targeted control served to check the activity of a sector nominally independent of state interference and with a reputation for democracy promotion and human-rights advocacy. Critical government insiders, who were opposed to the growing international presence, could also construe NGOs as foreign agents with hidden agendas, increasing the importance of close control. The treatment of NGOs as political actors rather than technical helpers was highlighted by the notable absence of British or large American NGOs, two countries with which Syria has had historically difficult relations, especially in the aftermath of the Iraq War. Instead, the NGOs allowed to operate represented a selection of relatively small French, German, Danish, Turkish, Spanish, Italian, and two small US NGOs.[34]

The entry of NGOs into Syrian territory contained a transformative element for Syrian state sovereignty and presented a difficult political issue for the government. The presence of a vibrant NGO sector would signal to the international community the Syrian government's tolerance of plurality and thus increase the impression of its representativeness and its sovereign credentials. Further, NGO activity would suggest that Syria had now arrived among those governed by the Washington consensus of liberal economic rule, an additional signal that the Syrian government was rational and interested in increasing economic dynamism and thus the welfare of its people.[35] In this way, NGO presence bolstered Syrian sovereignty vis-à-vis powerful states in Europe and in the United States, which, at best, could lead to the lowering of economic sanctions, mitigate the possibility of future military interventions, and lead to financial payoff in terms of donor money and other donations (as was already happening in 2009–10).

But for the maintenance of domestic sovereignty, NGO presence was much more tricky and possibly destructive. NGOs and their foreign employees could attract international attention to negative social, political, and economic conditions in Syria and undermine the credibility and legitimacy of state institutions, as Amnesty International and Human Rights Watch regularly did. Through constant, low-level reminders of state power, NGOs were made to fear that their operations could be easily shut down in case of official displeasure. Despite its openness toward aid money and socioeconomic development, the government remained adamantly against the development of a politicized civil society focused on transforming the relationship between the people living on Syrian territory and the Syrian government.[36] The civil society that the government's modernizers were trying to foster should rather bolster the regime's legitimacy by providing welfare and promoting "Syrian civilization."[37]

How to Distinguish State and Government in Syria?

Since 1970, the al-Asad family has controlled Syria's government. This government has in turn, over the decades, achieved a near-to-complete control of Syria's state institutions, including ministries, state industries, and the army. This overlapping of the government and state apparatus—formally distinct aspects of statehood—makes it difficult to disentangle centers of power in Syria. In the following paragraphs, I briefly explain the way the terms "government" and "state" are used in this book.

According to the standard political science understanding of statehood, a state is made up of various independent but interlinked components. These include basic elements such as a territory, a population, but also institutions and infrastructure, as well as the specific bodies designed to run the state, that is, the government. The individuals who staff the government are a further independent factor. The relationship between these different components is determined by the law, which enshrines their independence of each other.

On paper, Syria is a liberal nation-state in which elections determine the persons who temporarily control the government, which controls the state apparatus. But decades of al-Asad-dominated rule have led to a situation in which the law has ceased to function and state institutions are no longer independent. Rule has become personalized, and the persons who control the government can manipulate and use state institutions as they see fit. State security institutions no longer guard the law, but rather protect whoever controls them. Syria has experienced a gradual merging of government, state, and individual power. Yet despite this merging, it is, of course, still possible to discern the basic "material" that makes up the Syrian state: its territory, its population, and its infrastructure. These are all things that will last beyond the al-Asad government, albeit in possibly radically altered form. And it is in this sense that I speak of the Syrian state in this book. For example, one of the well-known characteristics of the Syrian government was its reliance on an extensive internal intelligence apparatus to monitor and intimidate the population. Key to the power of this apparatus was the lack of legal remedy against it, as actions by internal intelligence officers were beyond the law. No redress for transgressions against habeas corpus or other human rights were available, at least not along official paths. The patronage networks between government and intelligence personnel blurred the distinction between state and government to an extreme degree. Certain individuals controlled state institutions (such as the presidency) and state infrastructure (such as the security apparatus) to exercise their power. Through this process of personalization, these state institutions had now become part of the current government, or even individual rule, rather than representative of the state. Similarly, although intelligence services mainly monitored for criticism of government figures, the punishments meted out often made use of elements of state power, such as deportations, travel restrictions, prisons, or the withdrawal of licenses, or of public-sector positions or law courts.

The al-Asads' extensive ownership of the Syrian state also potentially confuses my discussion of sovereignty. In this book, sovereignty is discussed both in its abstract, international sense, which concerns the division of the world's territory into distinct states, and in its concrete, domestic sense, which concerns the reproduction of control and power over a population. The Iraqi migration crisis was heavily shaped by sovereignty in the abstract, which includes the belief that every person necessarily has to be a citizen of some state to exercise their rights, as well as sovereignty in the concrete, by how the Syrian government controlled the people under its power. Although as long as he remains in power, Bashar al-Asad's personal sovereignty is closely interwoven with Syria's state sovereignty, in this book I analyze this personal sovereignty as only one aspect through which the Syrian state was elevated to the most powerful actor position within Syria's domestic sphere.

Conclusion

The Syrian uprising brought into public view the dark side of Syrian politics, where political opponents are destroyed at all costs. Structurally, this attitude had existed for decades. But other elements of the revolution and the politics it may herald give rise to more difficult questions, including, paradoxically, the question of how thoroughly violent and despotic the al-Asad government actually was during times of peace. What does the dichotomy of authoritarian and liberal mean today in terms of state control over everyday life? This is a key question that the Syrian revolution forces us to address.

On the spectrum between authoritarian and liberal, the al-Asad government was considered by most Western analysts to be firmly on the authoritarian end. The absence of meaningful popular representation, the personality cult, the suppression of all political opposition, and the widespread use of an enormous surveillance apparatus indicated this. Yet a close observation of daily life in Syria before the war also revealed areas of life that were much less prone to regulation and control than in liberal democracies, where the combination of encompassing state efficiency with highly developed markets leaves almost no area of daily life untouched and unmonitored by state power.

In the powerful states of Europe and North America, public institutions ranging from national revenue services, residency bureaus, police files, and child protection agencies to state pension funds hold detailed information about citizens' private lives. Although legal barriers technically prevent the sharing of this information between state agencies, in cases of investigation or prosecution these barriers soften, and no citizen could be really surprised that the state holds vast knowledge of private activity—it is frequently collected by consent and openly. Yet in Syria, the state had not been developed to this degree of administrative definition and efficiency. It was not inserted in people's lives in a systematic and deeply invasive fashion. Although at a basic level Syria's public administration functioned well, the absence of personalized welfare systems or care or protection agencies meant that state bureaucracies held much less systematically organized knowledge about people's lives than in highly bureaucratized states and were much less intimately intertwined with people's everyday lives. There existed no systematic, regulated interface between state and citizen, which, on the one hand, left much more room for personal freedoms and personal chances to bend the state's power in one's favor, yet on the other hand also enabled despotic violence and oppression with no oversight or control.

This characteristic of the way state sovereignty appeared in people's daily lives in Syria became particularly apparent during the sudden influx of Iraqi migrants between 2006 and 2010.

Faced with Iraqi migration, Syrian state institutions were required to intervene on two levels: domestically and internationally. Observing these interventions made it possible to understand how Iraqi migration became an arena in which the spatial and social arrangements, on which state sovereignty is based, were created through constant activities. The domestic interventions relied on the existing mix of violence and laissez-faire politics to confirm the state's dominance over Syrian territory and the people living on it. This approach afforded Iraqis much wider leeway to thrive and integrate than is expected regarding migrants by the assumptions of a modern national state sovereignty. As long as Iraqis maintained the essential "red lines" that prohibited criticism of the government and led low-key existences, their success or failure in Syria depended more on their wealth, connections, and skills than on the fact that they held a different nationality. The constant affirmation of a united national population did not belong to the essential techniques of the Syrian government's domestic sovereignty construction. The (mythical) maintenance of representative politics, in which the government is an expression of national will, which is so important to liberal state sovereignty, was not important in Syria. As a consequence, neither was the systematic exclusion of migrants.

Nevertheless, in their interactions with the international actors who became involved in Syrian affairs as a consequence of the Iraqi migration crisis, Syrian government officials conformed to the norms set by modern national state sovereignty. At international meetings and in international publications, Iraqis were portrayed as a group of foreign citizens outside of the Syrian nation who had been generally accepted onto Syrian soil but remained fundamentally distinct. To manage this external population, Syrian officials claimed, Syria required the helping hand of international humanitarianism and donor states. By adopting this internationally accepted jargon and concept of migration and flight, the Syrian state performed in accordance with internationally hegemonic standards of liberal state sovereignty, in this manner boosting its membership in the international community and its recognition as a responsible government. Here, the construction of international space as the other side of state sovereignty's global structure became apparent.

This distinction between Syria's international state sovereignty, in which the appearances of liberal and nation-based rule were upheld, and Syria's domestic state sovereignty, which depended on nonliberal and nonnational techniques of rule, was striking. It pointed to a number of very important elements of the international order. First, it gave insights into how the construction of domestic and international spaces, a central element of state sovereignty, is achieved through and embedded in everyday interactions between governments, populations, and international organizations. Second, it confirmed the existence of an internationally hegemonic standard, or "ideal" of state sovereignty, that is shaped along liberal, national, and representative politics. This ideal, on such crucial institutions of international diplomacy as the UN are based, is the yardstick according to which a state's fitness and acceptability into the international community is measured. Despite the fact that domestically, Syrian state power relied on very different techniques, in international forums, it complied with the ideal. And third, it showed the particular ways in which postcolonial states navigate the demands of state sovereignty and the tensions that arise from the fact that their domestic arrangements of sovereignty do not match international norms.

3

UNHCR and Iraqi Migration

Parallel Sovereignty

One of the consequences of the sudden increase of Iraqi migration to Syria was a rapid expansion of the UN refugee agency UNHCR's operations. Previously, Syria had been largely isolated from humanitarian discourse and practice. UNHCR's framework and mandate reflect the internationally hegemonic ideal of liberal, national statehood and the social relations that underpin it. From 2007 onward, UNHCR introduced to Syria a parallel system of migration management alongside that of the Syrian government. In this chapter, I begin with an overview of UNHCR's operations in Syria and then make a political analysis of its resettlement and humanitarian programs. Throughout I seek to demonstrate that UNHCR's entire modus operandi is, ironically, based on singling out and exceptionalizing refugees. Compared with the Syrian government's laissez-faire approach to Iraqis, UNHCR thus set up programs that produced Iraqi identity as distinct from the Syrian population. The chapter concludes with some thoughts on whether and how UNHCR's projects blurred common understandings of authoritarian and liberal governance.

UNHCR, founded in 1946 to help manage the millions of displaced persons after the Second World War, is an organization in constant flux. It has undergone significant changes in the interpretation of its mandate in the past twenty years. Yet UNHCR's statutes, in particular the 1951 Geneva Refugee Convention, remain based on ideas of national statehood prevalent in the first half of the twentieth century. The UN founders understood the world as demarcated into powerful, clearly bordered nation states in which the government-citizen relationship is envisaged as one of protection and responsibility. UN documents of this time consistently speak of nations as the natural origins of states and political community.[1] But since the 1990s UNHCR has increasingly integrated with the global humanitarian sector, which merges economic deregulation, humanitarianism, and international law into a set of beliefs about how the world should be governed.[2] This approach is often portrayed by its proponents as *opposing* state sovereignty, for example, in the case of humanitarian intervention undertaken by the international community in a sovereign state to protect human rights or other matters considered to be threatened by state power.[3] But this is misleading. Instead of being opposed to state sovereignty per se, this approach simply favors one particular *form* of state sovereignty.

UNHCR has over the decades developed an enormous repository of knowledge about refugees and migration. The conclusions and programs drawn from this knowledge are distributed by UNHCR to wherever its activities reach. In this way the organization has created deterritorial and potentially global interventions into situations of migration that reduce the experience of migrants to a set of similar factors. UNHCR's interventions are, with regard to state sovereignty, teleological, as they contain very strong assumptions about what the correct relationship between persons and their government should be and about the rights that a citizen of a sovereign state should enjoy. These interventions also have hegemonic potential, as no other institution comes close to rivaling UNHCR in terms of knowledge, mandate, funds, or reach on matters of forced migration. UNHCR's written and spoken texts repeat the organization's commitment to human rights and its mandate to protect refugees from violence throughout. An analysis of these texts could thus conclude that UNHCR is a fundamentally liberal organization that aims to shape refugee lives in accordance with the Enlightenment ideals of citizenship and productivity. UNHCR's programs, as described in its own texts, amount to essentially biopolitical techniques that elevate refugees, broadly understood to be poor, deviant, and sick, to legal membership of society and prepare them to be handed over to the disciplinary apparatus of a sovereign state where, if they adapt their behavior accordingly, they will flourish.

In Syria, UNHCR's programs produced Iraqi identity in a way that revealed on the one hand its historical understanding of state sovereignty, borders, citizens, territory, and government. On the other hand, the programs also showed how far UNHCR had moved away from the narrow framework provided in the 1951 Refugee Convention. Formal UNHCR rhetoric categorized Iraqis in Syria as refugees, in need of broadly defined protection. This categorization displayed UNHCR's implementation of old-fashioned state sovereignty: Syria and Iraq were understood as two separate, sovereign territories whose borders clearly established distinct national identities and protective citizen-government relations. Once a citizen had lost the protection of his or her national government and had been forced to flee owing to this loss, UNHCR assumed that its intervention became necessary to enable the refugee to slot back into a system of state sovereignty, in which the individual floundered and floated as long as no state would offer protection by awarding the person a sovereignty-conformed identity.[4] Iraqis were cast in these terms by UNHCR Damascus.[5]

But in the nitty-gritty, day-to-day work of UNHCR's programs, protection for Iraqis translated narrowly into a concern for their physical welfare and for those matters that would enable them to become self-sufficient, economically stable persons: education and access to jobs. This very particular understanding of protection blended out any questions of political protection—in relation to which the Refugee Convention was in fact designed—and raised two interesting points: first, that UNHCR was adapting to the Syrian government's oppression of political freedom easily and rapidly, and second, that UNHCR's humanitarian discourse and conceptualization of refugees as nonpolitical bodies with chiefly physical needs made this adaptation astonishingly easy. This approach to Iraqi plight was linked very much to UNHCR's post-1990s expanded humanitarian role and its adoption of humanitarian governance techniques that depoliticized recipients of aid across the globe.[6]

The relevance of UNHCR's interventions in Syria lay not only in what they revealed about humanitarian values and ideas, a focus that has been developed relatively extensively in the literature.[7] In the Syrian context, these interventions also indicated that humanitarian actors were vehicles for the introduction of particular governance techniques that were previously absent from Syria. These governance techniques transported norms and ideas about state sovereignty and thus alluded to one mechanism through which the transformation of the politics on which state sovereignty is built in local contexts may occur in reaction to globally dominating ideas and practices. UNHCR's own reports about its Middle East operations showed how the organization was adapting to the characteristics of regional states, thus illustrating the intensely dynamic character of such transformations that do not, as is often assumed in critical literature, simply flow from the powerful metropolis into the postcolony, but through constant exchange.[8]

UNHCR's Operations in Damascus: An Overview

In 2006 UNHCR Syria operated on a budget of USD 1.4 million and out of a tiny office in downtown Damascus. In 2007, its budget exploded to USD 60 million, by 2009 it reached USD 130 million, and in 2010 it stood at USD 166 million. This was a staggering increase for any organization to manage in such a short time. In 2013, in the wake of the huge and devastating flight of Syrians, UNHCR asked for a budget of USD 1.4 *billion* to run the humanitarian effort inside Syria (the region-wide request exceeded USD 5 billion). In the short space of six years, UNHCR-led humanitarianism in Syria had gone from virtually zero to becoming one of the richest and biggest sectors in the region.

By 2010 UNHCR had developed three new main sites in Damascus. Their setup, detailed below, reflected the contradictory and ironic relationship of UNHCR and UNHCR employees with aid recipients, in this case mainly Iraqi refugees. The contradictions of this relationship will be familiar to most analysts of humanitarianism. Here, the continued existence of desperate people ensures the simultaneous existence of well-paid and prestigious jobs for expatriates, whose stated raison d'être is nevertheless the amelioration of the desperate people's poverty or fear. In Syria, as elsewhere, the most senior UNHCR employees were the furthest removed from contact with Iraqi refugees, a situation mirrored by the spatial organization of the UNHCR sites. The more lowly and badly paid UNHCR staff were either Syrian or Iraqi, and were most closely in contact with aid recipients—called "beneficiaries" in aid-sector jargon. During visits to UNHCR facilities I witnessed how difficult UNHCR employees often found it to deal with "beneficiaries," sometimes treating them as annoying petitioners rather than persons with a right to UNHCR's services. High in their upper-floor offices in separated buildings, senior UNHCR managers were shielded from any such stressful encounters.

In terms of this organizational hierarchy, the most important site was a newly built, modern, four-story office block on a main road in Kafar Sūsa, a rapidly developing area around 1 kilometer from Damascus center. The block was set around 50 meters back from the road in an unpaved building site of mud and rubble, and housed the central decision-making facilities of UNHCR in Syria, the offices of senior and middle-ranging UNHCR managers, meeting rooms, a cafeteria in a small garden, and, in the cellar, a small number of windowless and cell-like interview rooms. Entry to the building occurred through a metal gate and a reception area, where friendly receptionists sat behind two desks, asked visitors for their IDs, and handed out visitors' passes. The building's corridors and walls were richly decorated with UNHCR posters and advertisements displaying emotional portraits of refugees and words such as "courage," "hope," or "strength." Offices were set up in the familiar manner with desks, computers, and files, and the typical hierarchy of increasing office size and comfort according to managerial rank was visible.

The other two UNHCR sites, where the actual encounters between Iraqi migrants and UNHCR staff took place, were completely different in architecture and atmosphere. They resembled much more closely the harried atmosphere of the Syrian immigration authorities' run-down building in Baramka, lacking any pictures of happy refugees or the ordered interior decoration of the modern office. One site was located close to the central office block, though in a more removed and rundown site on a moderately busy side road. In this one-story building, simply constructed from corrugated iron, plywood, and tarps, UNHCR-registered Iraqis could seek different services each day of the week (Tuesdays, inquiries regarding resettlement status, Wednesday, legal aid, etc.). The center had a small, roofed outside waiting area and two separate entrances for men and women, through which one proceeded past a metal detector and into the waiting area, which had a warehouse feel (no pictures of hopeful refugees here) and rows of white plastic chairs. Although there was no cafeteria or garden, informal vendors offered soft drinks and snacks and there was a water fountain. As demand for services often outstripped the available space, a large crowd of dozens or sometimes hundreds of Iraqis regularly stood outside of the building waiting until the number they had been allocated would be called up, allowing them to proceed inside. This overcrowding and the long waiting times contributed to an atmosphere of disorganization and lack of consideration for the attending "beneficiaries."

The third main site consisted of a large warehouse complex 25 kilometers outside of central Damascus in the suburb of Dūma. This was where UNHCR conducted new registrations (the process through which Iraqis became recognized as refugees and received their protection paper) and where various kinds of clerks conducted the interviews with Iraqi families and individuals that were required during the registration and resettlement process. This facility, which at the time was UNHCR's largest registration facility in the Middle East and possibly the world, was also used for the distribution of food aid and consisted of warehouse halls, several large waiting rooms, and smaller interview rooms.

In addition to these main sites, UNHCR also ran a network of around eighty so-called outreach volunteers, all of whom were Iraqi women functioning as messengers between Iraqis and UNHCR. Each volunteer was responsible for a particular neighborhood and was in charge of alerting UNHCR to Iraqi poverty and of spreading information about UNHCR's programs by leaving her telephone numbers with local shopkeepers or wardens and by word of mouth.[9] UNHCR had developed this group in response to the absence of humanitarian NGOs, through which the organization usually conducts aid programs in a refugee crisis, when in 2007 it started responding to increased Iraqi migration. The lack of implementing partners in Damascus had left UNHCR initially without means to contact and collect information about the Iraqi community, making it difficult to target available assistance. As this lack was due to the Syrian government's reluctance to admit international NGOs to the country, the network of volunteers was an interesting sign of how state policies shaped

UNHCR's operating environment. The volunteers, who received a small monthly compensation for their expenses, met every two weeks at the UNHCR office. While speaking very highly of the volunteers and of the usefulness of this system, a senior UNHCR official also described it as heavily time consuming owing to the need to closely monitor the volunteers to prevent any abuse or misconduct.[10]

UNHCR was also indirectly present in the field through its funding of NGO programs, after the Syrian government began licensing such organizations in 2008. For example, UNHCR set up and funded six community centers in neighborhoods with Iraqi concentrations, which were later handed over to the NGO Danish Refugee Council and ran in cooperation with the Syrian Arab Red Crescent. These centers offered various training and counseling courses and sessions. UNHCR was the central funding vehicle for NGOs in Damascus. Finally, UNHCR also engaged in high-level and quiet diplomacy to lobby its position with regard to refugees and organized regional conferences and training workshops attended by government and other public officials.[11] By organizing charity concerts and festivities focused on the theme of Iraqi refugees the organization raised its profile among Damascene elites and the media. A biannual UNHCR Syria update, around ten pages long, provided regular statistics on recent developments and various puff pieces on the organization's activities.[12]

In 2010 UNHCR Syria employed around 200 staff, probably making it, according to one experienced UN consultant, the organization's second largest operation after Thailand at the time.[13] The resettlement program, discussed in detail below, was the largest service, employing around 60 staff, followed by the departments of registrations, community services, and protection. UNHCR's biannual update of summer 2010 states that it was at that time managing 151,907 Iraqis (54,054 families) who had registered as refugees since 2007. This presented a downward revision from UNHCR's winter 2009/10 update, which had reported 218,363 registered individuals (71,107 families). Although resettlement accounted for some of this trend (since 2007, 21,018 Iraqi individuals had departed for resettlement, according to UNHCR figures), UNHCR also "inactivated" the files of 15,900 individuals who had not had any form of contact with UNHCR during 2010, assuming that these persons were no longer resident in Syria.[14]

In UNHCR circles the Iraqi refugee operation, which also involved UNHCR offices in Jordan and Lebanon, was regarded as very new and exceptional, and indicative of the challenges that UNHCR had to grapple with in the Middle East and in relation to the issue of urban refugees, that is, refugees who do not reside in camps. These challenges included the lack of formal refugee legislation and UNHCR endorsement in Syria, Lebanon, and Jordan, and the precarious standing of UNHCR activities, which were tolerated rather than guaranteed. In this scenario, UNHCR could not roll out the international standard it liked to uphold, but had to negotiate with governments about how far they would adapt to such standards.[15] A further challenge was the fact that Iraqis in Damascus were obscured owing to their dispersion in the urban "jungle," which made it much harder for UNHCR to intervene than if they had been in camps. At that time, urban refugees, today a standard in the Middle East, were still considered exceptional and were the subject of a divisive special UNHCR policy.[16] UNHCR officials and publications repeatedly mentioned the absence of camps in Syria as a key difficulty, given that camps made it so much easier for UNHCR officials to assess, inform, supply, and control a refugee population. In addition, the large percentage of well-educated, relatively wealthy Iraqis in Syria meant that this was a refugee population harder to satisfy with regard to living conditions and more difficult to manage. In the words of one UNHCR manager working on the resettlement process:

> This is very different compared with an illiterate refugee population. These people ask questions and ask for information, they voice concerns and have expectations; they understand the process to a certain level. Also, this is the largest refugee operation UNHCR has and it is very different than a camp. . . . In a camp, I can go around, I know what is going on, but here it is not possible to know.[17]

This quote demonstrates the connection between *having knowledge about* and *having power over* a population and crystallizes the unequal relationship between UNHCR and the Iraqi population. UNHCR's anxiety about feeling out of control was due to its lack of information about the Iraqi population in Damascus. Similarly, Iraqi demands for information about UNHCR processes were attempts to obtain knowledge and power, and the unease expressed about this restful refugee population and attempts to empowerment vis-à-vis the organization showed UNHCR staff's limited desire to truly empower its "beneficiaries."

The irony that UNHCR was aiding often middle-class Iraqi migrants while many destitute Syrians remained beyond the organization's remit was not entirely lost on UNHCR managers. UNHCR and some of its partner NGOs made attempts to include Syrian internal migrants, most notably the poor farmers displaced to Damascus through the 2005 drought, into their work. By starting to speak and write about them as "internally displaced persons" humanitarian agencies fitted these Syrian poor within an established humanitarian concept and persona to whom certain knowledge and existing program templates applied. But at that time the Syrian government allowed only a limited expansion of humanitarian aid to the Syrian population. This only changed in 2012 when, after strong lobbying, the Syrian Arab Red Crescent (SARC) allowed UNHCR operations in aid of internal war refugees to begin inside Syria, although still under very close government control and not in all areas.

UNHCR ran four key operational units whose activities had a direct impact on Iraqi life: the registration unit, the community services unit, the protection unit, and the resettlement unit. The registration unit was in charge of interviewing Iraqis wishing to register and renewing their registration annually. To initiate registration, Iraqis would visit the center and receive an appointment by showing their Iraqi passport. In mid-2008, waiting time for the registration interview was two months owing to the large numbers of Iraqis wishing to register (an average of around eight thousand new registrations per month in 2008); however, by late 2009 the wait had been reduced to less than two weeks.[18] At the registration appointment, which all members of the family wishing to register were required to attend, Iraqis were asked to provide passports and Iraqi identity cards and fill in an application form, which requested information about the family's biodata, its previous situation in Iraq, and the reasons for departure in a narrative form. After completing the form and waiting for one's number to be called out, a Syrian UN clerk would conduct the interview based on the information provided in the application. In the official words of the UN, the registration interview served as the "first screening for special needs and identification of vulnerabilities."[19] Referral to and information about relevant UNHCR services could be administered through the clerk at this point. Photos were taken of each family member and each received a UNHCR protection document, valid for one year, and the family received a file number. The document, titled "Refugee Certificate," showed the owner's photo, name, nationality, date and place of birth, date and place of entry into Syria, and included a paragraph stating that the person had been recognized as a refugee by UNHCR and should, "in particular, be protected from forcible return to a country where he/she would face threats to his or her life or freedom. Any assistance accorded to the above-named individual would be much appreciated."[20] This document had to be presented to receive all other sorts of aid from UNHCR and affiliated NGOs.

The community services and protection unit cooperated to increase the broader protection space for Iraqi refugees in Damascus through identifying protection needs and developing programs to address them. This translated into running a variety of services via the above-mentioned community volunteer network, six support groups made up of Iraqis with a relevant background (for health, education, psychosocial issues, the elderly, people with disabilities, and unaccompanied and separated minors), twelve community support centers, and the UNHCR buildings at Kafar Sūsa and Dūma. UNHCR's 2010 "Regional Response Plan for Iraqi Refugees" reveals the extent of these community-based services and lists, including child-friendly spaces, vocational training, extracurricular activities and remedial classes for children, psychosocial counseling, adolescent empowerment programs, training of youth workers, life skills training, and support for victims of sexual violence.[21] UNHCR clerks and volunteers would alert Iraqis to these programs during any point of contact, or Iraqis could seek them out voluntarily. The protection unit, according to UNHCR reports, additionally focused on capacity building among Syrian officials involved in immigration through training and the provision of equipment, and raised awareness among the Syrian population on refugee issues.

Finally, the resettlement unit, at the time of research the largest unit in terms of staff, managed the complex process through which Iraqis were identified as qualifying for resettlement abroad and were matched with one of the participating resettlement countries.[22] If selected for resettlement, Iraqis received a permanent residency in the resettlement country as well as varying levels of financial and educational support, and thus, according to UNHCR logic, ended their refugee status. Resettlement was considered by UNHCR as one of three durable solutions to end refugee status, generally for the most vulnerable refugees, with selection criteria based on humanitarian and legal criteria. Whether a person would be considered for resettlement strongly depended on whether a third country had agreed to give UNHCR a resettlement quota for that particular group of refugees, and thus also on political questions. UNHCR documents and interviews talk about "filling quotas" or refer to estimates about how many persons could be submitted for resettlement in a given year, which were based on quotas provided by resettlement states. The availability of resettlement "places" therefore clearly influenced the selection process, and given UNHCR's urgent lobbying for more such places, it appeared unlikely that once a quota had been provided it would not be filled.[23] This presence of third countries in the resettlement process underscored that resettlement was a space of overlapping sovereignties.

In the case of Syria, each resettlement country informed UNHCR about the number of Iraqis it was willing to resettle in a given year and of any additional requirements. For example, Norway aimed to fulfil the 2009 quota to 55 percent with women.[24] UNHCR's task was to preselect and submit the required number of Iraqi files to the authorities of a country, but the final acceptance decision was made only after resettlement-country officials conducted a final interview with a proposed Iraqi; such interviews took place in Syria. The participation of various complicated bureaucracies and the sheer number of people and files involved meant that resettlement was a highly complex and work-intensive program. In addition, resettlement was high profile and controversial, and subject to much speculation and accusations of discrimination. This was partially because resettlement was so strongly desired by most UNHCR-registered Iraqis, and partially because of the deliberately opaque grounds by which files were selected and submitted. The long waiting periods between all decision-making steps, during which no information was provided to the Iraqi applicants, and which could stretch to months or even years, worsened the situation. The high work pressure on resettlement staff and the constant suspicion on all sides that Iraqis were trying to cheat their way into resettlement added to its contentiousness.

UNHCR's Conception of Statehood

UNHCR receives its mandate from the UN General Assembly. The aim of the mandate is to ensure the protection of refugees worldwide through various measures, including the lobbying of governments and the instructing of private organizations to assist in the task. The relevant UN documents define a refugee as a person who, owing to fear of persecution because of race, religion, nationality, membership in a particular social group, or political opinion, is unwilling or unable to secure the protection of his home country.[25] This definition sits, as do the documents as a whole, fully within the liberal, national ideal of statehood in which reified territories, borders, and populations are represented through the similarly fixed government technocrat who executes the will of the nation as embodied in a set of bureaucratic and legal rules. From this perspective, refugees are an anomaly, a living proof that the population-government-territory link has broken down or possibly never existed, resulting in the illogical situation that a government or a nation is persecuting its own people.[26] UNHCR and the 1951 Refugee Conventions sit like a band-aid on the international system, a corrective tool within international law, and as an afterthought following the realization that the firming up of postempire national sovereignty was creating exclusion and concentrated violence rather than islands of peace.

The inadequacy of the refugee convention, with its focus on the individual perception of fear of persecution, and its silence on situations of generalized violence, has been recognized.[27] The post-2003 Iraqi migration, in which many people fled the general insecurity that resulted from a mix of targeted persecutions, criminality, and the actions of the US Army, particularly highlighted the convention's shortcomings. But the key reason behind the convention's discrepancy with real-life refugee situations is its limited and normative understanding of statehood. If the convention would recognize that forced migration is not a result of the breakdown of a liberal, national state, but often a product of attempts to create it, and acknowledged that it often occurs in contexts where this form of politics is absent, it would call into question the entire universalizing system of international law and the United Nations, and its claim to peace, security, and human rights.

UNHCR in Syria did not apply international law by the letter. For example, the organisation accepted Iraqis as prima facie refugees, that is, it awarded refugee status automatically to every person from a particular region. Its particular notion of state sovereignty was observable in the organization's resettlement and humanitarian programs. To become deserving of resettlement abroad, which was regarded both by UNHCR staff and most Iraqis as the ultimate prize, Iraqis had to prove in great detail the foundations of their fear of persecution, their lack of (pro-Saddam and anti-West) political activity, and their poverty and suffering. The more vulnerable and lacking governmental protection a person was considered to be according to UNHCR criteria, the more likely resettlement and aid would be forthcoming. In other words, the more Iraqis lacked any of the characteristics of liberal citizenship, the more likely they would be regarded as true refugees and therefore in need of UNHCR's help. The intellectual puzzle and political relevance of this treatment of Iraqis in Syria by UNHCR lay in the fact that in Syria, the relationship between state, government, and population was not as assumed by UNHCR's concept of state sovereignty. "Citizenship," "governmental protection," and "nation" were all ideas only weakly recognizable from the lived experience of people on Syria's territory, whether they carried Syrian or Iraqi passports. Through its programs, UNHCR was transporting aspects of a liberal, national form of statehood into the lives of Iraqis living in Syria and into the Syrian political context.

UNHCR adapted to the Syrian scenario, but the knowledge and techniques it brought still created political contradictions and tensions. The Syrian state was not a signatory to the 1951 Refugee Convention and, from UNHCR's perspective, did not possess a modern asylum or refugee law.[28] Therefore UNHCR's mandate did not automatically extend onto Syria's territory. Instead, since 2003, the organization operated under a so-called temporary protection regime that was respected to a varying degree by the Syrian government. In practice this meant that the government permitted UNHCR's operations, cooperated with certain UNHCR efforts, and, for example, since 2010 accepted the temporary protection document that UNHCR provided to Iraqis as a reason to award official residency permits. Despite this last point regarding permits, it was noteworthy that during the time of my research, only one of around eighty Iraqi informants had obtained a residency permit through the UNHCR protection paper. All others had obtained permits independently of their registration with UNHCR, meaning that permits were also open to those Iraqis not registered with the organization. This point was important, as UNHCR's primary protection target was protection from *refoulement* (deportation and no option of legal residency), which, however, in Syria was provided or withdrawn by the state regardless of someone's status with UNHCR.

None of my Iraqi research participants attributed a strong protective element to the UNHCR document, in the sense that it would protect them from deportation. In fact, protection from deportation was not mentioned once in conversations and interviews about Iraqis' motivations to register with UNHCR. The reasons for UNHCR registration mostly concerned access to resettlement and aid, as well as a general hope that something positive might develop from this step.[29] UNHCR officials, Syrians, and Iraqis all believed that deportation of an Iraqi could occur at any time at the discretion of the government. Given the government's politics of toleration, interlocutors acknowledged that deportation was generally only likely if an Iraqi broke the law in some way.[30] As long as their papers were in order, many research participants felt secure from deportation in the political climate, again indicating that their residency in Syria had little to do with UNHCR registration. Iraqis frequently mentioned fear of a political reversal that would end the politics of toleration and would force Iraqis out of Syria. Such a change would be related to a change in Iraqi-Syrian government relations and not as an element within the remit of UNHCR. The fact that UNHCR registration did not play an important role in terms of whether an Iraqi was permitted to remain on Syrian territory or not pointed out UNHCR's ambivalent legal status and influence in Syria. Although it was possible that UNHCR's quiet diplomatic efforts contributed to the overall toleration of Iraqis in Syria, it was notable that since the organization's increased involvement in the management of Iraqis from late 2007 onward, the Syrian government had increased residency and visa restrictions on Iraqis. As argued above, it was possible to link these growing restrictions to transformations in the way the Syrian state ruled in response to the framing of Iraqi migration as a humanitarian crisis and the subsequent international involvement.

Onward Migration of the Fittest: The Resettlement Program

UNHCR's resettlement program categorized Iraqis according to vulnerability and provided them with an identity that supposedly conformed with correct state-society relations and citizenship. Inversely, the program demonstrated what kind of Iraqis were considered by UNHCR to be most nonconforming to proper citizenship and thus in need of resettlement, which was considered as a last-resort solution to become rehabilitated into the sovereign system. Resettlement was one of UNHCR's so-called three durable solutions to end someone's situation as a refugee; it was considered an important protection tool "when local integration is not an option, and voluntary repatriation does not seem viable or feasible in the near future," which was considered to be the case by UNHCR regarding the Iraqis.[31] Resettlement was also considered as a solution of choice when a refugee had "specific needs" that would not be met in the country of refuge, and for other reasons.[32]

Based on UNHCR's Resettlement Handbook, the organization had developed eleven categories of Iraqis who would be prioritized for resettlement. The profiles reflected a mix of heightened suffering ("persons who have been the victims of severe trauma"), of physically weaker persons or those less able to look after themselves ("older persons at risk," "unaccompanied children," "medical cases"), gender considerations ("women at risk"), and targeted persecution (due to a person's "religious or ethnic" background).[33] The categories also included the very situation-specific profile of persons who "fled due to their association with the Multi-National Force, Coalition Provisional Authority, UN, foreign countries, international and foreign institutions or companies and members of the press," and stateless persons.[34] Narratives and data that Iraqis were asked to provide during registration and resettlement interviews focused on identifying information related to these categories.

These profiles reflected UNHCR's twin concerns, first with vulnerability defined by humanitarian ideas focused on the physical body, and second with vulnerability defined as an "unclear" (from UNHCR's perspective) legal relationship vis-à-vis the state and government. The first concern could be traced to UNHCR's subscription to humanitarian discourse, as set out above, that casts refugees as persons with no means of employment or self-support. The second concern was linked to the organization's concept of "state sovereignty," according to which UNHCR's corrective intervention in a person's status became desirable if he or she did not enjoy, and could not in the future achieve, the kind of citizen-state relationship of reciprocal rights and duties that is the bedrock of the modern ideal of the state. Resettlement was regarded as a solution to both aspects of vulnerability: the granting of long-term residency status and the eventual option of obtaining citizenship solved the absent relationship with a state. The provision of government assistance in the resettling country, followed by integration into the labor market, completed the transformation into a self-governing human who contributed to the maintenance of a protective government through paying taxes and voting. Together, these steps were regarded as the successful provisioning of "protection space" to a refugee, who was resettled in a sovereign, stable, and peaceful realm. The resettlement program was a mechanism to eliminate the vagueness of Iraqis' status in Damascus. Iraqis' status was vague from the perspective of UNHCR because they were neither properly recognized refugees nor citizens nor fully stateless. This vagueness was regarded as a threat to Iraqi survival; however, perhaps more important, it threatened the stability of the political ideal of the state on which UNHCR's foundations rested (particularly in light of the fact that Iraqis did indeed survive in this vague state, many not very badly).

As set out above, the resettlement program functioned as a corrective tool through which an attempt was made to produce Iraqi identity and legal status in a way that conformed with the modern ideal of state sovereignty. From this sovereignty-conforming status, human rights, citizenship, peace, and stability (in short, protection) were supposed to flow, in accordance with the idea that a sovereign state was an ordered realm of law and rights. However, to qualify for the expensive and work-intensive resettlement process, resettlement candidates first had to be identified as having moved further away from the sovereign realm than any of their peers, by displaying poverty and suffering. Although UNHCR officials kept selection criteria secret, reportedly in order to avoid fraud, it was well known among my Iraqi interlocutors that signs of greater distress would increase the chances of being resettled. One middle-aged Iraqi man, complaining about the perceived randomness of UNHCR decision making and the general chaos and opacity of UNHCR operations in Damascus, stated this point when he asked, rhetorically: "Do I have to lie to receive resettlement, do I have to say that I was kidnapped and my wife was raped? They say that your story is not so bad, but they do not understand. People that lie receive resettlement."[35]

A further statement that demonstrated such awareness of UNHCR's decision-making processes came from another Iraqi man who was waiting to hear about his resettlement case and who stated:

> When we go to ask them about what is going to happen, they told us we have to wait until we . . . every family, it is like a queue. It depends on your story or your situation; it makes them deal with you first. There are other families, maybe they came after us, but their circumstances makes the UN deal with them before us. It depends on their opinions and their ideas.[36]

Interlocutors whose relatives or who themselves had held positions in Iraq's former army under the Saddam regime were aware that this placed them in an awkward position vis-à-vis the resettlement requirements. Two middle-aged female interlocutors, whose husbands had both worked in the army (as a doctor and a pilot, respectively), suspected that their respective delay and rejection from the resettlement process was linked to their spouses' previous positions. The fact that one of the men had vanished on the Syrian-Iraqi border, in all likelihood murdered for his army association, showed the potential life or death impact of UNHCR's judgment about people's deservingness of resettlement.[37]

The resettlement program considered Iraqi identity within selected aspects of Iraqis' experiences and self-understanding. Although violence, fear, injury, poverty, dependency, weakness, and support of the US-led invasion were all recognizable elements, among many others, of Iraqi experience and life in Damascus, participation in the resettlement program turned these elements into defining features of Iraqi identity and they were prerequisites to being selected for the (often) highly desired move abroad. Even as UNHCR clerks recognized that this perception was highly distorted, the structural requirements embedded in the stated "priority profiles" ensured that resettlement remained focused on identifying these vulnerabilities. By producing Iraqis as huddled masses of beings that had been cast outside the protective realm of state sovereignty, and who through resettlement could access this realm again and achieve safety, UNHCR produced and performed successfully the narrative that state sovereignty in its modern, liberal manifestation was the right, just, stable, and peaceful form of power and social-political organization. This mise-en-scène of sovereignty could only be achieved by ignoring the many ambiguities that Iraqi existence in Syria introduced into the sovereign ideal, by the simple fact that many Iraqis existed quite well without a citizen-state relationship that would qualify as such from UNHCR's perspective. UNHCR's ignorance about other aspects of Iraqi existence in Syria, elaborated below, was astonishing and thorough.

The resettlement program also contained a judgment on Iraqis' place in the Syrian body politic. As UNHCR considered resettlement viable only if local integration was not an option, Iraqis examined for resettlement were necessarily understood as unintegrated in Syria and, in their present circumstances, unintegratable. This notion was often repeated in UNHCR rhetoric, both in official statements and interviews, and always extended to Iraqis in general, not just those being examined for resettlement. Speakers and interlocutors pointed to two key facts when making this argument. Integration was considered not possible because Iraqis received only temporary residency permits and because Iraqis were officially prohibited from working. These facts again clearly reflected UNHCR's two central concerns about refugees, namely, their lack of a stable relationship with the state and their inability to care for themselves. Iraqis' status, in UNHCR's view, cast Iraqis outside of the Syrian body politic, as they were assumed to stand in a fundamentally different relationship to the

Syrian state than persons with Syrian papers. The following paragraphs will argue that this understanding of Iraqis was possible only by viewing the Syrian context through the lens of a nation-based, representative politics and by ignoring that Syrian state sovereignty was constructed through very different social relations, governance strategies, and techniques. Government protection and a reciprocal citizen-state relationship did not form part of Syrian statehood in the way that the sovereign ideal stipulated. By basing its programs on this ideal, UNHCR imported related ideas and techniques onto Syrian territory, creating a conflicting narrative about where Iraqis stood in relation to the Syrian state than did the situation that presented itself through daily observations.[38]

When confronted with the observation that signs of Iraqi employment and investment were evident around Damascus, many interlocutors (both from UNHCR and not) would stress that Iraqis could seek work only in the informal sector, in unskilled jobs, and that Iraqis easily became victims of exploitation owing to their lacking legal status. The clearly widespread Iraqi employment was thus portrayed as temporary and precarious, as an emergency survival measure, rather than as a sign of residency, stability, and successful organization. The most striking aspect of this assessment was its blatant and peculiar blindness toward the reality of labor, authority, citizenship, and state—in short toward the reality of daily life—as it presented itself in the Syrian context. Lack of security and precariousness was a central governance strategy through which the Syrian government enacted the state's sovereignty to the people living on its territory. One key technique through which this precariousness was produced was to impose official prohibitions, while at the same time tolerating systematic and widespread transgression of the official rule. In this way the possibility of state intervention was always allowed for, though it was never clarified when such an intervention might occur.[39] This technique, combined with a low supply of jobs and poor education facilities, meant that precariousness and at least latent feelings of insecurity were constant factors for many people living in Damascus, especially regarding employment and income. The regional instability, highlighted during the 2006 Israeli attacks on Lebanon, followed by the 2008 attacks on the Gaza Strip, strengthened this feeling even among Syrian interlocutors who held attractive and relatively well-paying jobs.[40] In the Syrian context, "protection" in UNHCR's sense of physical safety, enforcement of one's rights, and economic independence flowed much more from personal wealth and from useful personal connections to state employees and otherwise powerful persons than from the judiciary or from the government. This applied to all people living on Syria's territory, be they Iraqi or Syrian. Dozens of observations and interviews confirmed that successful Iraqi employment, business activity, and investment depended much more on such matters than on their secure or insecure relationship with the Syrian state.

A similar analysis may be made in reference to the often-repeated statement that Iraqis were allowed to work only in the informal economy and were prone to exploitation. Although it was true that Iraqis could not access public-sector jobs, which in Syria included wide swathes of the economy and large parts of the health and education sector, there was no further indication that other parts of the job market remained systematically closed to Iraqis. In addition, the formal sector (i.e., jobs in which a closer government inspection was likely, such as education or health) was not fully closed to Iraqis, as was indicated by the private Iraqi-run university on the outskirts of Damascus that had been open since 2005, staffed and headed by Iraqi faculty. One of my interlocutors, a natural scientist, was visiting Damascus for several months for the specific purpose of seeking a job at this university; his worries focused on the competition and made no mention about possible troubles about work permits.[41] Further, the vague term "informal" did not carry a clear meaning in the Syrian context, where official and nonofficial spheres were blurred to a high degree. The fact that many Iraqis were working in jobs beneath their level of education or in worse jobs than they had held in the past was disappointing and sad, but not highly different from the situation experienced by many Syrians I encountered. Although Iraqis occasionally seemed to be paid substantially less than Syrian employees for the same tasks, this was not the case across the board, as many observations and conversations indicated.

Another interlocutor, an Iraqi woman in her late teens, reported on her search for work and how she had learned about a juice factory where

Syrian Kurdish girls squeezed pomegranate with bare hands while sitting next to large, burning-hot cauldrons, earning around USD 5 per day. Through this encounter the Iraqi woman learned that Kurds in Syria were in a "bad situation" and were denied citizenship. The job in the juice factory would have been under such bad conditions that my Iraqi friend decided against it.[42] A further research informant, an Iraqi man in his early twenties, was actively searching for work in a number of fashionable restaurants in the old city, where some of his Iraqi friends were employed. The wage he expected to earn, around USD 160 per month to begin with, would be the same as Syrian employees. However, it was noteworthy that this informant was not hired because his residency permit had expired; the restaurant owner told him that once he obtained a residency, he would hire him (a work permit was not mentioned).[43]

Daily life in Syria challenged UNHCR's assumptions about the way state sovereignty worked in other areas of "protection" and the key issues of residency and freedom of movement. The lack of a formal relationship with the state, which in UNHCR's logic translated into a lack of protection, did not distinguish Iraqis in the Syrian context. Protection was not a key element of the state-citizen relationship in Syria, where the state's sovereignty was built on different strategies of coercion and social relationships.

One of the most pertinent issues when considering the alleged absence of Iraqi freedom of movement and residency, assumed by UNHCR to be an issue of official state matters, was the fact that persons who had drawn the negative attention of state agents were regularly prohibited from or harassed when leaving the country by the Syrian government. As mentioned in chapter 2, this situation applied to various interlocutors of mine: a Syrian middle-aged male government critic, an Iraqi woman who had been questioned by intelligence agents because of her links with foreigners, and a young Syrian man who was dodging military service. A further Syrian acquaintance, a man in his late twenties who had been living abroad for many years, faced trouble when trying to exit Syria after visiting his relatives. After repeatedly having to pay bribes and mobilize contacts to leave, he decided not to visit again despite important family occasions, as he was too worried about the consequences: in effect, the Syrian government had banned him from returning to Syrian state territory. These observations show that, when on Syrian territory, state affiliation was not a crucial determinant for "protection." Freedom of movement from and to the territory was not a sovereign-citizen right for persons with Syrian documents that could be systematically upheld under certain conditions. Syrian state agents, owing to arbitrary circumstance, could easily treat two "citizens" differently in terms of protection and freedom of movement.[44]

Certain observations about the resettlement program also scuttled notions that a legal residency permit in a "correctly" sovereign state would result in "protection." Hardship, and other issues, led a small (and unknown) number of Iraqis to return to the Middle East after having received the long-awaited resettlement.[45] Once resettled in the United States, Iraqis received financial support from the US government for the first months. After this period, food stamps were provided; however, rent and other expenses had to be covered by Iraqis themselves. This process clashed with UNHCR's focus on resettling the most "vulnerable" refugees, who were often persons who would find it most difficult to obtain employment and economic independence abroad. Here, UNHCR's narrative that legal residency in a "properly" sovereign state would result in protection for the "huddled masses" was most clearly revealed to be problematic. The returning Iraqis were also living evidence that the particular definition of "protection" enshrined in ideas and laws about modern sovereignty had important limits in practice. Although protection covered violence stemming from certain types of persecution, it did not extend to physical harm resulting from poverty, and thus revealed its historical and ideological ties to capitalism and liberal values about self-governance. The issue also highlighted that the belief in an imagined nationhood as the basis of state sovereignty resulted in exclusions and barriers faced by migrants, and it pointed out that in Syria the state had not assumed control over the broader and more inclusive identity of "Arab," even though this meant a slacker control of borders and territory. Further complicating any assumed link between citizenship and protection, UNHCR's financial and food aid for Iraqis inside Syria was perceived and portrayed as unlimited, unlike the temporary state support received abroad after resettlement.

As UNHCR sought to create the protection space that Iraqis were apparently lacking because of their foreignness in Syria, the organization created benefits and services that were not available to Syrians via the Syrian government. In this somewhat ironic situation, UNHCR conceptualized "Iraqi" and "Syrian" as distinct categories of persons, based on the sovereign ideal of citizenship as a person's defining characteristic, in a way that the Syrian government did not. This absence of protection space for Syrians again called UNHCR's assumptions about sovereignty and citizenship into question, as vulnerable Syrians, be they women at risk, elder persons at risk, or persons facing persecution on political grounds, had no recourse to enforce their assumed right of protection as citizens. A conversation with a Syrian acquaintance who was an astute observer of Syrian politics stressed this point. When asked about what she considered a key difference between the situation of Syrians and Iraqis, she answered that "the state did not care about the human rights of either its citizens or the Iraqi refugees; whether they lived or died, the state did not care. But the Iraqi refugees had various organizations that were representing them in Europe, in the United States, and in the United Nations, such as UNHCR and the aid organizations. So in that sense they had someone speaking for them and there was a spotlight on them (unlike ordinary Syrians)."[46]

Together with other humanitarian actors, UNHCR contributed to a transformation of the space in which the Syrian government could produce the state's sovereignty, both toward the people living on its territory and toward the international community. As already alluded to, UNHCR's humanitarian programs played a crucial role in these transformations; they are the focus of the next section.

UNHCR's Assistance Programs: Caring for the Most Vulnerable

UNHCR's assistance programs demonstrated the organization's institutional belief in liberal values of self-government and the liberal subject, and they hinted at the connection of these ideas to the ideal of national state sovereignty. Nevertheless, it would be a mistake to establish an easy dichotomy between UNHCR as a liberal actor and the Syrian state as a despotic actor. As the last section of this chapter will argue, UNHCR's governance techniques showed that in terms of violence, there was no neat divide between liberal and authoritarian forms of power. Considering UNHCR's humanitarian programs, it is important to note that at no point did Iraqi emigration result in the widespread misery associated with tent camps and forced marches of people carrying their belongings.[47] No camps for Iraqis had been established in Syria, neither had homelessness visibly increased in Damascus in association with Iraqis. In early 2007, during a meeting with UNHCR in Damascus when no significant programs yet existed, the community services officer recounted how she gave a (then unusual) cash handout to the most desperate Iraqi man who had approached UNHCR, who told her that he had no accommodations and was considering sleeping in a park. In prewar, middle-income Damascus, where visible signs of extreme poverty were scarce and considered indecent, this man was considered to be in a crisis. The explanation for the rapid expansion of humanitarian programs should be rather sought in the particular politicization of Iraqi migration through US and European advocacy groups, and the consequent expansion of funding for such aid programs.[48] This money, coupled with the intrinsic expansionism of humanitarian agencies, was always fundamental to setting up the various new interventions analyzed below.

Given their breadth, the humanitarian programs provided a rich ground of analysis; this section concentrates on two aspects. First, it addresses the question of the targeting of the programs, the meaning of their focus on certain areas of life and not others. Second, it analyzes the political transformation these programs hinted at and the changes to the Syrian state and its sovereignty that they entailed.

As discussed, a crucial aspect of UNHCR's raison d'être was its portrayal of Iraqis as weak, dependent, and unable to make themselves, through their own efforts, into persons who could pass as citizens (and therefore as sovereign, adult humans). Without the existence of vulnerable Iraqis, there would have been no justification or reason for UNHCR's press releases, funding appeals, job announcements, program designs, or cooperation with NGOs or with the Syrian state.[49] The figure of the vulnerable Iraqi was the bedrock of UNHCR policy in Syria. It was therefore no surprise that this figure was ever present in nearly all UNHCR Syria publications and programs.[50] Between 2007 and 2010, UNHCR Syria leaflets, plans, and funding appeals always referred to several key areas of humanitarian intervention, which portrayed the Iraqi refugee population as lacking in these areas of life. The referred-to areas were: delivery of basic food items, financial help, health care (including psychosocial counseling), training and remedial education, special help for single women, and special help for victims of sexual attacks and torture.[51]

The importance of the agency's aid varied according to an Iraqi's situation. Whereas a small number of interlocutors described it (especially the financial aid) as crucial to their existence in Syria, others were happy to take food aid and educational courses as a bonus, and still others dismissed it completely, stressing the bad quality of the food aid, which they sold. Some interlocutors, who were single men and did not qualify for aid, spoke about times when they had needed support and did not understand why UNHCR would not provide it, and still others refused to register for aid out of pride.

Yet the image of Iraqis that emerged from UNHCR publications did not in the least reflect this plurality of attitudes toward aid provision. Aided by photographs, these documents portrayed Iraqis as persons who, owing to unspecified developments, were too poor to have enough food, were not able to earn a living, were unprepared for the future, and were sick and in psychological distress or in social distress (single-women households), or were victims of cruel and sexual violence. There was a strange silence about the causes of the Iraqi plight. Apart from occasional and vague references to persecution by unnamed perpetrators, Iraqis could have easily been the victims of a natural catastrophe that had led to a wider state collapse, an event of "higher force" for which no human agency was to blame. The responsibility of the US-led coalition forces and Iraqi politics for the Iraqi flight was thus veiled, as was the complete failure of the stated goals of the war, such as "bringing democracy to Iraq." By eliminating the historical and political context of Iraqi suffering, UNHCR achieved a depoliticizing of its "beneficiaries"; being nonpolitical or apolitical is, in humanitarian discourse, a necessary prerequisite for a person to be deserving of aid.

In the case of UNHCR, presenting its "beneficiaries" as nonpolitical also allowed for its image of neutrality to be upheld. The use of technical and medical language in this categorization of Iraqis ("trauma," "at risk," "gender-based violence") also contributed to a strong distraction from the political processes and political violence that were contained in Iraqis' experience.[52] Although it was thus relatively clear that UNHCR's humanitarian programs were biopolitical in effect and produced Iraqis as vulnerable, politically neutral, and passive agents, it was much harder to pin down the political transformations of statehood and citizenship contained in them.[53] The humanitarian programs in Syria were linked to the powerful, globalizing discourse of humanitarianism in general, and they embedded Iraqis into forms of governance that not only transcended Syrian territory but were also deterritorial, in the sense that they drew legitimacy from ideas presented as universal and neutral: human rights, compassion, and solidarity. However, the social relations created by humanitarian programs—between Iraqis, between Iraqis and Syrians, between Iraqis and UNHCR officers, and between Syrians and UNHCR officers—were power relations and relations of governance and influence, and were decidedly not neutral. These relations, through which money, ideas, and identities flowed, created new understandings about what it meant to be Iraqi, what it meant to be Syrian, and what the meaning and power of Syrian state or Iraqi state sovereignty was.

The creation of "Iraqi refugee vulnerability" as an arena of intervention produced a new space of encounters in which Syrian state sovereignty, Iraqi identity, and the influence of humanitarian actors were renegotiated and transformed. As Iraqi "vulnerability" was a factor in determining access to welfare services and resettlement, it very concretely influenced a person's (physical and imagined) location within a state's territory and population, and thus his or her position vis-à-vis the state's power. The characteristic "vulnerability" produced through humanitarian programs had a transformative power because persons understood as such were slotted into particular programs that changed their location in the sovereign system. Further, it affected Iraqis' modes of behavior and self-governance, as certain Iraqi practices were rewarded and others not. Like the resettlement program, the humanitarian agenda cast Iraqis as external to the Syrian body politic and as outside of the Syrian state's responsibility.[54] In combination with Iraqi "vulnerability," this justified and explained the intervention of UNHCR on Syrian territory and the lives of the population living there, that is, the intervention of UNHCR into areas of life normally strongly understood as belonging to the state. Intervention would have been much harder to implement had Iraqis been presented as agents with (political) potential for activism or indeed action of any significance on Syrian territory, as this would have merited stricter government control to maintain state sovereignty. By producing Iraqis as passive, neutral, and not possessing any means of intervening in Syrian affairs, it was possible that UNHCR's interventions became understood as similarly neutral and based on universal human values.

Although it would be tempting to argue that UNHCR was simply taking over areas of governance usually associated with the state and transforming Syrian sovereignty in this way, UNHCR's interventions rather pointed out that the organization was creating spheres of governance that had not been part of the Syrian repertoire of sovereignty-creating techniques before. Given the lax institutional separation between Syrians and Iraqis enforced by the Syrian government, arguably UNHCR's humanitarian discourse about Iraqis was crucial for producing "Iraqi refugees" as a particular field of governance, which had a transformative effect on how the Syrian state entered this field. This was most clearly visible in the way that the international focus on Iraqi migrants as a humanitarian crisis and in need of global attention opened the space for Syrian government officials to perform Syrian state sovereignty to external audiences. International conferences, UN committees, journal and press articles focused on Iraqi refugees as a platform on which Syrian public figures acted out Syrian state sovereignty in terms of power (Syrian control over refugees), stability (Syria as safe haven for refugees), morality (Syria as a generous host), and membership of the international community (Syria participating in the international effort to help the refugees).

As mentioned, the Syrian government gradually increased restrictions on Iraqi immigration simultaneously with the humanitarian focus on the matter. Until late 2007 Iraqis entered Syria without visas and obtained residency relatively easily; from then on visa requirements and residency procedures gradually tightened. Clearly, many issues contributed to this complex development, including government anxieties about border security and popular discontent about Iraqi immigration. But the growing restrictions were also a sign that the Syrian government was transforming its management of Iraqis according to ideas and practices about how borders and states should divide populations. The humanitarian management of Iraqis, which was practiced mainly by European and US NGOs, and the UN, at least appeared to have had an influence on the way the Syrian government transformed its sovereignty-producing techniques toward Iraqis. The continuing entry restrictions in 2009–10, when public attention in Syria and globally to the Iraqi issue was waning, as well as the acceptance in 2010 by Syrian state agencies of the UNHCR protection paper as a means to obtain residency, pointed to this.

This growing cooperation between UNHCR and Syrian state and government agencies, which has continued to flourish, was particularly pronounced in UNHCR's aid programs. It indicated an increased convergence of interest and approach between the two institutions. For example, in 2009, UNHCR signed a cooperation agreement with the Syrian Women's Union, a government organization, to jointly operate centers and programs for Iraqi women at risk. The opening celebration of the first jointly operated center in Kafar Sūsa (Damascus) saw speeches of senior members of both UNHCR and the Syrian government. Although their rhetoric remained quite different, their agreement that the existence of Iraqi refugee women merited cooperation on the aid effort and on the type of help offered to women showed a merging of interests on the matter.[55] Similarly, in 2010, UNHCR announced a memorandum of understanding (MOU) with the Syrian Ministry of Social Affairs and Labor "to strengthen the services provided to vulnerable refugees, particularly women at risk, unaccompanied and separated children, minors in juvenile centres, refugees with disabilities, and the elderly."[56] In the field of health, UNHCR cooperated closely with the Syrian Arab Red Crescent (SARC), a quasi-government institution. SARC operated several clinics that delivered primary health care services to registered Iraqis, and it transferred them to public hospitals if necessary. Treatments for Iraqis were subsidized by UNHCR, and in 2007 and 2008 the organization funded SARC with over

USD 6 million, which also highlights the financial incentives provided to Syrian actors to comply with UNHCR's processes.[57] Given that SARC created a new computerized database to record UNHCR patient information, its personnel would have necessarily been exposed to UNHCR's selection criteria and categories of vulnerability and, further, would have participated in the production of Iraqis as vulnerable refugees in line with the sovereign ideal.

In turn, UNHCR's implementation of its humanitarian agenda was also affected by Syrian government demands and by the government's approach to Iraqi migration. At the most basic and important level, the unofficial and open attitude of Syrian authorities to Iraqi presence, settlement, and economic activity strongly limited UNHCR's scope and depth than if Iraqis had been forced to live in camps, deprived of all means to make a living.[58] Further, the fact that the Syrian government was not a member of the refugee convention and that UNHCR operated only under a temporary agreement placed the organization into a situation in which its operations were dependent on governmental tolerance. This dependency must count as an explanatory factor for UNHCR's consistent and lavish praise for the Syrian government, which was not otherwise often mentioned in the same breath with phrases such as "principles of human rights," "protection," or "humanitarianism."[59] Despite UNHCR's constant emphasis on human rights rhetoric, in no instance did the organization appear interested in crossing Syrian government "red lines" on matters of political freedoms, that is, freedom of speech and so forth. Although UNHCR did offer a free legal aid clinic to Iraqis and worked on a very small number of detention cases, the UNHCR employees I encountered displayed the same deference to government repression of certain political topics as most other persons in Syria.

The contradictions between UNHCR's approach to managing Iraqi migrants in Syria and that of the Syrian government return the focus of discussion to the opposition of liberal and authoritarian government. One of the arguments running through this book is that this dichotomy, which is based, inter alia, on a differentiation of how such governments apply violence, is not as stark as is often understood. The management of Iraqi migration in Syria by authoritarian and liberal actors demonstrated this differentiation's limits. Ultimately, distinct regimes of violence appear to be instead differentiated by whom that violence is visited on, and how visible this violence is made, rather than what kind of violent is used. To a smaller degree, the type of violence used is also a differentiating factor. An analysis of UNHCR's governance from the perspective of violence demonstrates that it contained a mix of liberal and violent techniques that blurred the perception of UNHCR as a chiefly liberal organization.

UNHCR: Liberal and Authoritarian

In Syria, UNHCR's treatment of Iraqis showed a mix of liberal, violent power that produced Iraqis not as "beneficiaries" but as unruly, deviant, and potentially dangerous persons that had to be disciplined and punished. Occasionally, UNHCR's apparently liberal techniques of categorizing and humanitarianism were responsible for life and death decisions, for example, if a person associated with the former regime were refused protection from persecution or if the nonprovision of aid to a person led to their return to Iraq.

UNHCR's more violent treatment of Iraqis was visible during direct encounters between UNHCR staff and Iraqis at the processing center in Kafar Sūsa, where often dozens or hundreds of Iraqis waited outside. One day I accompanied an Iraqi acquaintance to this center, where she was hoping to obtain information about her resettlement file. We arrived at around 7 am in the morning to obtain a paper slip with a number that would ensure entry on that day; although the center opened at 9 am, it was known that there were not enough numbers for everyone, and for this reason it was necessary to queue early. No proper waiting area adorned the entrance, and soon two to three hundred people crowded around it, leaning where possible against concrete blocks or fences that dotted the undeveloped site. From 9 am onward, ten people at a time were allowed entry through a narrow doorway, which was monitored by a male Syrian UNHCR employee. As the day wore on and the heat increased, with no shade to stand in and no opportunity to buy food or water, the crowd, which was separated into men and women, became restless, and people pushing toward the entrance were shouted at angrily by the UNHCR staff. After around five hours' wait, my friend and I stood on the dusty sidewalk, trying to lean against a fence to relieve our weary legs and feet. We had now been shouted at several times by a harassed-looking UNHCR employee who asserted several times that people without a number should go home, that there were no further numbers that day, and that persons from outside Damascus would not be served at this site.

I noticed that men were processed much faster than women and assumed this was because a male crowd would likely become aggressive and demanding more quickly. Several women harangued the UNHCR guard about the long wait and their exhaustion as a result of standing in the sun. I observed how a Syrian army officer intervened several times, in one instance raising his voice to an older woman who could not stand in the sun any longer and had questioned being treated badly; her indignant assertion that "they were not Jews" made my friend laugh. The presence of the officer made the waiting women nervous; in one instance I overheard him ask if one of the women had a residency permit. Eventually we were allowed inside. After a brief discussion about my presence, I was allowed to accompany my friend as an exception to the rules, though requested to sit at the back of the waiting room, where I received additional attention from the various guards. At the end of an incredibly exhausting and demoralizing wait of about six hours, my friend had a 5-minute audience with a UNHCR employee, who looked something up in computer electronic database and told her that there was no news on her resettlement file. That was it, we returned outside.

The experience of the day sat very uneasily with UNHCR's rhetoric of refugee rights and protection that I encountered during interviews with UNHCR staff and in UNHCR publications. It showed that when the presumably passive and unprotected "huddled masses" of refugees were demanding and proactive, UNHCR's approach could turn disciplinarian and threatening. Caught in their organization's discourse on the sovereign ideal and humanitarianism, UNHCR staff seemingly had no rights-based solutions once the refugees' behavior upset and undermined the rhetoric.

UNHCR had no means of punishing Iraqis who cheated the organization or broke any other rules, other than withdrawing support, and the organization's lack of any form of detention or police apparatus showed important limits on its use of violence. To identify Iraqis who cheated or lied, UNHCR had developed instead a system of unannounced visits to beneficiaries' homes to check their identities, and it tried to cross-reference information through interviewing family members separately or checking different databases. Iraqi interlocutors complained about the intrusive nature of the interviews, and reported on very personal questions asked separately of spouses (presumably designed to spot false information, although this was not always recognized or believed by Iraqis, who experienced such processes as harassment). UNHCR staff was deliberately opaque about the organization's procedures and about why certain questions were asked, documents requested, or further interviews requested. This strategy, reportedly intended to prevent fraud, left Iraqis in the dark about the reasons for UNHCR's requests and therefore also without significant room to react to them other than be passively compliant in the hope that something positive might come from them. The lack of information about significant events such as resettlement, dates of final interviews, and departure resulted in a situation of living in limbo and increased dependence on UNHCR. By means of the access UNHCR provided to other states and citizenships, the organization itself wielded a degree of sovereign power, even if the final decision rested with the resettlement states.

To outside observers, the violent aspect of UNHCR's operations was completely hidden, as it could only be witnessed by overcoming significant hurdles and engaging in close observation of day-to-day interactions between clerks and Iraqis at the ground level. UNHCR rhetoric overwhelmingly stresses its liberal strategies, and the design and setup of its Damascus sites separated foreign visitors from the messy direct-service provisions to Iraqis. Only through accessing sites normally reserved for Iraqis (and to achieve such access without a UNHCR chaperone was tricky) was it possible to witness the full range of UNHCR interventions as they appeared in Iraqi day-to-day life.

Conclusion

UNHCR's management of Iraqi refugees in Syria revealed the kind of political rationality contained in its framework and operations, including the kind of statehood and state-society relations considered correct from its perspective. UNHCR's programs created contradictions in Syria, where the Syrian government implemented Syrian state sovereignty through social relations and population management techniques different from those practiced by UNHCR. UNHCR's institutional commitment to the ideal of the territorially stable nation-state as a basis for state sovereignty can be found in its statutes and in the Geneva Refugee Convention on which it is based. These documents, written shortly after the Second World War, imagine the world as a community of distinct states, each with a government representative of its citizens. The assumed normal government-citizen relationship is one of protection and mutual obligations. In the exceptional circumstance that this order breaks down, a citizen might become a refugee, now floating unprotected between sovereigns and in need of a new sovereign identity. UNHCR was created with the mandate to help refugees reaccess a sovereign space.

Far from static, UNHCR programs and policies have continuously changed the interpretation of its mandate. In the past twenty years, UNHCR has evolved into an organization with a broad and more interventionist humanitarian agenda that extends to the provision of food, health, psychosocial care, financial aid, and education services, far beyond making available passports and resettlement. Its approach casts refugees as "vulnerable" by reason of the absence of a legal, documented relationship with a sovereign state and of liberal self-governance (in the sense of an inability to make oneself independently into a financially stable, healthy, and orderly person). UNHCR's programs are keyed to rectifying these two absences in the lives of refugees. These notions of "sovereignty" and "citizenship," on which UNHCR's programs in Damascus were based, did not correspond to the way the Syrian government managed Iraqis and integrated them into the Syrian body politic. The Syrian government's toleration of Iraqi migrants meant that their presence was based on a precarious stability that depended more on individual wealth, skill, connections, and luck than an official relationship with the state. Governmental protection and citizenship in the sense of mutual obligations were not a defining feature of the way the Syrian government conducted Syrian state sovereignty.

Through its programs, UNHCR produced Iraqis as vulnerable and passive refugees outside the realm of any sovereign protection, and ignored many aspects of Iraqi life in Damascus that pointed to integration, self-help, and stability. These programs disregarded several key elements of the Syrian government's sovereignty-producing strategies, such as the creation of official prohibitions that were continuously disregarded unless an inopportune person needed to be controlled. This strategy applied, for example, to Iraqi employment, which was officially prohibited but in practice widely tolerated. In line with its assumptions about refugees, however, UNHCR constantly portrayed Iraqi employment as illegal, precarious, and temporary.

UNHCR's programs opened up a political and social space for humanitarian intervention and for the Syrian government to produce Syrian sovereignty in this space. UNHCR's interventions in Iraqi migrant life in this manner did not weaken Syrian sovereignty, but did have a transformative effect on how Syrian sovereignty appeared in relation to Iraqi migrants and on Iraqi migration as a humanitarian crisis. On the international stage, Syria's portrayal as a generous host of Iraqis confirmed Syria's sovereignty according to the sovereign ideal. On Syrian territory, cooperation between government agents and UNHCR, as well as increasing residency and visa restrictions on Iraqis, pointed out that the Syrian government was adapting its governance techniques to this ideal. Finally, an analysis of UNHCR's resettlement and humanitarian programs found that although UNHCR's techniques for managing Iraqi migrants were mainly liberal, they also contained a degree of disciplinary power and violence. This observation calls into question the frequently made distinction between liberal and authoritarian actors or regimes, usually distinguished by the presence or absence of violence and freedom.

4

International NGOs and Iraqi Migration

Humanitarian Sovereignty

Beit al-Aqqad, a glorious fifteenth-century Mamluk house, reveals itself suddenly via a tiny wooden door set in a high wall lining the narrow market streets of old Damascus. The building, which fell into severe disrepair during the twentieth century, was lovingly renovated by the Danish Ministry of Science, Innovation, and Higher Education over the course of four years, and eventually reopened in splendor as Damascus's Danish Institute in 2000. Beit al-Aqqad's huge marble courtyard and raised loggia are decorated with fountains and framed by two stunning mosaics of colored stone that delight the eye. It is an oasis of calm and, intriguingly, sits on the ruins of a large Roman amphitheater dating from the first century AD. Beit al-Aqqad's foundations reach back two thousand years.

As the Danish Institute, Beit al-Aqqad hosted some of Damascus's most memorable cultural and academic events of recent years, including wonderful world music concerts and Syrian film nights. The Danish Institute opened a small library of academic books for researchers and fellows staying at the Institute. While researching in Syria in 2009 and 2010, I would occasionally visit this library. One day I had a brief conversation there with an employee of a Scandinavian NGO, recently arrived in Syria. He explained that he was busy setting up programs for Iraqi and Syrian youth including remedial education classes and extracurricular activities. The wider focus of his organization was "democratization," but because this was a "no-go area" in Syria, they did not include this aim into any of their proposals or reports. Though of course, he added with a smile and a wink, this was the NGO's real interest, to develop democratic awareness and empowerment for their "beneficiaries" via the back door.

Looking back on this conversation after the Syrian uprising, the presumptuous assumption that Syrians and Iraqis required training to understand their political rights and "democracy" appears ridiculously misplaced. Yet as an opening anecdote to explain the work of INGOs in Syria, it is useful because it captures well the opportunities, clashes of mentalities, and contradictory knowledge and assumptions that the work entailed. International NGOs (INGOs) and their foreign employees generally knew little about Syrian politics when they arrived in the wake of the Iraqi refugee crisis. This was not unusual: many aid workers frequently change countries and are not regional experts. Instead they carry with them the particular, standardized knowledge of a humanitarian emergency response. As emergency aid is supposed to fill the gap that an overwhelmed state government cannot momentarily fill, managing relations with a strong and controlling government was not a standard repertory of INGO planning, yet became an important one in the Syrian context.

In Syria, the "emergency" of Iraqi migration veered heavily from other mass migration crises, mostly as it was unfolding in a middle-income country with a relatively high standard of living. Here, many of the international aid sector's standard refugee-aid projects did not prove to be a good fit. INGOs occasionally acknowledged the exceptionality of the situation, but mostly they cheerfully charged ahead with their blueprints and tropes about refugee needs and "vulnerabilities," and about the origins of (and solutions to) refugee plight. The peculiar contradictions, sometimes risible, sometimes more serious, this created in the daily lives of Iraqis as well as of Syrians are the focus of this chapter. As will be argued throughout, these contradictions, apart from their explanatory value regarding political conditions in Syria shortly before the outbreak of the uprising and war, are revelatory about the type of power contained in humanitarian assistance. Again, the analytic lens of state sovereignty will provide the thread of my argument, for as observations and interviews found, unlike common assumptions about INGOs, they did not stand opposed to state sovereignty. Instead, they were opposed to *certain forms and expressions* of state sovereignty, whereas others they regarded as natural and correct. In this manner, INGOs were indeed agents of a particular type of statehood and a particular type of politics and power, which they transported into the Syrian context via their programs.

The rapid-fire development of an INGO sector on the "virgin" territory of Syria, which happened between 2007 and 2010, was particularly revealing for a number of reasons. Before the onset of the Iraqi crisis, only a very small group of national and international NGOs operated in the country. None of them focused on providing humanitarian emergency aid, but rather on development or human rights. For example, a small Italian INGO called Movimondo ran health projects for women, or the Syrian NGO Thara focused on women's rights. The Syrian Human Rights Observatory, which emerged as one of the most important news sources about human rights violations during the subsequent conflict, in 2009 already ran a small office in Damascus. In addition, a number of so-called quasi-NGOs (quangos) had been developed with the personal and financial support of Asma al-Asad, the wife of Syria's president, during the first decade of Bashar al-Asad's rule. At least half a dozen of these nominally independent organizations existed, and they focused on women's and children's issues and fostered entrepreneurship and rural development. However, the arrival of humanitarian emergency INGOs was unprecedented.

In the two decades since the end of the Cold War, humanitarian emergency INGOs, and in particular those focused on refugees, had developed into highly professional actors. This meant that by the time they arrived in Syria, they approached this new market with highly fixed views about how an aid operation should and would function. Forced migration was a particular subcategory of emergency suffering, part of the aid portfolio, and was also the object of fixed expectations and ideas in the INGO worldview. With this background, INGOs approached Syria with assurance and were confident they had the knowledge and power to help and improve the situation.

The Syrian government's inexperience with accommodating such highly skilled humanitarian players was important. Unlike many of the contexts that aid organizations work in, in Syria they encountered a state that, though inefficient and slow, could mobilize intimidating surveillance and control over any social area. Also, although many countries in which aid INGOs work are characterized by illiberal or nonliberal politics, in many cases their governments have at least learned to speak the language of universal human rights and basic needs, which eases their cooperation with the aid sector. In Syria, this was not (yet) the case. Official Syrian rhetoric remained full of actively nonliberal rhetoric, including anti-Israeli, pro-Palestinian statements, and portraying Western powers as dangerous imperialists with bad intentions, and human rights activists as a national security threat and as spies and infiltrators. The adaptation of Syrian officials to the sudden presence of an enormously wealthy, largely Western humanitarian sector was significant in terms of the transformational power that humanitarianism contains. It also revealed the limits of this power: for the surprisingly smooth, and unquestioned, adaptation of INGOs to the Syrian government's rules of engagement, and their adoption of the widespread attitudes of fear and acquiescence, showed how humanitarianism's technical approach to political problems enabled adaptation. Mostly, the humanitarian sleight of hand that was performed to define certain types of Iraqi suffering as "nonpolitical" and their own aid activities as "neutral" papered over any potential problems of cooperation.

This chapter describes how several INGOs embedded themselves in relationships of bureaucracy, money, emotion, and violence that partly constituted statehood in the Syrian context. The empirical evidence presented in this chapter shows that the observed INGO activities indeed contained a will and power to transform the way Syrian state institutions govern. But INGOs in Damascus were also forced to stray from their accepted beliefs and practices, adapting to those of Syrian state agents. Power was closely enmeshed with convictions, money, and fear, and worked subtly through personal and institutional contacts. Most INGOs I encountered regarded their projects as remedies for problematic aspects of Iraqi lives.[1] This problem-solving attitude, in which knowledge was understood as a legitimation and responsibility to intervene, was contradicted by the fact that despite their efforts, INGOs did not possess significant information about the Iraqi population and were prevented by the Syrian government from acquiring such knowledge. INGOs in Damascus therefore based their projects largely on *assumptions* about the Iraqi population that flowed from established ideas and tropes about refugees, which were closely connected to modern, national, and liberal ideas about state sovereignty.[2]

The term "international NGO" is vague; this vagueness was reflected by the diversity of organizations that could fall under this label and that appeared in Damascus as part of the Iraqi aid effort. In this chapter, I define "INGOs" as organizations that are independent of governments and whose funding, expertise, staff, and operations are multinational. Within this group, I make one further distinction. First, I discuss professional INGOs, organizations with a long-standing track record, full-time employees (both expatriate and local), and professional fund-raising and PR departments. Examples of professional INGOs working in Damascus included, for example, The Danish Refugee Council, Première Urgence, or Secours Islamique France.[3] Second, I discuss volunteer INGOs, organizations with a multinational staff, funding, and knowledge structure, but with small operations that rely on nonpaid volunteers. These had often sprung up as a personal, spontaneous reaction of its founders to Iraqi plight and lacked any significant form of back-office to handle external funding or PR issues. Examples of such INGOs working in Damascus included, for example, The Iraqi Student Project, Native without a Nation, or Bidna Capoeira. Whereas professional INGOs maintained official relations with state institutions and were registered, volunteer INGOs lacked any official status and, if at all, maintained unofficial contact with government representatives. The struggle between professional INGOs and Syrian ministries in particular over how to run aid programs highlighted that INGO activities posed a potential threat and a potential building block for the construction of Syrian state power. The presence of INGOs promised financial reward, the upgrading of public infrastructure, and a legitimacy boost for the state domestically and internationally. On the other hand, INGO presence could also signal internationally and domestically that the Syrian state was a developing country in need of foreign intervention to sustain basic elements of the state.[4]

This chapter is based on direct observations of INGO activities in Damascus as well as conversations with Iraqi migrants, foreign and

Syrian INGO staff, and UN staff. The first section of the chapter gives a broad overview of INGO activity focused on Iraqi refugees in Damascus. The second section analyzes in greater detail the activities of professional INGOs that were officially registered with the Syrian state and were characterized by the ideas and language of professional humanitarianism. The third section concentrates on volunteer INGOs, and the fourth section concludes the chapter.

International NGOs in Damascus: An Overview

The link between post-2003 Iraqi migration to Syria and the sudden and unexpected expansion of INGO presence in Damascus has been noted repeatedly.[5] This expansion, made possible chiefly through the lobbying efforts of American INGOs, was also linked to political developments in Syria, such as a growing openness among prominent government figures toward INGOs and their role in economic development. But clearly, the rapid and large-scale funding provided by Western states to UNHCR for its Iraqi program, and UNHCR's need to find implementing partners to run projects, increased the pressure on the Syrian government to allow the registration of INGOs.[6] Consequently, by 2009, fourteen INGOs were established as partners to UNHCR in Damascus in addition to around half a dozen active church organizations (with international links) and a small number of private or less official international organizations.[7] No public register for organizations working with Iraqi migrants existed, and despite an increasingly streamlined registration process, INGOs still maintained various channels with the state to authorize their activities.[8] My research collected information on ten very different INGOs. On two occasions, I was able to conduct repeated and intensive participant observations, on four occasions in-depth interviews plus limited observations, and at other times information was collected through informal conversations and interviews with INGO staff, aid recipients, or third parties.

INGOs diverged in their programs, staff, and setup, but a common thread was that their operations established Iraqis as recipients of either goods or services. The standard explanation and justification for their presence was that Iraqis needed assistance to survive, to lead meaningful and healthy lives, and to prepare for the future. Numerous INGO reports along these lines were published.[9] This needs-based view of Iraqi life was also the standard argument with which INGOs underlined funding requests, and was the general perspective that INGOs had on refugees worldwide. In terms of setup, larger INGOs generally maintained a head office in central Damascus but implemented their projects in Iraqi-populated suburbs such as Saida Zainab, Jaramana, or Yarmuk, more rarely also in cities outside Damascus such as Homs and Aleppo. Smaller, less formal INGOs were run from private flats, church facilities, or with no central location. INGO programs covered the entire gamut of standard aid programs: medical help, education, leisure activities, and the building of infrastructure (new schools or hospital facilities).

Accessing INGOs in Damascus proved difficult. Contrary to my expectation, the sudden enlargement of the INGO sector had not made research in Syria easier. Instead, many INGO employees, especially in large organizations with little experience in Syria, were too worried about state surveillance to meet me, despite the very general and noncontroversial focus of my research. Although initially frustrating, these experiences became valuable information in their own right, as they expressed ways of control and self-preservation exercised by INGO employees and related to questions about Syrian statehood.

An unusual feature of INGO activities in Damascus was their inconspicuousness. In humanitarian crises, INGO names are often displayed prominently on cars, buildings, and signs; however, INGO logos were absent in Damascus. All INGO locations that I visited were unremarkable and found in low-key buildings and apartments. But to a careful observer with some experience in the country, the novel presence of INGOs in Damascus was nevertheless noticeable, most prominently in the expensive cafes and restaurants in uptown Mālkī or the old city. INGOs had brought a new type of foreigner to the city: the humanitarian expert and aid worker. On my previous stays in Damascus, conducted annually between 2005 and 2008, the foreigners I had met consisted mainly of language students, diplomats, and nonhumanitarian professionals. Now I encountered people in their twenties and thirties trying to establish their international INGO careers, and older, experienced humanitarian workers. Their knowledge about Syria frequently involved a mix of keen interest, a lack of access to local information, and surprisingly confident opinions. Syria was beginning to offer job and career opportunities in the humanitarian field, which placed it among a particular group of "developing" or "postconflict" countries, conceptually a huge departure from the idea of Syria as an isolated member of the axis of evil and inimical to Westerners. This subtle shift in perception among internationals indicated the connection between a state accepting foreign aid and being accepted as a member of the international community. Syria's acceptance of the international humanitarian sector implied the introduction of good and responsibly state-society relations and bolstered its international standing. This connection between the humanitarian sector and global forms of political organization is summarized by the medical anthropologist Omar Dewachi, who argues that "humanitarian interventionism, as part of a transnational mobile network of deployment of people, ideologies and markets has become the link between transnational forms of domination and local political practices."[10]

Professional INGOs in Syria

One of the few professional INGOs that responded to my request for an interview was the International Rescue Committee (IRC), one of two US-based INGOs operating in Damascus.[11] The interview took place at IRC's inconspicuous office behind a main road in central Damascus, a typical French-style Damascus flat with wide stone floors and high windows located on the first floor of a four-story building. Three employees, two Syrian, one European, provided me with an overview of the organization's activities with Iraqi refugees, which consisted of projects in the education sector. IRC was renovating and improving a number of schools in deprived suburbs and offered remedial classes to Iraqi pupils.[12] Three main ideas emerged from the interview. First, that Iraqi pupils faced problems when trying to attend school in Syria; second, that Syria was a new and difficult context for IRC to operate in owing to control from state institutions; and third, that funding constraints and opportunities were a central concern for IRC. The expatriate director conveyed a business-like attitude and focused on the managerial challenges faced by IRC such as obtaining funds, hiring staff, and compliance with government regulations. One of the Syrian staff explained that there were around 1.5 million Iraqi refugees in Syria and that 60 percent of Iraqi children did not attend school, adding:

> As you might have read, Syrian schools suffered from overcrowding. First, the Iraqis face many challenges when it comes to schooling. For example, with the English language, in Syria we start in year one, whereas in Iraq they only start in year seven, so there is a very big gap there. Then there are the financial problems; this is probably the biggest problem. Often children have to work and families live off their wages.[13]

This rhetoric closely reflected the language and information about Iraqis on IRC's website and in press releases and reports.[14] Iraqis in Syria were presented as troubled and in desperate need of the world's attention and aid. IRC's language, compared with that of other INGOs, was extreme in this regard, although it nevertheless represented broadly the tone of most INGO publications on Iraqi refugees. For example, IRC's February 2010 report titled "A Tough Road Home" included the following descriptions of Iraqis:

> *Neglected Populations*
>
> Host governments and the Government of Iraq have done little to ensure that these young men and women have any access to meaningful job training or economic opportunities. The longer they remain refugees, the greater the possibility they could become a "lost generation"—and a potential threat to regional stability. Young, unemployed men grow frustrated by their inability to provide for themselves or their families. Returning refugees are leaving young people behind in host countries because in Iraq they would be at risk of being arrested or forcibly recruited by militia groups.
>
> Victims of sexual violence and those with psycho-social needs resulting from war-related trauma require targeted and timely interventions if they are to become fully functioning and contributing members of a society, be it in Iraq, a country of first asylum or a resettlement destination. The UNHCR and other bodies have noted the near universal

> experience of serious and debilitating trauma among the Iraqi displaced. The Commission urges the development and adequate funding of psycho-social services for Iraqi displaced wherever they may be.[15]

The Danish Refugee Council's website depicted Iraqi life as follows (similar wording could be found in the organization's quarterly reports):

> *Humanitarian Needs*
>
> Due to their illegal status, the Iraqi refugee population in Syria is facing a difficult situation being both illegal and out of funds, and their possibilities of living a decent life are limited. The influx of refugees has created additional inflation and pressure on the job market in the country. Criminality has increased, and prostitution of young Iraqi women in need of cash support has become a reason for resentment by the host community. The Syrian education system is also struggling to cope with the increased numbers of children and access to secondary or tertiary health care systems for Iraqis with chronic diseases is very limited.[16]

Finally, the website of Terres des Hommes Switzerland, which supported a number of health projects in Syria, carried the following description:

> *Regional Assistance to Iraqi Refugees*
>
> The Iraqi groups who have taken up temporary refuge in Syria and Jordan are in great distress. They have very few rights and no access to adequate services, in particular in the field of psychology. However, this is where their needs are greatest because of the trauma experienced during the war, while fleeing and also during their stay in the country which has taken them in. TdH is providing psychological and social help to these children and their families in Jordan, where it has opened a centre. Two partner relief organizations are working in Syria.[17]

All of these descriptions of displaced Iraqis focused exclusively on the negative elements of Iraqi life and migration experience. They cast Iraqis as problematic, potentially dangerous, and in need of correction.

The repeated focus on psychological and sexual trauma located Iraqis' problems firmly inside their own minds and bodies. This implied the need for interventions that targeted Iraqi lives and individuals rather than the external, political circumstances that were contributing to Iraqi poverty. Unsurprisingly, this was indeed the form that projects of large, international INGOs took. The reports repeatedly referred to the apparent "illegality" of Iraqis in Syria and their lack of rights. The act of migration to another state and the existence as a refugee was portrayed as an existence of last resort. INGO rhetoric reduced the extremely varied existence of Iraqis in exile, which also included successes, opportunities, strength, health, and self-help, to that of suffering and weakness. In these texts, the natural and ideally best location for Iraqis was the territory of Iraq and the sovereign space of the Iraqi state, and it was only highly exceptional circumstances that had undone this natural and baseline situation.

Returning to the IRC interview, the second important matter raised during the interview concerned ICR's interactions with Syrian state institutions. When I asked whether I could visit one of their projects, IRC's expatriate director warned me: "This is not a regular environment for INGOs. I will request approval and I'm sure that there will not be a problem, but we will have to see. In a different context we would take you along and show you everything, but here. . . ."[18]

From the perspective of the IRC, Syria's working environment for INGOs deviated from the norm owing to the relatively heavy monitoring conducted by state institutions. This once again pointed out that INGO assumptions about what a state's role in society should be, and normally was, were influenced by abstract notions that did not correspond to the Syrian context. The IRC interlocutors explained that their actions were closely monitored by officials from the Ministry of Education, with whom they met every week to discuss progress and to request approvals. After broad approval had been received, further requests had to be made regularly even for small activities such as distributing leaflets to inform Iraqi students about projects.

The schools that IRC was rebuilding and renovating were located in the suburbs Harastā, Qudsīa, and Bīla. They had been selected by the Ministry of Education rather than by an independent needs assessment.

Regarding information and statistics about Iraqi pupils, according to which the schools had been identified (Syrian government statistics were notoriously poor), IRC staff explained that it was not easy to get information, as the statistics of the ministry were old, and that IRC used a mixture of government and UNHCR statistics for its purposes. The knowledge and figures about Iraqis, which IRC staff so confidently provided, thus appeared largely as assumptions rather than empirically researched. In this particular case, IRC's choices and projects were so closely related to those of the ministry that the boundary between governmental and non-governmental was extremely blurred.

IRC's experience emphasized the particular way through which public space was lived and constructed in the Syrian context. In a liberal political framework, INGOs form a part of an international civil society located in the public space, a realm of activity protected from state influence by law and an active citizenship. This relationship between state and public can only be ensured through a vibrant civil society active in the public space.[19] As the IRC's experience showed, these notions were not applicable in the Syrian context, as the Syrian government clearly treated INGOs as political actors that needed to be controlled. Indeed, as will be highlighted below, state institutions used the new public sites developed by INGOs (community centers, training courses) as new sites in which to perform the state's sovereignty.[20] The close monitoring and control exercised by Syrian ministries over INGO activities and knowledge was described in an insightful report by the Middle East Institute:

> The [INGO] registration procedure reflects the weight of the Syrian bureaucracy and the government's desire to keep the activities of foreign entities under control. The procedure is as follows: INGOs are first to seek accreditation from the Ministry of Foreign Affairs. One condition to be accredited is to present proof that the organization is fully funded. The second step is to submit a project proposal to [the Syrian Arab Red Crescent] SARC without being able to a conduct preliminary needs assessment. After SARC approves the proposal, it signs a Memorandum of Understanding (MoU) with the INGO. The MoU was particularly challenging for the first INGOs that signed agreements with

> SARC: these agreements included the obligation for INGOs to share a common bank account with SARC, and the need for SARC's approval for any disbursement or the payment of 2% of the INGOs' budget to SARC in compensation for expenses related to the partnership. A few months later, these financial arrangements were lifted after SARC realized that they were time consuming, impractical, and unacceptable by donors and INGOs. However, other restrictive terms of the MoU have remained in place: SARC enjoys oversight of the INGOs' recruitment process, meetings between INGOs and any other organizations is subject to SARC's approval, and so is communication with journalists or researchers.[21]

These restrictions partly explained the reluctance of INGO representatives to meet with me. But more important, they showed that professional INGOs transported norms, ideas, and behaviors onto Syrian territory that were new to state officials. Further, they provide an insight into how clashes over the way to do things could lead to changes in practices and beliefs on both sides—resulting in new micropractices that could gradually produce social and political transformations to the way state sovereignty was exercised in Syria.

It is of interest to consider the motivations of both INGO and Syrian state officials to engage in these struggles. For professional INGOs, there appeared to be a publicity value in having been one of the first INGOs to set up operations in Syria. For example, The Danish Refugee Council prominently presented its work in Syria as pioneering on its website and in PR material; similar statements were found in publications of IRC and the International Medical Corps, emphasizing that their operations were among only a few others in Syria. Entry into Syria allowed INGOs to portray their work as groundbreaking, which presumably enhanced their profile with the public and donors. The availability of funds and UNHCR's call to INGOs were other important factors that pushed professional INGOs into Syria.

Regarding the motivations for Syrian officials to engage with INGO procedures, apart from the fact that many would have been ministry officials carrying out decisions made by their superiors, access to resources such as jobs and money acted as incentive. The involvement of Syrian officials in the hiring of INGO staff, including, according to informal conversations with expatriate INGO employees, deciding on individual appointments and salaries, meant that such jobs became part of patronage networks. Expat INGO staff, for example, believed that some of their Syrian colleagues were giving up parts of their salaries to the persons who had arranged their jobs. Further, the investment of INGOs and UNHCR in the Syrian health and education sector, occasionally without proper financial oversight, created substantial flows of money and jobs for Syrian companies. A rather shocking 2009 internal UNHCR audit of its Syria operations found a stunning lack of control of funds provided to Syrian public hospitals, which resulted in a system of double-bookings and submissions of bills without proof of services over hundreds of thousands of dollars. Such flows of money clearly created significant interest on the Syrian side to keep the humanitarians on board.[22]

But the relationship between professional INGOs and Syrian state institutions remained tense. Authorities heavily controlled new public spaces developed by INGOs, which included community centers or women's shelters, that offered unprecedented programs focused on the inner life of individuals, such as psychosocial counseling or parenting skills. These new forms of social organization and interventions included new governance techniques in which the Syrian state appeared in various forms. For example, the existence of foreign and Syrian INGO staff, and spaces associated with INGOs, created new sites in which state officials demonstrated the state's presence in these newly created domestic spheres. INGO activities thus did not weaken the sovereignty of the Syrian state over its territory, but did change the way this sovereignty could be performed and experienced.

Professional INGO programs introduced a strict conceptual distinction between Iraqi and Syrian aid recipients, and their project proposals and reports stipulated percentages for both. This practice elevated nationality, a key organizing principle of state sovereignty, to new importance.[23] Establishing percentages of Iraqi and Syrian aid recipients who were to profit from certain projects was linked to ideas about "do no harm" principles, according to which aid projects focused exclusively on Iraqis could have fueled resentment from the host population. Particularly in education projects, the continued distinction made between Syrian and Iraqi children, the latter described as the reason for the overcrowding of schools even though of course they had often arrived in Syria as toddlers, was striking. To use the example of Première Urgence's description of its school rehabilitation program, in an announcement concerning the completion of two new school buildings:

> These two schools, with a capacity to host 1.050 pupils, will allow the development of a response to the overcrowding of Syrian public schools and will promote the enrolment of Iraqi refugee children. Over 33.500 Iraqi children are enrolled in Syrian schools and over 75% of these are attending schools in the greater Damascus region. . . ." We are proud of this result and are now eagerly looking forward to the creation of educational programmes with the support of the Syrian Ministry for Education, with the goal to ensure the future of Syrian and Iraqi children," explained Sandra Bachrach, Première Urgence's chief of mission in Syria.

In this text, Première Urgence is not simply concerned with easing the lives of disadvantaged children, but is also focused on promoting a continuing distinction between Iraqi and Syrian children. The reference to overcrowding and the figures, percentages, and locations of Iraqi children imply that Iraqi children are somehow alien to the Syrian education sector. Given that the existence of "alien" Iraqi refugees was the raison d'être for INGO presence in Syria, promoting their distinction was in fact existential to these organizations. This observation again points out that INGOs working on refugee issues were closely bound to the exclusions linked to nationalism and liberal statehood, rather than standing outside or even opposed to such exclusions.

Turning now to the final key point arising from the IRC interview, the following and last section on professional INGOs considers the relevance of their seeking of and dependence on third-party funding. The IRC interlocutors made several key references to the relationship between funding and their programs. IRC's focus on education was explained by the statement that most INGOs were focused on education, as "this is where the funding is and the need." Healthcare, on the other hand, was "90 percent taken care of by SARC [Syrian Arab Red Crescent] and funding for healthcare goes to them." At the time of the interview, IRC was looking to add fourteen staff members to the existing ten employees to cover an increased number of project in 2010. In reference to the expansion, the IRC director stated: "Last year, the number of Iraqi children registering in schools was so much lower, so it was very difficult to justify any increased funding for this and the donors were very reluctant to fund any more projects. The latest information from the MoE [Ministry of Education] is that they are expecting more children to register, so this should mean that there should be more funding forthcoming."

Relying on the potentially wonky statistics of the Syrian Ministry of Education in order to decide on the allocation of millions of dollars of funding was concerning in and of itself. More relevant for an understanding of the new political situation introduced by international aid to Syria was the particular interplay of foreign donors, INGOs, and Syrian state institutions that the IRC director's statement implies. The power of donors' assumptions and the funding flows also became apparent in an interview with a program manager at Terre des Hommes. Terres des Hommes presented a slightly special case, as a Syrian branch of TdH Lausanne had been active in Damascus for decades, originally focusing on helping refugees from Palestine. TdH Syria and TdH Lausanne became involved with Iraqi refugees in 2007 when UNHCR was looking for any established organizations that would be able to implement Iraqi refugee projects.

RESEARCHER: Are TdH projects limited?

PARTICIPANT: Yes of course. It all depends on the funding. After the end of the project we provide a report and we discuss the possibility of renewing the project or not. According to the report and the result, the target achievement of the project.

RESEARCHER: Are most Iraqis that come to you registered with UNHCR?

PARTICIPANT: No, no. That depends . . . some. Last year we had a regulation that we cannot help any Iraqi if he is not registered in UNHCR. But this year, when we start a new project, one of the project funding from the EU, they set a regulation that the project has to target Iraqis not registered in UNHCR.[24]

Funding is the most fundamental aspect to professional INGOs operations: no funding, no projects. Unlike some of the smaller, informal INGOs to be discussed below, professional INGOs had to pay staff salaries, office rents, and administrative overheads, and they required large amounts of money. UNHCR and INGOs did not provide detailed breakdowns of their budgets; however, some documents allowed for a rough idea of the figures involved. The Danish Refugee Council in the fiscal year ending September 30, 2009 spent around USD 4.6 million on its projects in Iraq, Syria, and Jordan. The IRC had a budget of around USD 6.4 million for the Middle East in 2009; in 2010 this figure grew to around USD 9.8 million.[25] These figures were dwarfed by UNHCR's budgets for Syria of around USD 167 million in 2010 and around USD 130 million in 2009 (some of which would have gone to DRC and IRC).[26] The European Union donated around EUR 37 million in 2009 for the Iraqi refugee issue (extraordinary, as standard annual funding to Syria amounted to around EUR 30 million).[27] Even if the highest estimates for Iraqi refugee numbers of 1.5 million would have applied (UNHCR never registered more than around 250,000 Iraqis as refugees in Syria), these budgets were large, amounting for UNHCR alone to around USD 1.5 per day for each registered Iraqi refugee in 2009.

These flows of money dedicated to "nongovernmental" efforts to manage Iraqi migration show perhaps most clearly that INGO practices were indeed part and parcel of the global, social, and material relations that transported a particular political rationality. In the case of Iraqi migration, INGOs filled an institutional gap, allowing a multitude of states to intervene on Syria's territory to focus on a mutual interest: that Iraqi migration would not destabilize the territorial and social divisions on which the stability of states rested.[28] The global flows of money created a web of connections between foreign states, the United Nations, Syrian state institutions, and INGOs. The trajectory and acceptance of the funds through and across boundaries of territory, bureaucracy, culture, and, indeed, sovereignty, and their link to the implementation of certain ideas (education for Iraqi children in Syria, for example), highlighted that money was a crucial transporter of norms, but also showed how governance techniques, including those linked to sovereignty, were transmitted through humanitarian aid.

Volunteer INGOs

In addition to the large, professional INGOs described above, by 2010 a number of smaller organizations had set up projects for Iraqis that were neither officially registered with the Syrian government nor relied on professional staff. These organizations did not maintain regular, close contact with Syrian ministries and their staff generally possessed a deeper, more intuitive knowledge of Syrian government red lines. As they were more able to navigate these, they tended to be more open to meeting me as a researcher and allowing me to participate in and observe their programs.

The volunteer INGO that I had closest access to, and that was the most intriguing of all, was an organization called Iraqi Student Project (ISP). ISP was the creation of an elderly, retired couple from the United States, and aimed to help gifted Iraqi high-school graduates receive scholarships to liberal-arts colleges in the United States. Apart from a single paid employee in the United States, where ISP was registered as a non-profit organization, this INGO was funded entirely through the couple's small retirement income from the US social security system and donations of time and money from a small group of supporters in the United States and Syria. ISP was run out of the couple's rented two-bedroom flat in central Damascus, which functioned as a private residence and a work space where volunteer teachers—often American or British TOEFL teachers working at the American Language Institute close by—gave classes to prepare the selected students for their study and life in the United States. ISP originated from its founders' engagement in the US peace movement and their protests against the 2003 invasion of Iraq. After spending two years in Damascus studying Arabic and learning that many young Iraqis in Syria could not attend university because of expensive fees, they decided to create ISP, which was modeled on a project that had been developed during the Balkan wars of the 1990s.[29]

The key fascination that developed from my participant-observation at ISP concerned the intense and complicated power dynamics between the elderly directors, the volunteers, and the Iraqi students. After several severe conflicts at the organization, in which students were expelled from the program for unclear reasons, I became aware of the sharp power imbalance between directors and students that operated underneath the organization's studiously maintained egalitarian and peaceful veneer. Given this chapter's focus on how INGOs contributed to the construction of particular forms of statehood, the following paragraphs tease out how the relationships encountered at ISP could be traced to state-related boundaries and exclusions.

ISP's selection process was based on several standard items, such as holding Iraqi nationality, not having been accepted for UNHCR resettlement, having a good school record, and expressing an interest to return to Iraq after finishing college to contribute to the country's future. In addition, selection depended on assessments of the candidate's family environment and his or her psychological stability and potential for coping alone in a foreign country. The two directors, through home visits and interviews, carried out these assessments in an informal manner. If selected, candidates joined a program of classes and were subjected to continuing, informal monitoring by the directors and volunteer teachers. Should a student be considered "not ready," he or she could be required to complete a further year of program or could be expelled at any time.

The following excerpts from field notes illustrate the personal nature of these assessments and report a conversation with one of the directors about several of the students:

> He [the ISP director] talked about Firas and how he was such a great kid. "This guy's essays, they are just so good, his use of English. . . . If I could speak directly to any of the people in admissions at the colleges, I would really tell him to take this guy, he's just going to take off and flourish over there." It's clear that Firas is one of the director's favorites and I just can't get it out of my head that it has to do with his pretty tough story: 1.5 years in poverty in Jordan, during which he was alone with his father and had to take care of the household etc.
>
> He named Radi as one of the students that he had some doubts about having the maturity to success "once he is alone over there." Although he acknowledged that Radi was very passionate about his subject and very good in class in getting the others to participate, he somehow doubted that Radi had the toughness to "hack it" once out there in the States by

> himself. I was quite surprised by this assessment, as Radi lives on his own in Syria and is managing his affairs by himself, and though there is indeed something quite "young" about him, I personally definitely found him quite tough and grounded.[30]

The two directors' personal views held enormous sway over the students' future. Most students considered their success in the program to be monumentally important. One Iraqi young woman described how, at the time she was being considered for ISP, her alternative option would have been a job as a waitress in one of the new malls of Damascus, which highlights how the chance to complete a university degree in the United States was an extremely desirable exit from a dead-end existence in Syria. This desire to succeed, coupled with the arbitrary and personal control exercised by the program directors, created pressure on the students to conform to the directors' expectations. The following extract from a conversation with one of the Iraqi students, which occurred in the immediate aftermath of the sudden and unexpected dismissal of another student, highlighted this situation.

> The thing with Hussein was such a shock. With Huda, ok, it was kind of predictable that they wanted to kick her out, but with Hussein it was a complete shock. Everyone likes him, he is such a friendly and smart guy. And they did not give him a warning. After this, everyone feels insecure, no one knows what is going to happen.
>
> I feel so afraid now. Do we have to depend on her moods? Everything can change, I don't know how to behave so that she likes me. Today when she said something about my trousers, I thought, oh no, I'm not going to wear these trousers again. Does she not like my hair the way it is? Does she not like my nose today? Or if I write an essay that she does not like. . . . First we were under pressure in Iraq, then we were under the pressure of the Syrian government when we don't know whether they will kick the Iraqis out, and now we are under the pressure of ISP.[31]

But ISP's personal relationships were also fused with wider political relationships that strongly shaped the power dynamics at the organization.

In the above quote, the student likens the ISP directors' power to former pressures she experienced in Iraq and Syria that had been exercised by governments. Materially, the power exercised by the ISP directors was directly linked to their US citizenship, which bonded them to the US government and pension system that provided them with the money required to run their organization. Their security and power, stemming from their US citizenship, was inversely reflected by the insecurity and weakness of the ISP students, whose Iraqi citizenship bonded them to the Iraqi government, which provided them with neither opportunities nor money. The ISP directors' ability to intervene in Iraqi students' lives, and to decide their future, was afforded them by the political and social organization of statehood. Astonishingly, the fact that the directors' strength was thus directly linked to the source of power responsible for the students' displacement and impoverishment was lost on most of ISP's foreign volunteers, and was, indeed, initially lost on me. To the students, it remained highly obvious. I learned this during an interview with one of them, who responded in a scathing tone when I pointed out the personal sacrifices that the ISP directors were making to run ISP. Bitterly, she stated:

> But they are the fault of all our problems! They have made all the problems for us, in Iraq, not only now, but for decades! [Their sacrifice] is so little, compared with the problems that they created for us. They [the directors] were part of this peace group, this silly thing. . . . They want you to be dependent on them, they want that you ask them for help all the time, they like it when you are weak. They don't like it if you are independent. But last year I was honest with them and then later they turned this against me and used it as an argument not to send me to college.[32]

ISP students were frequently encouraged to express their national pride as Iraqis, and maps and numerous books about Iraq's rich history were displayed in the ISP flat. But representations of Iraq as a place of destruction and hopelessness also abounded, in contrast to which the United States appeared as a safe haven, the only chance for these students to lead meaningful lives. The ISP directors were frequently cynical and critical about US politics in the Middle East, but strongly celebrated other instances of US culture, such as the peace movement, which they remembered fondly, and the civil rights campaigns, and encouraged the students to celebrate these too. One striking instance of such a celebration occurred on Martin Luther King Day 2010. To mark the occasion, the directors had invited everyone to watch two episodes of a TV series on nonviolent resistance, as well as a video of King's "I Have a Dream" speech. Afterward, a discussion of the films took place. Practicing animated but respectful discussions was a key element that ISP students were expected to learn in preparation for the US college system. The following section documents part of the discussion.

DIRECTOR A: Does anyone have any comments or questions?

STUDENT A: There is a comparison with our situation in Iraq. We need to rebuild our country together. How can you change a country by yourself alone, but if we put our hands together that will change our country. We have Sunni, Shi'a, Christians . . . but we are together, we have to put all this aside, we need to bring knowledge from America, after that we will be able to rebuild our country.

[In response to these comments, Director A sighs and claps her hands.]

STUDENT B: There has to be a strategy and planning together, these movements just didn't happen, there needed to be a national understanding, that is what they were striving for. That is the toughest part. The endurance that they had, amazing, that was the most amazing to me.

STUDENT C: Common in both movements was the decision not to go ahead with violence, even if they abuse you, then they will feel that they did something worse to you and you should look them directly in their eyes.

DIRECTOR A: Notice that it was women and girls AND men.

DIRECTOR B: Yes. "We will use our capacity to absorb violence to the same extent as their capacity to commit violence": Talk about something so much harder.

STUDENT D: Usually if someone is attacked the other will counterattack, but with nonviolence you drain the will to attack.

DIRECTOR B: Gandhi is so famous, but has anybody ever heard of this guy? (Holds up a book titled *Nonviolent Soldier of Islam*).[33]

As the discussion died down, one of the directors picked up a guitar and began singing "We Shall Overcome," a famous US protest song from the civil rights movement, urging everyone to join in. At one point, the director changed the words of the chorus to: "deep in my heart, I do believe, we shall live in peace—ya Iraq," therefore making an explicit connection between the nonviolent civil rights movement in the United States of the 1960s and contemporary Iraq.

The selection of videos and the subsequent discussion clearly urged the Iraqi students to draw parallels between nonviolent movements in India and the United States and the situation in Iraq; whenever a student said something along these lines the directors demonstrated agreement. Even from a superficial political and historical analysis, this comparison was, of course, ludicrous. But for the arguments at stake in this article, the situation provides a snapshot of how the translation of the values of liberal citizenship and state government into an illiberal context, via the humanitarian aid sector, worked in the nitty-gritty of the everyday. Here, education was combined with real material incentives (the opportunity to study in the United States) to train students in the particular form of the "good life" that the organization's directors believed in and that is an important element of liberal, domestic politics in the United States. This situation stood in marked contrast with the Syrian (and Iraqi) context, where the open discussion of any form of politics, let alone different forms of protest or social engagement, were taboo and did not form part of the educational curriculum. Differences in opinion and criticism of Syria's politics were not met with educational and material persuasion, but with harsh violence and punishment.

Also along other lines, students were encouraged to abandon certain cultural traits, and there was a narrow framework of behavior that made someone a "good ISP kid." The following extracts from a conversation with the ISP directors develop some of the complex understandings of the United States and Iraq as separate spaces that were present throughout the ISP programs, and how they were linked to distinct forms of behavior and knowledge:

DIRECTOR A: The students get taught for one year by voluntary teachers to improve their English and to prepare them for the way teaching is

> done in the US. In Iraq, students generally learn information off by heart and reproduce it in the text. In the US, they have to learn critical thinking and analysis and to write good essays. There are classes every day. Once a week my wife [one of the directors] does a writer's workshop that focuses on essay writing skills.
>
> For many Americans it is an experience to meet an Iraqi. It becomes a real place for them. One of our students was at immigration when the officer stopped short at the passport and did a double take, then expressed surprise that this girl, who does not wear the hijab and wears modern clothes, could be from Iraq. "You can walk around like that in Iraq?" Yes you can. "Is that a tattoo?" Yes. "You can have a tattoo in Iraq?" Yes you can.[34]

Iraq and the United States were understood at ISP as two distinct educational spaces in which knowledge and knowledge production functioned and were understood and valued differently. In order to succeed in the United States, the students had to abandon aspects of their previous "Iraqi" learning and acquire new modes of knowledge and thinking. Modern statehood closely links knowledge production to questions of legitimacy and government. Distinct epistemologies connect citizens to the imagined sovereign in a particular way and establish the citizen's home state as different (and better) than all other states; the fundamental boundaries of security and global hierarchy are established through discourses about what constitutes valuable, useful, dynamic, and creative learning and knowledge, as much as through other media.[35] In this sense, knowledge and education have been added to oaths of allegiance and religion as ways of connecting populations with their rulers.

The distinct forms of Iraqi and US knowledge became visible at ISP seminars, during discussions about representations of Iraq and the schooling the students had experienced in the past. My recordings of numerous classes showed that, of course, Iraqis did indeed learn critical thinking in Iraqi schools, though its form and content was different than in the West, where it could be dismissed as anti-Western propaganda. Most of the students reflected critically themselves on the image of a rapacious and imperialist United States waiting to steal Iraq's oil, as they had been taught in

Iraq. Crucially, these observations demonstrated that knowledge and its content were linked to territory and government and were a form of power controlled by state institutions, through which the state's boundaries and the unity of its government, population, and territory were created and demonstrated. To fit in and succeed at US colleges, Iraqi students had to acquire the modes of knowledge production intimately tied to US statehood that indicated US territory as a separate physical and conceptual space. It was remarkable that the ISP directors considered it necessary that their students (who had already been preselected according to criteria of education and personality that would conform with US college life) receive months of training to achieve an appropriate standard. Their experience of several students failing in the United States had taught them that students needed much more than English-language training to make it.

In a different way, education also played a central role for the activities of the small organization Native without a Nation (NWN), created and run principally by an Iraqi man called Firas. NWN's activities, such as workshops for children and teenagers, home visits to depressed or hard-up families, and Skype exchanges between Iraqi and US youngsters, had developed out of Firas's personal social activism since his arrival in Syria in 2006. Further, NWN ran a website on which Iraqi teenagers could publish their stories and art. A small group of US-based supporters helped organize the Internet exchanges with a school in upstate New York, and funding consisted of occasional donations of equipment from friends and small cash donations.[36] Although NWN's projects helped mostly Iraqis, thus making a distinction based on national identity, the organization's close focus on personal narratives, friendship, and nonjudgmental compassion made it an example of international solidarity that did not depend on reconstructions of the state boundaries or the categorization of people into populations of citizens. In this sense NWN activities themselves stood outside the edifice of statehood, although, of course, they took place within its context.

Perhaps because of Firas's own in-depth experiences with UNHCR's and the Syrian state's and donor states' harsh categories and exclusions, NWN's activities focused on the personal disposition of the persons involved in the projects but did not use them to categorize or connect them to official procedures. No a priori assumptions were drawn about people's needs. NWN's website presented peoples' stories without judgment-laden introductions or texts about the situation of Iraqis as such, their illegality and so forth. Many narratives concerned memories of violence experienced in Baghdad, but many also articulated instances of empowerment and independence. One of Firas's stated aims was to develop a platform for young Iraqi people to express themselves freely in their own words and thoughts. The following quotes, taken from the website, illustrate the diversity of these:

> *Othman Abd al-Rahman Mohammad:*
>
> My name is Othman Abd al-Rahman Mohammad. I am an Iraq pupil and I am proud of being an Iraqi. Despite the fact that I live in my second country Syria, I love this country so much as well as its generous people.
>
> I love to study in a perfect way. I love my school, my family and my relatives who are away from me due to the cruel circumstances. I also love helping my father with the housework.
>
> *From Noor, Muna, and Anfal:*
>
> Since the first art show we had in Damascus, we felt admiration and encouragement from the audience to continue painting, and talk about the mixtures of colors. We were often asked if we ever went to art schools. The answer always is "We never studied art, it's just what we do and like to do. We do express what we feel and we convert it on our paintings." . . . At the end of the meeting we agreed that we have to be strong and keep getting better.
>
> We noticed the difference between the first and last art show, our paintings became stronger and more expressive through the subjects and the colors. Every painting had story. Now we are preparing for another art show, with new paintings, new stories, and new style. We will never stop looking forward. We will never be silent.
>
> *Mustafa, age seventeen:*
>
> I will never forget that accident. I no more want to be in Iraq so that I don't have to face any of this again. That doesn't make my situation

> any easier as I have heart failure and the medical care is basically non-existent. All I hope for is to know my future after registering with the UNHCR as a refugee.[37]

The state is not absent from these self-representations, and boundaries, both physical and imagined, structure the thoughts and practices of these young people. However, the key point was that NWN's activities did not depart from these boundaries in the way other INGOs did. They did not contain regulations or classifications according to people's official position vis-à-vis states. NWN's semi-spontaneous interventions relied on in-depth personal knowledge of persons who were interested in receiving support. Rather than aiming to guide or change these lives in any particular direction, this support created small instances of success or positive feelings, which empowered people to continue struggling against the often overwhelming way in which power was affecting them. By ignoring statehood's frameworks in these small ways, NWN's practices used an alternative lens through which Iraqis in Syria were not consistently recast as outsiders, but simply as fellow humans. A similar dynamic could be observed during the web conferences that NWN organized between Iraqi youth in Damascus and a school class in upstate New York. These conferences, held around every six months, were conducted via Skype and included video calling so that the partaking individuals could see each other. During the calls, the children and teenagers would introduce themselves and show each other artwork they had made or narrate items they had recently studied. The focus on shared, enjoyable activities among individuals (rather than on divisive, negative experiences of imagined collectives) created a basis of understanding of one another's humanness regardless of territorial, governmental, and population divisions.

Conclusion

Despite growing poverty in Syria in the early years of the new millennium, especially in northern villages and in urban slums, up until the mid-2000s international NGOs played no significant role in the fully government-controlled aid effort. Iraqi migration changed all that. It was a crucial catalyst that set Syria and the surrounding region on course to becoming one of the world's major international humanitarian aid markets. This chapter described the activities of some of the first international emergency NGOs to begin operations in Syria in 2008, and analyzed their relationship to the construction of state-related boundaries and exclusions. Today, in 2016, hundreds of aid INGOs are working in and around Syria, mostly for Syrian refugees, writing projects, implementing programs, setting up offices, hiring experts, arranging glossy fund-raising material, and mailing it off to hundreds of thousands of recipients across the globe.

The Syrian conflict has politicized and split the international aid effort. Even though all of the professional INGOs mentioned in this chapter continue to work in now war-torn Syria, they do so on different sides. The IRC, for example, was abruptly ordered by the government to leave Damascus in 2010 for unclear reasons. In 2014, the government announced more explicit rules of engagement for foreign INGOs. INGOs are now only allowed to provide aid in areas under government control. Areas under rebel control cannot be serviced, which enforces a collective punishment on anyone living there. Most INGOs agreed to this and continue to deliver aid in partnership with the Syrian Arab Red Crescent, a government-controlled institution. The only large organization to pack up shop in response was Mercy Corps, essentially privileging its operations in rebel-held areas at the expense of projects in areas under government control. Since closing its office in Damascus, Mercy Corps has developed large cross-border aid deliveries from Turkey, servicing rebel-held areas around Aleppo and Raqqa. Here, we again meet ICR, which joined the cross-border efforts in 2011; in 2014 those efforts reached a volume of over USD 70 million, dwarfing ICR's previous Iraqi refugee projects inside Syria. The Danish Refugee Council, Première Urgence, and Terres des Hommes today, in 2016, continue their operations from Damascus. This means that together with UNHCR and several other UN agencies, only a handful of INGOs deliver aid inside the government-held areas of Syria's contested territory, although this aid has hugely expanded in volume. A small, immensely valuable aid economy has developed under the close control of the Syrian government, which has, evidently, improved its knowledge and ability to manage the humanitarian aid sector since the Iraqi refugee crisis.

The arrival of INGOs in Syria and their growing interactions with government and society demonstrated the transformational power of the language of human rights and humanitarian protection, of nondiscrimination and empowerment, which appeared absurdly opposed to the illiberal politics of the Syrian government. But INGOs' drive to expand, and their scramble to be among the pioneers of Syria's aid sector, cowed them into a submissive, dependent attitude toward authorities, to the extent that the label "nongovernmental" became questionable, despite their international and seemingly independent origin.

The international aid sector consists of a huge variety of actors. Despite behaving surprisingly similar according to their shared humanitarian mode, INGOs differ in size, in nationality, and in operational focus. They work according to a much more entrepreneurial style than the United Nations, actively seeking out opportunities for funding and new programs, and are keen to present themselves as forerunners in responding to newly arisen crises. Their expatriate staff often includes younger and less experienced aid workers who earn less than UN officials but also enjoy a lower degree of security protocols and more freedom to hang out and live among locals. Unlike UN agencies, which had maintained small offices in Syria for decades and could expand on existing channels to government officials, the communication and cooperation between INGOs and Syrian authorities had to be developed from scratch. The resulting interactions, social programs, and spaces, all new to Syria, showed that the humanitarian management of migrants, based on the language of universal rights, could actually reduce the range of actions available to Iraqis far more than the ostensibly illiberal Syrian state. In particular, the humanitarian stage-managing of Iraqi subjectivity, and the representation of this subjectivity to international audiences, condensed it to a narrow set of experiences to be answered by a similarly narrow set of political solutions.

This narrowness of the international aid sector's understanding and response to forced migration in the Middle East must raise concern at a time in which this sector is expanding rapidly and wielding budgets in the billions of dollars, which are translated into projects targeting millions of displaced persons. In what ways is the interaction between foreign-aid actors and regional states developing, and how are local politics adjusting to the migration management via aid? Recent developments point toward growing political restrictions against migrants, both through complete border closures, as in Jordan, and through new visa requirements, as in Lebanon. In Jordan, Syrian refugees are increasingly concentrated in two enormous camps that are jointly run between UNHCR, INGOs, and the Jordanian police. Both camps operate on a system in which aid management combines with state security controls to extremely restrictive effect. Here, both the Syrian and the Jordanian government's increasingly "effective" harnessing of the international aid sector for their own security aims depressingly points toward a development in which regional states are integrating the most restrictive aspects of humanitarian refugee management while even the last remnants of its emancipatory and rights-based approach fall by the wayside.

5

Western Donor States in Syria

Layered Sovereignty

The previous chapters argued that the programs of UNHCR and international NGOs treated Iraqi identity and life in Syria according to a particular vision of statehood based on an assumed unity of territory, population, and government. This chapter focuses on the politics of Western donor states, whose funding made the humanitarian programs possible in the first place. Paradoxically, the international effort to refit Iraqis into a territorial and national state system included a host of extraterritorial interventions by foreign states into Syria. Here, donor states' actions simultaneously defied the state boundaries that humanitarian programs strove so much to uphold and re-create. To control the boundary-undoing activities of Iraqi migrants in Syria, Western donor states intervened across multiple territories and populations. Ironically, the construction of a state-centered politics, of fixed territories and nations, thus relied on transborder practices of control. Western donor states channeled their interests and influence via international NGOs, as chapter 4 showed. This chapter shows that the International Organisation for Migration (IOM) and UNHCR, both state organizations, played a similar role.

Western donor states' interventions into the Iraqi refugee crisis also highlighted that certain states could be "more sovereign" than others, according to material or moral criteria. The field of Iraqi migration made visible the existing hierarchies among nominally equal states, in which travel to "superior" sovereigns appeared as a prized gift that could be granted or withheld.[1] These hierarchies appeared in Syria via the material and organizational power brought to bear by Western donor states. Far from creating anarchy among equals, state sovereignty produced a layered process of governance in which human beings could influence one another according to their association with differently powerful states.

More than anything, therefore, the involvement of foreign states in the management of Iraqis on Syrian territory highlighted that "the domestic" and "the international" were conceptual spaces, and thus not fixed in their meaning and even location. For example, Western donor states were able to shape Syria's domestic space without upturning the façade of equality among sovereigns. Whereas certain practices, by powerful sovereigns, were thus able to traverse "domestic" and "international" space and negated their existence, other practices constructed them as separate and punished those who dared cross them. The acceptance or rejection of practices crossing the domestic and international divide were related to hierarchies of power: while Iraqi migration activated an international response to "correct" the contradictions that this migration created for state boundaries, the cross-border interventions by Western donor states were treated as unproblematic.

Foreign states' interventions in Syria showed that effective bureaucratic systems powered by sophisticated technological hardware were very powerful tools to manage a disparate population of Iraqis. Unlike the Syrian state's bureaucracies, which were shot through and thus weakened by corruption and personal relationships, Western donor states' bureaucracies implemented an abstract logic beyond the influence of even powerful and rich Iraqis. Dominant statehood was contained in and constructed through impermeable bureaucracies that ruled according to hidden laws and whose judgments had to be accepted as they were handed down. The importation and exercise of such techniques into Syria emphasized the hierarchy between those states wielding sophisticated technical apparatuses and those ruled by less structured and less disciplined administrations. The Syrian state conducted no elaborate preselection of Iraqis entering its territory, rather governing all persons on its territory similarly through techniques of insecurity and surveillance. Donor states, on the other hand, engaged in highly elaborate routines to select those Iraqis who would qualify as potential members of their citizenry and who they would bind themselves to in a relationship of rights and duties. This comparison pointed out that state-society relations in the United States and Europe relied more heavily on the myth of democratic representation and that of the public's ownership of the state. In Syria this myth was of much less importance for the continued functioning of the state.

This chapter begins with an overview of Western donor states' interventions into the Iraqi refugee crisis in Syria. The IOM and UNHCR served as gatekeepers and agents, and donor states' governments also engaged in direct activities through, for example, their own immigration clerks. The second part of the chapter analyzes the interventions of two important donor states, the United States and Germany, respectively. Although the United States of course was considered to hold special responsibility for Iraqi flight, the German government had opposed the 2003 invasion of Iraq and already hosted a significant Iraqi diaspora. Via a comparison between these two states' politics toward Iraqi migration, the chapter argues that their interventions had two effects: first, they affirmed the statehood of all involved states, and second, they affirmed the role of Iraqi migrants as problematic outsiders in need of rectification. Discussions about the end or continuation of nation-states in times of globalization are put to rest by arguing that waxing, waning, and paradoxical state practices are crucial elements of domestic and international statehood.

Western Donor States and Iraqi Migration to Syria

During field research, casual conversations with Iraqi research participants and Syrian friends frequently turned to the topic of life in the West. Many had relatives and friends living in Europe, the United States, or Canada and were hoping to emigrate themselves. The UNHCR resettlement program and the immigration programs of different governments presented opportunities.[2] The pros and cons of each option were pored over and explained. Complaints about perceived discrimination were discussed, and conspiracy theories about the reasons behind certain questions and requirements of immigration officials were circulated.

Emigration has been an important element of Iraqi society for decades and many Iraqis in Syria had worked or studied abroad.[3] Many of my interlocutors were aware of its positive and negative aspects.[4] Nevertheless, many (though by far not all) of my Iraqi research participants and acquaintances had pinned all their hopes on emigration. Syria offered little opportunity for higher education and no economic security to achieve a lifestyle on par with the prewar situation in Iraq. This fostered a belief, in particular among university-educated Iraqi families, that Syria did not offer a good future for their children. Further, the worry that the instability in Iraq would continue in the long term, as well as a desire to join relatives abroad, and sometimes sheer youthful curiosity about the world and a desire for adventure, all fueled Iraqis' interest to migrate further. Western territories and nations thus featured prominently in Iraqis' thoughts about their future plans and lives. These entities were associated with hope, but also with overwhelmingly strong borders, which manifested in visa requirements, passports, interviews, letters of rejection, and sheer distances and cost of travel, all contributing to feelings of humiliation and powerlessness. These feelings were illustrated by the following quote from an interview with a young Iraqi man who compared his previous travel experiences to his current predicament:

> And most important, the Iraqi, when he traveled, for example, we traveled a long time ago, we were respected. In the airport, at the borders, by the state—wherever we went we were respected. Now, there is nothing like this at all. Wherever we go, there is no respect. You are Iraqi? What's that, Iraqi. Go, no . . . when we went to the airport, maybe they let our passports through immediately—now, if they hear Iraqi, you have to wait until last. Because you are Iraqi. Why is it like this? Wasn't the basis, when they entered, the liberation of Iraq?[5]

The reduced acceptance of Iraqi passports as *libre passage,* and the consequent lack of freedom of movement, were a very tangible demonstration of the reduced clout of Iraqi citizenship and the Iraqi state. It demonstrated the lack of respect and reward that formal association with the Iraqi state received from other, more powerful states and confirmed the lack of interest of Iraqi state institutions for the fate of its citizens abroad. Growing travel barriers instructed Iraqis that their citizenship was worthless, and planted the idea that as an Iraqi, it was necessary to obtain the protection of another government, even though emotionally the idea of abandoning one's nation might be controversial and painful. The idea that a better life was possible abroad, and the hurdles that foreign states created for people with Iraqi papers, created a hierarchy between states and their citizens. Those Iraqis wishing to emigrate were forced into a position of trying to comply with the numerous requirements of the more powerful (and desirable) sovereign, and of waiting, often for months or even years, for a decision without knowing what factors would influences its outcome.

The UNHCR resettlement, and other immigration programs, such as skilled migrant schemes, family reunification, or asylum claims, offered various opportunities for onward travel from Syria. These programs involved direct interventions of foreign state officials on Syrian territory. Although all required, at some stage, a "confessionary moment" by Iraqis in front of a foreign official, in which any and all questions about a person's life and conduct were permitted, the exact routines required by different states varied.[6] The United States, for example, relied heavily on the IOM to further process those Iraqis who had been preselected by UNHCR clerks for US resettlement. In Syria, the IOM ran a refugee processing center exclusively for the United States, where IOM staff concluded a range of services for the United States Refugee Admission Program (USRAP). For example, IOM conducted interviews to double check eligibility and identities, obtained additional biographic data, and worked to "elicit testimony of past persecution" in a "chronological narrative." It promised to enter "all required bio-data into the US State Department Worldwide Refugee Admissions Processing System (WARPS) database."[7] Further, IOM staff would request the necessary security name checks from US government agencies and provide on-site assistance during "adjudication circuit rides," which was the term for visits to Syria by Department of Homeland Security (DHS) officials. During these visits, officials conducted the final checks and decisions on resettlement files. IOM was in charge of "scheduling refugee appointments, managing case files, distributing DHS/CIS decision letters at the conclusion of the circuit ride, and supervising interpreters."

IOM effectively functioned as an outsourced branch of US government ministries, and channeled activities of the US state, which were carried out on Syrian territory and had a direct impact on the population living on this territory.[8] This channeling of US power via an international organization had the effect of veiling the presence of the United States, which became more clearly visible only in the very last step of the process when officials from the DHS arrived for their "circuit rides" to interview Iraqi applicants and provide a final decision. Here, IOM functioned as an institutional gatekeeper between boundary-defying state practices that contradicted Syria's territorial exclusivity, and that in fact created a situation of layered statehood in which the officials and politics of several states influenced the lives of the same people, living on the same territory, in a very direct way.

The United States was the only state to rely so heavily on the IOM. Other donor states, such as Germany or Norway, were more inclined to trust the UNHCR selection process, as their officials did not create additional steps through the IOM, but directly interviewed UNHCR-selected Iraqis. Officials from these states communicated their preferences for potential applicants to UNHCR before preselection took place, when they announced their state's so-called resettlement quota, that is, the number of Iraqis to be accepted in a given year. For example, Norwegian officials informed UNHCR managers that they wished to receive 60 percent women through their quota, and Germany's sectarian request for Christian Iraqis was publically rejected by UNHCR—however, then resurfaced, reformulated as Germany's particular concern to resettle "religious minorities" (considered especially vulnerable).[9] Through these requests, the influence of donor states in the domestic sphere and politics of Syria could have momentous impact on the lives of individual Iraqis. As in the case of IOM, UNHCR's gatekeeper function served to blur the power of individual donor states and presented the resettlement process through a single prism of humanitarianism and generosity.

Apart from offering onward migration opportunities, donor states financed the enormous aid sector aimed at Iraqis by channeling funds to UNHCR, the Syrian government, and, to a lesser extent, international

NGOs (who mostly received their money via UNHCR). Donor states sent hundreds of millions of dollars annually to Syria from 2008 onward, with the stated aim of improving Iraqi lives and helping the Syrian state cushion the financial burden of hosting Iraqis.[10] These donations allowed UNHCR to pay monthly stipends to Iraqi families, enabled the World Food Programme to distribute bi-monthly food packages, and led to renovations in the Syrian education and health sector. Such money also paid the high salaries of foreign-aid workers as well as the lesser salaries of the dozens, if not hundreds, of Syrian staff that the humanitarian sector employed. Further, it lined the pockets of Syrian businessmen who provided, for example, the food packages or were involved in associated transport services. The funds thus contributed to diverse social and economic developments in Syria, including new networks of patronage and corruption.

UNHCR and NGO publications systematically veiled the origin of the funds that made assistance to Iraqis possible. This absence of communication corresponded to a lack of awareness among Iraqis about who funded the aid and resettlement programs.[11] One participant was convinced that the social security funds received by Iraqi migrants in Sweden came directly from the Iraqi state. Rather than emphasizing and advertising their involvement and donations to Iraqis, donor states provided no information to Iraqis about the impact their decisions were having. The chief mechanisms through which donor aims were achieved were international institutions and NGOs, which outwardly appeared as independent, international actors without any particular state affiliation. The fact that their actions and decisions were strongly influenced by, or formed a cohesive apparatus with, donor governments was very difficult to perceive and document for outsiders. Yet state officials, both Syrian and foreign, international aid workers, and media held privileged knowledge about the institutional structures through which aid money was obtained and distributed. Whereas internationally, the Syrian government's request for and acceptance of foreign financial support allowed Syrian officials to participate in a range of discourses and activities that demonstrated Syria's ability to behave like a respectable state, domestically, hiding the origins of this money allowed the continuation of an unencumbered Syrian domestic space that, conceptually, remained the exclusive domain of the Syrian state.[12]

International awareness of donor state involvement created a further paradox: while hosting Iraqi migrants constructed Syria as a generous state and nation, the acceptance of foreign funds to deal with this migration also identified Syria as a country in crisis and located it closer to being a developing country than a fully fledged sovereign state.[13] Donor states' influence on crucial turning points in Iraqi lives in Syria created a real and imagined web or layer of state power for Iraqis to navigate. The opacity surrounding donor states' involvement only heightened the effect of this power by keeping Iraqis waiting and guessing about which element of their identity to emphasize when approaching any particular aid program. Through their funds and resettlement quotas, donor states supported the humanitarian portrayal of Iraqi migration. But research participants' reports on intrusive and aggressive questioning by UN and donor state officials revealed the application of naked power and the treatment of Iraqi migrants as dangerous security risks and financial burdens. Resettlement and aid processes combined donor states' caring and threatening policies, and emphasized, at different times, different aspects of Iraqi existence as suited those policies and processes. In fact, the crucial power of all the states involved in Iraqi migration was to construct, portray, and represent Iraqi lives selectively and as official channels and interests saw fit. A rich mix of mechanisms emphasized some and veiled other facets of Iraqi lives in Syria, including the highly selective manner in which Iraqis themselves chose to portray themselves when interacting with those in power.

The following section details the involvement of two important donor and resettlement states, the United States and Germany. In addition to considering these two states' activities in Syria, the analysis will reflect on the intertwining of domestic political debates about Iraqi migration with the techniques used by state officials abroad.

Germany and Iraqi Migration

Back in 2010, Germany was a small- to medium-sized player in the international aid response to the Iraqi crisis. This would radically change five years later, when hundreds of thousands of Syrians would begin arriving in Germany as a result of the Syrian war. In July 2010, 2,046 Iraqis were resettled from Syria to Germany, compared with 14,250 to the United States, 907 to Australia, and 102 to France.[14] Aside from resettlement, the other main route for Iraqis to access Germany at least on a temporary basis was by claiming asylum; in 2010, 12,093 Iraqis claimed asylum in Germany, of which on average around 50 percent would receive at least some form of temporary leave to remain.[15] The regulatory process through which Iraqis first approached German territory was decisive for the consequent treatment they received. For example, whereas UNHCR resettlement resulted in a very stable residency status and generous monthly benefits, "regular" asylum seekers remained in a much more precarious situation.

At the same time that the German government decided to participate, for the first time, in UNHCR's resettlement program, thousands of existing Iraqi asylum seekers in Germany began having their residency permits revoked, mostly after years of living in the country. German authorities operated a complicated and contradictory jungle of laws and bureaucratic procedures to address Iraqi immigration. Different agencies and authorities operated independently across different state bodies and became mobilized according to the different ways in which Iraqis arrived on German territory.[16] German statehood, its bounded territory and population, emerged out of a web of human interactions that nevertheless were all guided according to a particular political rationality, and through their outcomes created the German state's particular form of organization.[17] Iraqi migrants, in Syria, in Germany, and in transit between them, presented the human bodies on which this organization could be visited and carried out.

In Damascus, Iraqi research participants regularly mentioned Germany as a possible destination for onward travel. For example, three interlocutors had acquaintances or relatives living in Germany. In two cases, relatives had been resettled, and in another case, they had migrated many years ago. One afternoon, conversation at the house of an Iraqi family, which was desperately waiting to be resettled, turned toward Germany. The parents spoke about the case of a single, female friend who had been resettled in Germany, as described in the following field note extract.

> He spoke at length about the chaos and lack of transparency of the UNHCR operations in Syria. . . . More than once the case of one of their friends was mentioned, who received resettlement in Germany—and came back after a month, taking the immigration stamp that is valid for three years and then coming back to Syria because she did not like it in Germany. "She does not need it!" the wife exclaimed, and the husband repeated this story as an example of the perceived randomness of the resettlement choice.[18]

Here, Germany's resettlement of a woman from a religious minority (she was Christian), who met the humanitarian criteria of helplessness and fear, was essentially revealed as a fake. The presumptions that the woman in question was persecuted in Iraq and unable to integrate in Syria proved incorrect, as ultimately she preferred her vague residency status in Syria to the presumed proper status in Germany and was willing to regularly travel to Baghdad. Resettlement, which provided a three-year immigration status in Germany as well as an income from the German state, simply served as an additional security strategy should political developments in Syria and Iraq worsen. Here, the two distinct spaces and relations of Syrian and German statehood were leveraged to the maximum advantage of the lucky resettlee, though far from the way they were designed and imagined by the humanitarian community. The Syrian mechanism of broad but unpredictable tolerance and the highly selective but (temporarily) guaranteed existence in Germany created a layered and unpredictable system of governance. For at the same time that some resettlement applicants got lucky, others, such as the family mentioned above, were left waiting desperately for years and experienced the other side of donor states' Janus face: that of unfettered, not-to-be influenced, secretive decision making, and of exclusion, barriers, threats, and violence.[19] Limiting the number of Iraqis accepted for resettlement and keeping the criteria and mechanisms of choosing applicants secret established several key elements of donor state's power: the power to care, the power to select, the power to exclude, and in the extreme case, the power to decide over life and death, which, in the worst case, could be a consequence of nonresettlement. Crucially, donor states had sovereign, unquestionable power, as Iraqis could not seek any justification for decisions, could not question or influence the resettlement criteria, and could not even find out many basic facts about the processing of their resettlement file.[20]

While the involvement of Germany in the management of Iraqi migration on Syrian territory highlighted Germany's projection of international power, it was also closely linked to processes and decisions taken within Germany's domestic space. At the same time as German engagement in Syria intensified, German authorities began revoking the refugee claims of Iraqis who had migrated to Germany many years ago, whose claims had been awarded in recognition of their fear of persecution from the Iraqi government. German authorities interpreted refugee law to allow such revocation if the conditions that had previously justified the claim had disappeared owing to "significant and permanent changes." The removal of the Saddam government was considered such a change, and one that removed the repression that had justified Iraqis' claims and status in Germany.

Despite public criticism from UNHCR and the unique position that the German practice presented in the European Union, between 2003 and 2011 around 20,000 Iraqis living in Germany had their refugee status revoked.[21] Paradoxically, this withdrawal of permits happened at the same time as newly arriving Iraqis in Germany received leave to remain and were recognised as having a legitimate asylum or refugee claim.[22] Also, permit withdrawal did not lead to systematic, forced deportations of Iraqis from Germany, although a fraction of those with revoked permits *were* deported. Between 2003 and 2006, around 100 Iraqis annually were forcibly deported from Germany, according to government statistics (the reported total for this period was 473).[23] Forced deportations became possible only when a number of regulatory conditions were met, and even supporters of the massive permit withdrawal, such as Germany's conservative party, the Christian Democratic Union (CDU), acknowledged humanitarian reasons for not deporting Iraqis into the conflict zone of Baghdad.[24] But beyond actual deportation, the revocation of refugee status signaled to German society that this person no longer had a right to be under the protection of the German state and no longer held any special connection with the German nation, territory, or government. German responsibility for the permitless had ceased, and these persons became, according to German officialese, *ausreisepflichtig*, roughly translatable as "legally obliged to depart." In 2011, the European Court of Justice broadly confirmed the legality of Germany's position.

Comparing this mobilization of statehood with that of the Syrian state toward mass migration is highly revelatory of their differing state-society relations. In Germany, state power was exercised via a set of laws whose power stemmed from their presumed democratic origin, as an expression of popular will. These laws were strengthened through entrenched bureaucratic processes, which required detailed training and knowledge to implement, and which even minor errors or deviations could derail. Applicants were assessed according to and made to fit within a small bandwidth of knowledge, which erased nearly all possibility for individuality and difference beyond its categories. In classic Weberian style, the bureaucratic state took affect, emotion, and anything deemed to be part of private life out of the equation, as the law, assumed to have been developed out of a democratic and rational process, was considered as the morally correct and rational choice. Deporting Iraqis back into a war zone in this manner became a "necessary evil" required to uphold the overall morality of the law and stability of the state—even though, very obviously, materially it would not have mattered one iota to the stability of Germany whether 473 Iraqis remained on its territory or not. As the previous chapters showed, application of Syrian state power to Iraqi migrant life could not have been more different. Even after Syrian authorities began investing any resources *at all* into managing Iraqis as different, state procedures remained extremely haphazard, changeable, and very much subject to individual intervention, communication, and negotiation. Ironically, across the board, this awarded Iraqi migrants in Syria a much greater flexibility and space to live as locals than did the "iron cage" of German bureaucracy, with all its restrictions on work and education and its inflexible paperwork.

The power of law could also explain why the contradiction of revoking some Iraqis' permits, at the same time as other Iraqis were being granted asylum, could continue without threatening legal cohesion.[25] The rejection of previously accepted Iraqi refugees affirmed the German nation as a homogenous group of persons with unique links to German territory and government. The legal expelling of Iraqis via recategorizations and the issuance of letters and documents marked the internal boundaries of the nation, affirming its power over strangers.[26] The granting of asylum to new arrivals and the highly publicized German participation in UNHCR's resettlement program, on the other hand, affirmed Germany's international role as a great and generous power. As in Syria, Iraqi migration served as a field through which domestic and international spaces of German statehood could be translated into practice and made tangible and real.

The press coverage surrounding the arrival of the first Iraqi "resettlers" to Germany emphasizes how this particular international affair boosted Germany's international status as a great and generous power. UNHCR spokespersons lauded Germany's effort, stating that "Germany is providing a very positive example which we hope will inspire other European countries to consider resettling Iraqi refugees during 2009."[27] Another UNHCR representative added, "Germany has set an important example to ensure that especially vulnerable Iraqi refugees can plan their future life in peace and safety. The resettlement of these refugees is a valuable contribution to international refugee protection and the commitment and support received by the German authorities and civil society deserve our explicit appreciation."[28] In stark contrast to the treatment meted out to those Iraqis threatened with deportation (and indeed those deported), the first 120 resettled Iraqis received a personal welcome from a federal minister, who welcomed them with the words "we have prepared everything to make you feel comfortable."[29] In a related statement, Germany's national ombudsman for integration called on the population to receive Iraqis with "open arms," as it was a principle of humanity to quickly help people seeking protection. The message to refugees was to be "you are welcome."[30]

This highly staged performance projected Germany's international influence and served to affirm German power and participation in international affairs. Once again, the actual number of received Iraqis, a maximum of 1,500 via UNHCR, were negligible in terms of social or economic impact. It was their symbolic value that mattered, as well as the field they provided to set in motion a range of state practices that reconstructed and affirmed the German state as the ultimate arbiter inside and outside Germany. Here, "overlapping" state sovereignty did not simply refer to a situation in which actions by different states took place on a single territory. Instead, overlapping sovereignty rather explained, in a slightly crude metaphorical way, the way in which the practices of different states necessarily intertwined and influence one another. The manner in which the Syrian state included Iraqis in its population and territory gave opportunities for the German state to exercise its power. In conjunction with the hegemonic ideal of statehood, functioning as a yardstick of correctness, legitimacy, and stability, these overlapping constructions created a dynamic hierarchy in which those states who performed most perfectly could draw resources from this performance, which also legitimized their intervention into the spheres of less well-performing states. Tellingly, the interactions and negotiations preceding Germany's accession to the resettlement program took place between officials from Germany and UNHCR without the involvement of the Syrian state.[31] Without further investigation about the actual daily-life situation of Iraqis in Syria, German officials accepted that Iraqis in Syria faced no prospect of integration, which legitimized German intervention. Germany's power to intervene resulted directly from the judgment that Syria's "protection" of Iraqis was nonexistent or at least insufficient. The superiority of German statehood also emerged from the particular understanding of the term "protection" as a legal connection with a state, which Syria did not offer, and was thus linked to the different ways in which the German and Syrian state exercised their governance. The apparent fairness and transparency of Germany's bureaucratic apparatus, offering stability and integration, was contrasted with Syrian randomness and instability, a judgment that was, as demonstrated by the experience of Iraqi interlocutors, often nullified in daily-life experience.

Yet Germany's superior qualities as a state could not have been performed had there not been many Iraqis who were extremely keen and willing to be resettled to Germany. The fact that many Iraqis explained their willingness to resettle as the hope for stability and material support, as well as better life chances for their children, showed not only that the performance of German sovereignty was successful but also that the

German state indeed governed those people qualifying for citizenship in a way that promised greater prosperity and personal freedoms. This governance, which was linked to far-reaching and complex differences between the Syrian and German state, was part and parcel of the German state's success and strength, and reflected the Syrian state's much weaker success in establishing itself as the key focus of loyalty and identity for the people living on its territory.

The United States and Iraqi Migration

Between January 2007 and July 2010, the United States was the most important recipient of Iraqi resettlement cases from Syria by far. During this period, 14,255 Iraqis departed from Syria to the United States via UNHCR resettlement. In addition to resettlement, Iraqis living in the Middle East could apply to special immigration programs for people who had worked for the US Army. From within US territory, Iraqis could also claim asylum. According to US government statistics, from 2008 to 2010, inclusive, a total of 50,676 Iraqis were given immigration status, UNHCR resettlement cases thus making up, on average, one-quarter of the total.[32]

Given these numbers, it was not surprising that the United States was the most frequently discussed immigration option among my research participants. Participants analyzed the pros and cons of different US cities as well as conflicting information about the financial support refugees might receive, which frequently changed and differed according to the state of residence.[33] Although interlocutors hoping for resettlement to the United States sometimes expressed a muted excitement about traveling, the general attitude was that of long-term waiting amid uncertainty whether the hoped-for announcement, and eventually the tickets, would truly arrive. UNHCR (or IOM) informed Iraqis only *days* before their departure that their resettlement date was due—sometimes after years of waiting. Questions about the discomfort that Iraqis might feel when being offered resettlement to the country that many perceived to be at the root of Iraq's problems were only rarely raised. This was particularly ironic in cases when Iraqis described the actions of US forces as closely connected to their fear and ensuing flight. In fact, Iraqis often indicated that they considered it the United States' responsibility to help Iraqis, and thus had no problem with accepting US aid or resettlement, indeed sometimes regarding it as their right. The following quotes demonstrate this perception.

> OK—they wanted to change Iraq for the better. But now we haven't seen anything good at all. There is nothing good. OK—America entered Iraq and is not concerned about the situation of the Iraqis, what is happening with people, every day thousands are killed, a million have died, they are displaced, forced to leave their work, their work—all these things are not important to them. But when they entered at the beginning it was all to liberate Iraq. So yes, they are responsible to support Iraqis and to give them help because they have done this. It is necessary that they carry the responsibility.[34]

One young woman, when asked about the personal sacrifices that some Americans were making to help Iraqi refugees, said: "But they are the fault of all our problems! They have made all the problems for us, in Iraq, not only now, but for decades! . . . But it is so little, compared with the problems that they created for us."[35]

On first glance, such willingness to accept US responsibility confirms the liberal idea of responsible governments offering "protection." Similarly, the acceptance of continued US intervention in their lives and the acceptance of US territory as a place of safety and peace affirmed the narrative of the United States (and Europe) as superior sovereigns. It is important to note, however, that underneath these affirmations, other ideas raised in interviews and conversations pointed to a very different belief among Iraqis about what responsibility meant in this situation and where it stemmed from. A number of responses and opinions indicated that interlocutors understood it in a more paternalistic or perhaps absolutist way that had different implications for how state-society relations should and would be lived.

A further extract from the interview drawn on above states: "For example, why is the father responsible for the family? Isn't it that the government, which is bigger, is responsible for the people? Yes, it is necessary, they are responsible. They have to support and help Iraqis and find a solution for them."[36] This expression of a fundamental distinction and separation between government and people also appeared during casual conversations. One Iraqi interlocutor reflected on how governments of European countries cared for their citizens abroad, in the case of arrest, for example, whereas Middle Eastern governments did not, thereby expressing an understanding of governments as caretakers over whose actions people had no control. Intrigued by an apparent lack of understanding of how taxes and public finance worked in Syria and Iraq, I occasionally asked Iraqi acquaintances about who they considered to be the owner of public spaces such as roads and parks. Invariably, the answer was that these items were owned by the government. These answers pointed toward a perception of statehood shaped in a political context in which the notion of "citizens," "civic responsibility," and the government as "representative" of the population did not appear. Iraqis' clearly had experience of fundamentally different social relations underpinning the state than those espoused by the rhetoric of aid organizations and donor states. Yet in a further ironic twist, the lack of transparency and the effective randomness of the resettlement procedure meant that the power it expressed was very close to the unfettered sovereign power that Iraqis had experienced in the past, either from their own government or from foreign occupiers. Interlocutors remained highly aware of the politics of their migration and considered it as the very basis of their relationship with the United States. Unlike the underlying logic of the resettlement program, which focused on forging new US citizens out of resettled Iraqis in order to allow them access to secure, sovereign space, Iraqis did not consider themselves in this way. Rather, the United States was considered as a type of patron who, after intervening disastrously in Iraqi lives, now must take responsibility to help.

As in the case of Germany, the US involvement in managing Iraqi migrants in Syria emphasized how imagined borders between domestic and international space were created and how these distinct spaces encountered each other. US involvement in Iraqi migration was closely linked to the 2003 invasion of Iraq and its increasingly disastrous aftermath. Iraqi refugees were the living proof of this failure. As has been noted by Geraldine Chatelard, the foremost analyst of Iraqi migration in the last decades, it was US-based NGOs that first raised global awareness and understanding of Iraqi flight as an unprecedented refugee crisis. Their lobbying in Washington, DC, created a "global refugee agenda" that was closely linked to US domestic politicking, as it was a highly marketable reminder of the Bush administration's problems in Iraq.[37] The plight of those Iraqis who had supported and helped the US Army, and had lately become targets as a result, placed extra pressure on the US government; in response the special visa program for such persons was created. The successes and failures of this program were monitored by the media, as was the fate of displaced Iraqis in general.[38]

Thus, in the field of Iraqi migration, the United States appeared simultaneously as the reason for Iraqi insecurity as well as a rescuer of Iraqis. The Iraqi asylum programs became a place where these two roles coincided: an Iraqi who had fled violent acts committed by the US army could now receive safe haven in Dearborn, Michigan. Amazingly, rather than dispel the mythical understanding of a secure "inside" domestic space that is fundamentally distinct from a dangerous "outside" international space, Iraqi flight and resettlement to the United States ultimately affirmed this distinction. But how was this possible? If actions by US state officials and soldiers on the "inside" had clearly contributed to making the "outside" dangerous, how could the separation between domestic and international be upheld? The maintenance of these conceptual spaces despite very apparent contradictions pointed on the one hand to the power of the "territorial trap" intrinsic to contemporary beliefs about the way statehood is rooted in defined territory.[39] On the other hand, it demonstrated how the contradictions were solved: via the narrative that the preexisting dangerous outside (Iraq) proved too dangerous even for the essentially pacifying hegemon (the United States). This narrative underpinned much of the analysis of the US engagement in Iraq and the perception that the United States suffered from a so-called military "overstretch."[40] But despite being a powerfully suggestive story, it blended out the historical involvement of other states, including the United States, in these "outside" places and successfully upheld the idea of territorial exclusivity, which should be and was broken only in self-defense when the dangerous "outside" threatened the peaceful "inside" (which was, of course, how the 2003 invasion of Iraq was justified).[41] It further explained how the potential instability that Iraqi refugees presented for the integrity of US statehood could be successfully nullified through the resettlement and asylum programs, by which US territory could be again confirmed as a source of peace and stability. In this sense, the US involvement in managing Iraqi migrants in Syria (and the Middle East region) had to be considered as a state-affirming involvement despite its extraterritorial character. As briefly described above, this extraterritorial character was partly obscured through the reliance of US ministries on the IOM to conduct large parts of the emigration process.

At the time of field research in 2009, diplomatic relations between Syria and the United States were improving, although the United States did not have an ambassador to the country. The resettlement of Iraqis required, as the last step, an interview with an officer from the US Department of Homeland Security (DHS), who thus had to be physically present in the country. DHS committees regularly visited Syria for this purpose and interview appointments depended on their schedules. The final interview with a DHS official was the "make or break" moment of a resettlement case, as all the previous selection by UNHCR clerks and IOM officials could be nullified by the decision of the DHS interviewer. Correspondingly, Iraqi interlocutors expressed nervousness and excitement once the DHS appointment had been announced. One Iraqi friend told me about a dreaded DHS official, known among his Iraqi friends as "Barbara," who had rejected many Iraqis on grounds of "credibility." According to my friend and other informants, "credibility" was the most common reason for rejection; this would be indicated on the rejection letter simply by a tick in a small box titled "credibility." Interviews, which were completely unpredictable and could be both highly intrusive as well as quick and superficial, were set up to detect such a lack of credibility, for example, by interviewing husband and wife separately.[42]

It struck me as peculiar how the United States appeared personified in this official named Barbara. As a human being, "Barbara" was a precise yet moving and temporally unstable location of US sovereignty, physically deterritorial but, through her US citizenship, conceptually linked to and representative of US territory. As a gatekeeper for Iraqi access to US territory and the nation, "Barbara" also presented a moving border post that would only sometimes appear on Syrian territory to allow for a crossing of this border. In this way, the role played by Barbara summarized and went to the heart of the fiction of modern statehood and its fixation on territory, population, and government as an inseparable entity.

In addition to its presence in the resettlement process, the United States played a role in managing Iraqi migration through the vast amount of funds it provided to the aid effort. The United States was by far the largest funder of UNHCR's total budget, contributing around five times more than the two next biggest donors, Japan and the European Union, each. In 2010, the United States contributed around USD 712 million, Japan USD 143 million, and the European Union 118 million, out of a total of around USD 1.9 billion in contributions.[43] With regard to UNHCR's operations for Iraqi refugees in Jordan, Syria, and Lebanon, US funding covered an even larger percentage. A 2009–10 report indicated that the United States funded between 40 and 50 percent (and possibly more) of UNHCR's budget for the region.[44] In Syria, this money created the gradually growing aid sector.

The difficulties involved in digging up information about US financial contributions to UNHCR's individual country budgets demonstrated well how the institutional channeling of extraterritorial state practices hid overlapping sovereign jurisdictions. Although contributions to UNHCR's budget were heavily weighted toward a handful of states, the organization presented itself as a unitary and international actor and as a neutral representative of all its member states and, by extension, their populations. Notably, in public communications, UNHCR very often praised the Syrian government for its cooperation; however, it never expressed thanks to its biggest donor, the United States, for its continued and crucial support. Here, the filtering of US money through UNHCR's structures served to veil US financial intervention in a territory considered to belong to an enemy state by many US politicians, who regarded the growing budgetary support to UNHCR with suspicion.[45] Sending Syria millions of dollars in aid money at an improving but nevertheless low point in diplomatic relations could have drawn criticism, especially as the expanding humanitarian budget clearly also benefited the Syrian government, which was facing an economic crisis. UNHCR's organizational structures veiled and neutralized the expansion of donor states sovereign space onto Syrian territory.

Conclusion

Western donor states contributed to Iraqi migration through their funding of aid programs and by offering different forms of onward migration to Iraqis. Paradoxically, the "managerial" efforts to reintegrate Iraqi migrants into the state system involved significant transborder interventions, which themselves undermined state boundaries. Donor states' extraterritorial interventions were channeled through international organizations such as UNHCR and IOM. Both of these organizations served as gatekeepers and international border guards for donor states' participation in managing Iraqi migrants. Not only did UNHCR and IOM negotiate the terms and conditions under which donor states would conduct their interventions, but they also conducted the preselection of Iraqi resettlement candidates and a host of bureaucratic and security measures required by the immigration policies of donor states. This form of gatekeeping and institutional channeling made it possible to blur the nitty-gritty involvement of donor states in Syria and presented the aid and resettlement process through a single prism of humanitarianism and generosity by an abstract international community.

To provide further insights into how the involvement of donor states nevertheless managed to uphold a distinction between domestic and international, the chapter detailed the involvement of Germany and the United States. As the German government had opposed the invasion of Iraq and did not participate in it, the question of direct German responsibility to assist refugees did not arise. Still, Germany's high-profile lobbying of European states to accept displaced Iraqis via UNHCR resettlement delivered a boost to Germany's international sovereignty, as it confirmed Germany as a location of peace and compassion. Germany's unprecedented participation in a UNHCR resettlement program was publically lauded by UNHCR in press releases, and the first resettled Iraqis were welcomed to Germany by senior German politicians to a media fanfare. Yet this construction of Germany's international sovereignty was contrasted by the ironic fact that *in parallel*, thousands of Iraqis in Germany, who had previously been accepted as asylum seekers, had their residency permits revoked. The revocations were justified by the argument that the conditions in Iraq that had previously resulted in a justified fear of persecution for these Iraqis had permanently changed through the US-led invasion. The revocation of permits affirmed the boundaries of Germany's domestic space, through which the nation had to be continuously made visible in order to maintain the physical manifestation of the nation-state. The contradictory treatment given to different Iraqi migrants approaching the German state via different bureaucratic channels also emphasized how this nation was constructed through a maze of regulatory procedures and management techniques rather than through a single locus of power.

US participation in resettlement and aid was more directly linked to the failure of the US-led war to stabilize Iraq. Iraqi refugees were a living proof of this failure, and US lobby groups pressured the government to help displaced Iraqis, especially those who had become targets for assisting US forces. The involvement of the United States thus expressed a contradictory situation in which the country was at one and the same time the source of Iraqi insecurity and protection. Fascinatingly, the resettlement and asylum programs ultimately neutralized this tension, as US violence was understood as being performed in dangerous spaces considered outside of the US domestic state. Theories about US military "overstretch" displayed this approach, which continued the myth about the United States as an essential source of peace and order. Allowing Iraqi migrants access to US territory in this way did not contradict constructions of US statehood, as Iraqis could still be considered to access the peaceful realm of the United States without the acknowledgment that their benefactor at the same time had destroyed their stability in the first place.

The perspectives and opinions of Iraqi interlocutors about resettlement, humanitarian aid, and sovereignty were also considered in this chapter. In particular, the acceptance by interlocutors of US responsibility to assist Iraqis, rather than an outright rejection of further US interventions in their lives, was described. In several interviews, Iraqis described the United States as a paternalistic power that had intervened disastrously in their lives and now had the responsibility to offer what little improvement could be had. In these statements, the relationship between government and population was viewed as a form of sovereign paternalism in which the government's actions were broadly independent of the will of the people, but could be judged as good or bad. This portrayal indicated perhaps that the states of which Iraqi interlocutors had experience (mainly Iraq and Syria) relied much less on the myth of popular representation as a technique of upholding domestic sovereignty.

6

Iraqis in Syria

Individual Sovereignty

My Iraqi group of research participants consisted of around eighty persons. The group included individuals with highly divergent lifestyles and personalities, ranging from the devout, motherly, and smiling friend with six children, to the high-strung, eccentric, and gay fashion designer, to the confident, flirtatious, and jolly teenager. It included individuals scarred by recent violence who could not reconcile themselves with life in exile, as well as persons quite happy with their life in Syria. A key experience drawn from interviewing this group was that Iraqis in Syria reflected the whole range of existence present in Iraqi society, and that the reasons for flight and continued exile were diverse, even if they frequently involved violence. Violence and crime had become so widespread in postinvasion Iraq that it did not amount to a targeted persecution of this or that group, but to a breakdown of social order that affected people across class and religious boundaries. The diversity among Iraqis in Syria, and their reasons for remaining in exile, reflected this violent breakdown, but also wider social developments that pushed and pulled Iraqis to migrate, not least the simple opening of the border and the newly found relative ease of travel.[1]

The wide variety of lifestyles within my relatively small group of research participants made short analytical shrift of classifying Iraqis according to age, gender, class, or any of the other standard sociological markers. My participants mirrored the richness of human existence and their experiences formed part of the paradoxical conditions of life organized according to modern statehood. In this chapter I show how a diverse group of Iraqis navigated these paradoxical conditions and how precisely the richness of their human existence was transformed by the demands of power.

The range of Iraqi stories, opinions, and reflections presented in this chapter also delivers a more nuanced analysis of "Iraqis in Syria," a category wielded rather generally until now. Remaining with my line of argument, Iraqis' personal experiences are analyzed with regard to their relationship with the state, with Iraq, with Syria, and with notions such as "nation" and "territory." I seek to demonstrate how research participants undermined or confirmed the constructions of statehood applied to them. Through highly individualized responses to various state-related forms of control, participants' frequently spoiled not only the hoped-for effect of power, but also the images and reputations of the state and nonstate institutions applying it. Compliance with power transformed Iraqi lives in their most intimate aspects. Biopolitical techniques, aimed at shaping Iraqi life rather than threatening it, blurred any distinction between public and private, extending the space of what is generally understood as "public" politics.

Without significant time spent hanging out with research participants and writing daily detailed field notes, it would not have been possible to glimpse and document the fleeting moments in which the effects and contestations of power manifested themselves. Ethnographic participant observation, as a "fly on the wall" approach to research, made such moments possible. Although interviews helped to flesh out context, they could not help me understand the daily-life effects of the different state constructions present in Iraqi life. Only one of the key observations presented in this chapter was collected through an interview.

The style of writing and analysis in this chapter thus makes heavier use of the ethnographic data collected during field research and slightly differs in style from previous chapters. Research results are clustered around three themes: (1) conformity, (2) contestation, and (3) disobedience and deception. The first theme, conformity, analyzes changes in Iraqis' behavior and self-governance in reaction to bureaucratic structures related to their migrant status. This section argues that these bureaucratic structures served the (re)construction of the state (stipulating a homogeneous and healthy nation, for example) and was based on neoliberal technologies of risk management and control. The effect of these structures was to create particular exclusions and barriers, according to which Iraqis had to change their daily-life behavior so that they could become accepted, for example, as immigrants to the United States. The second theme, contestation, highlights how Iraqis manipulated the categorizations and exclusions that were applied to them by aid organizations in Syria. Although contestation did not amount to open resistance, such actions nevertheless weakened the efficiency with which conceptual exclusions could be translated into lived reality. They were a form of Iraqi agency that spoiled the characterizations of weakness and passivity thrust on them by humanitarian rhetoric. This section also highlights moments in which the randomness of sovereign decision making, ostensibly based on fairness, knowledge, and justice, was revealed. Finally, the third theme, disobedience and deception, focuses on moments in which Iraqis directly and openly expressed analyses and opinions that protested against the way they were being governed.

Conformity

The most visible incident of conformity that I came across during fieldwork concerned the father of a lovely Iraqi family with six children who lived in very poor conditions close to my flat in the Jaramana suburb. Through the activities of an Iraqi social activist called Firas, this family had been put in contact with some foreigners who were impressed by the artistic talents of the family's two eldest daughters, who had exhibited in several art exhibitions in Damascus and abroad. The family, here referred to as the Abu Mahmud family, could not return to Iraq owing to the hostility of the wife's family to her mixed-religious marriage, which had surfaced since the onset of violent sectarian strife in Iraq. Now they were hoping for resettlement to the United States, a process they had been working and waiting on for several years. One of the reasons for the long delay had been Abu Mahmud's health and weight problems. Iraqis with no relatives or friends in the United States to act as their resettlement sponsors were allocated such a sponsor, for example, a charity or a refugee support group. Yet such sponsors were reluctant to receive people with potentially expensive health problems, which were flagged during the mandatory health check that was conducted during resettlement registration.[2]

One afternoon when I was visiting the artistic sisters, the parents returned and we started speaking about resettlement. Abu Mahmud explained that the year before, a doctor had conducted the resettlement health check on him. At that time, he had weighed 120 kilos and had been a heavy smoker. As a proof, one of his daughters brought an old photograph, showing a very round, heavy Abu Mahmud. The doctor had written a report to the IOM, stating that Abu Mahmud's health was very bad; this had very much complicated the resettlement procedure and caused a severe delay. However, since that time, Abu Mahmud's health had vastly improved; he had lost a lot of weight through a program of daily running and exercise, and now Abu Mahmud was one of the skinniest men I knew in Syria. He had quit smoking and ate much more healthily. After one year, Abu Mahmud returned to the same doctor, who then issued a report that his health was fine and that he could travel. So now everything should have been ready; Abu Mahmud did not understand what was causing the delay. He called the IOM and UNHCR quite regularly, but did not receive any substantial news. It had been eight months now since the post-weightloss resettlement interview. Both Abu Mahmud and his wife repeated how the waiting was tiring them and causing a lot of worry.[3]

Thinking about and analyzing the structures, ideas, and individual actions that led to Abu Mahmud's physical transformation reveal a complex, transnational web of actors and of power: the US healthcare system, perceptions of risk management and statistics about cardiovascular disease combined with ideas about productive human life, the individual power of the doctor to issue the report, and biological controls on the possibly diseased outsider before he or she was allowed to access national territory.[4] The techniques of power that enticed Abu Mahmud to improve his health revealed a curious mix of what Michel Foucault refers to as "disciplinary" power and that what he broadly called "securitization" or "biopower." The disciplinary element was present in the selective procedure, according to which being overweight and smoking not only prevented

Abu Mahmud but also his whole family from being resettled. Yet as Abu Mahmud was free to choose between remaining fat or being resettled, there was also a distinct laissez-faire element in the process.[5] Also, the overall goal of the procedure, namely, the acceptance of only relatively healthy people into the United States, was indicative of modern ideas about the healthy body politic and biopolitical population management that Foucault has so well described as first emerging in Europe during the eighteenth century.[6] But the arguments of Abu Mahmud's potential sponsors, that accepting an overweight man was too great of a financial risk, spoke much more about neoliberal developments, in which more and more elements of social life previously controlled by the state become ruled by market logic and risk calculations. There was no guarantee that an overweight man would become sick or that his slimmer version would remain healthy; these were calculations based on knowledge of health statistics and cost analyses of differed ailments, similar to those regularly carried out by health insurers. Abu Mahmud's lifestyle change thus was clearly linked to, and only explainable in reference to, modern and neoliberal forms of power and ideas about state and nation, and it was directly connected to techniques of power that maintained modern state sovereignty in the United States.[7]

Another important area of conformity I encountered related to obtaining a residency permit from the Syrian state. Although there appeared to be few instances of Iraqis being deported for not having such a permit, almost all research participants made significant efforts to obtain one and keep it up to date. One possible explanation for this was that the residency permit was the only clear bureaucratic performance that Iraqis could undertake to demonstrate that they were willing to conform to the rules laid down by the Syrian state, and in this way demonstrate their allegiance and legality. Yet the permit was also necessary for interactions with the humanitarian sector and to receive health care and schooling, and was occasionally asked for by potential employers. This latter point was highlighted during the following episode. One of my Iraqi interlocutors was a very hip young man in his early twenties called Hasan, who was the only Iraqi I knew who did not appear very concerned about the residency permit. One day Hasan was visibly excited and happy because he had received an offer to work as a waiter at a popular bar in the old city, a pleasant place at which he had spent much time as a customer. He had asked the Syrian owner for work and had been told to come to the bar that night at 7:30. Hasan said that he was happy because he very much needed the money and because it was a good place to work. Hasan was mainly concerned about what to do with his hair, which he wore in a large, curly Afro, as the bar owner had mentioned that he might have to tie it back. Humorously, we discussed several options. Hasan was extremely vain about his hair and received much positive attention for it, especially from foreigners and, more important perhaps, from girls, so I could see that he understood his hair as a physical feature that made him special. Hasan speculated that maybe after two or three weeks he would be able to just leave his hair as it fell naturally, which I told him I doubted, since it was probably a health regulation or something similar. He also stated that he wanted to tell the owner that it would be better if he drank some alcohol at work, as he worked much better then. Not much, Hasan added, just two or three glasses of Arak, then he was more lively and active. Amused, I cautioned him that that might not be something to float immediately, and also expressed skepticism about whether he would really work better after having drunk. I said that if I were him I would tell the owner that of course I would do anything with my hair that is required, and of course I never drank while on the job, and so on, which in turn made Hasan laugh. As the afternoon wore on, I noticed Hasan checking his watch several times, and eventually he left early to ensure that he would be at the bar at 7:30.

Later, at around 9:30, I was at a friend's house, having been invited to watch a movie. She had told me on the phone that Hasan was coming as well, which surprised me. Sitting on her wonderful terrace overlooking the old city of Damascus and the Mount Qasīūn, she told me that she had bumped into Hasan on the street and he had been very excited about his new job. Then she bumped into him again half an hour later, and asked him why he was not at the job. She said that there had been a problem because Hasan had only an expired residency permit. Hearing that, I felt terrible, as I knew how excited Hasan had been about this new opportunity; at the same time I worried that maybe there was a bigger problem relating to the permit. Eventually, Hasan turned up and told me what had happened. The owner of the bar had asked for his passport, and asked him about his residency permit. Hasan told him that he indeed had a permit, but that it was expired. The owner replied that Hasan needed a valid permit to work with him, and also that he would give his details to the government. Hasan seemed to be unclear about what that meant. He said that he would renew his permit the next day, and that the owner would then employ him, on the other hand, he also said that apparently the other Iraqis working at the bar had some sort of official piece of paper saying that they were allowed to do so. Overall, during the conversation Hasan seemed confident that he could work out the permit issue, saying more than once that he would sort it out the next day. I asked Hasan what had happened with his permit and why he had not renewed it. He told me, lowering his voice and switching partly to English, that his permit had expired one month ago. He had then not renewed it because he thought that he was going to "travel" (that is, be resettled) anyway. I later pressed him a bit on this, and he told me, again lowering his voice, that he had not known for what reason he could claim a permit after the old one had expired, which had been for "health reasons." Hasan thought that he could get a new permit through his two younger siblings, who were in school, which was a reason the whole family could obtain a permit. So he had called his parents and asked when they would be renewing their permit; it turned out that they were going to renew it in two months. So he decided to wait and go renew it with them because then he would get a one-year extension. But now, because of the job, he would go and get one the next day. "Kuss Ukhta al-Iqama!" he exclaimed.[8]

Similar to the Abu Mahmoud episode above, Hasan's story revealed intertwining relations of power at different levels of the state and social apparatus. It highlighted once again how the Syrian government did not use ironclad bureaucratic and legal procedures to enforce the Syrian state's sovereignty. Hasan had been confident to live for several months with an expired permit until an opportune moment arose to renew it conveniently. Had he been able to ensure no contact with Syrian officialdom, his plan would have probably worked without problems. Yet by finding a job, he entered an area of life of greater concern to Syrian state institutions and thus increased his risk of becoming visible to government officials. Hasan's expired permit was not picked up by a ministerial software system programed to issue a letter to his registered address or to automatically cancel benefit payments, as it would have in a state with a high level of technology to manage its population. Instead it was noticed by a potential employer who owned his business and who refused to hire Hasan without a valid residency permit. This refusal might have been a risk-management strategy, as certain ministries and security services occasionally conducted raids of businesses to check for foreign workers, presumably as a way to demonstrate concern about the labor market (there was some public discontent that Iraqis may be taking Syrian jobs) and to create opportunities to solicit bribes and remind business owners of the state's power. Hasan's potential employer, the bar owner, was perhaps aware of this risk and sought to minimize it by only employing Iraqis who had a valid residency permit. Interestingly, no mention was made about an work permit, even though Hasan's passport, like that of all Iraqis, had a stamped sign stating that he was not allowed to work in Syria. Once again, the state's presence in Syria was created through ambiguity of rule, which necessitated a constant and time-consuming investigation of the current state of regulations, and which created a very different effect of statehood than that of transparent, if unbendable, legal or bureaucratic rule.

The personal "micro" occasions described above showed that the "making visible" of the state (be it Syrian or foreign) as an ultimate force to comply with occurred in Iraqi migrant life via different techniques of power and in different local contexts. This knowledge advances the theoretical understanding of how exactly the political order of statehood is maintained as a durable form of political organization, and how states can rely not just on a variety of state-society relations, but also can adapt to transformations in the distribution and character of power. Understanding that the political order of the state can exist in the context of very different social relations between population and government furthers conceptual and political clarity on the relationship between the abstract ideal of the state and the varied, messy, and contextual reality of statehood in physical life. While governments may mobilize and reference the ideal in a variety of ways to construct their state's sovereignty in some instances (especially during practices in spaces designated as international), in others, this ideal may be hardly recognizable from practices used by the same government to enforce its state sovereignty in other areas of life.

The following section looks at how interlocutors consciously contested and discussed certain managerial systems applied to them as migrants, and the sovereign exclusions that these systems contained.

Contestation

The most frequent complaints by research participants concerned UNHCR. This was not surprising, given that UNHCR was the most highly visible aid provider and made highly publicized claims that it was there to help Iraqis. Also, it is important to note, public complaints about the Syrian government's treatment of Iraqis were subject to self-censorship. Nevertheless, UNHCR's lack of transparency surrounding its decision making on matters of extremely high importance for Iraqis raised frustrations. The following paragraphs discuss instances in which research participants contested categories and ideas applied to them, or they describe actual clashes between Iraqi migrants and those governing them. These observations serve to analyze and understand yet again elements of the power and violence contained in the governance of Iraqi migration and their relation to the (re) construction of statehood in the context of Iraqi migration.

As mentioned in earlier chapters, for around three months in 2010 I worked as a volunteer teacher for a small NGO, teaching a seminar to a group of six Iraqi students between eighteen and twenty-two years of age. The seminar focused on different representations of Iraq in academic and popular texts, and discussions often concerned questions of nation and statehood. One afternoon, toward the end of a session, I asked the students whether they themselves felt Iraqi and how they defined their identity. The responses turned out to be very mixed. One young woman, who had already lived in Syria for five years, very clearly stated that she definitely felt Iraqi and was proud of her Iraqi identity. Another young woman, Rana, who had arrived in Syria only several weeks ago, was the most outspoken in saying that she did not identify herself as Iraqi. Rana passionately questioned why people should have an identity attached to them just because they were born in a certain place. She felt that she had not found a place that was "home" yet and that home was a place where you felt good and where you liked the ways of society. Iraq and being Iraqi for her was all about the traditions that curtailed her life. I asked her whether it was nationality and not nationhood that precisely transcended these traditions, but she did not agree. Rana was very vocal in expressing her dislike of being associated with a place whose rules and way of life she did not agree with. Rana's friend Widat, who had also only left Baghdad two months ago, tended to agree with her.

The other students put up some resistance against Rana and Widat's position. Hamud said that in other places people would treat you as a foreigner, to which Rana answered that one had to wait and see whether this would really be the case. Hamud responded that here, in Syria, one could already see that this was the case. Another student called Amir probed Rana, asking her: "Then, where is home for you?" to which Rana simply answered that she did not know yet where her home was, as she had not found a place to call home. An intense discussion developed, as each student clearly felt strongly about this question of Iraqi identity. It was interesting how the majority of the students tried to convince Rana, who was openly straying away from Iraq, that indeed she was an Iraqi at heart and should acknowledge and celebrate this nationality. Yet Rana remained unconvinced. Further, it was notable (yet inconclusive), that Rana and Widat had both experienced more time in Baghdad after the occupation and had only recently been introduced to the experience of being migrants, whereas the rest of the group, who expressed strong feelings of being Iraqi, had already spent several years in Damascus. Rana's emotional distance from Iraqi identity and Iraqi nationhood not only went against dominant feelings of patriotism and national pride prevalent among Iraqi interlocutors. By questioning the necessity to develop positive attachment to the place one was born in and associated with, she contradicted one of the most fundamental assumptions of the sovereign ideal. By openly admitting that she had not yet found a place she was willing to attach herself to so closely as to base her identity on it, she indirectly called for a right to choose one's nationality, in the emotional and patriotic sense, according to preference. This perspective stood in complete contradiction to the assumed unity of territory, population, and government at the heart of the sovereign ideal.

Another interesting episode from these seminars occurred on a different afternoon when a remarkable discussion was sparked during the reading and deconstruction of an extract from *The Lion in the Sand* by Gerald Butt. The book contains the memories of an upper-class British man about life in the Middle East during the mandate period in the 1920s. I had chosen the text as an example of, from my perspective, dreadful orientalist portrayals of the Middle East. To my astonishment all students in the group stated that they had enjoyed the text, partly because it was easy to read. They had found the reading enjoyable and funny. I hid my surprise (if not to say shock) and asked the group what they had liked about it. Several students pointed out various instances in which the author described positive aspects of Arab behavior, for example, the ability of Arabs to distinguish between a government and a person who was a subject of this government. This observation referred to a section of the article describing an anti-British riot by schoolboys, during which the boys' British teacher decided to flee. During the teacher's attempt to depart, his car stalled. In response, the rioting boys swarmed around the car to help the teacher, pushing his car home while chanting anti-Churchill slogans.

Whereas I had interpreted this passage as a patronizing example of illogical and silly behavior by Arabs, the students perceived it as an example of Arab kindness and ability to distinguish between a person and their government. Reflecting on this question, a small discussion ensued about the students' relationship with Americans and the US-led occupation of Iraq. Some students argued that their relationship with Americans was good, and separate from the policies of the US government. A student called Amer pointed out that he had ninety-six American friends on the social networking website Facebook. But Hamud argued that if he saw an American as a soldier, he was against him, and that an occupying force could never respect the culture of the country that it was occupying—simply by the fact that it was an occupying force. This position received some support. Karima also came out strongly against the Bush administration, as it had been its decision to occupy Iraq. Partly because of instructions received from the directors of the NGO on behalf of which I was teaching, which included avoiding overtly political discussions, I steered the discussion back to the text.

The second point that the students used as an example of how *The Lion in the Sand* described Arabs in a positive light was the book's consistent representation of Arabs as highly generous and hospitable, which delighted and surprised the European colonialists. The students expressed some pride in this "Arab" trait, which they agreed with. As I was keen for the students to consider the text more critically, I tried to steer them toward applying some of Edward Said's methods of analysis, which the seminar had discussed the week before. Further, I asked the group about what they had learned about the colonial period in school (both in Iraq and Syria, as some students had attended secondary school in Damascus), which brought on some interesting points. Clearly, the students felt some embarrassment talking about their former education. Some started by making general statements such as, "it was all negative, they [the British and the Americans] were the thieves who wanted to steel our oil, who were going to take away our culture and so on," adding discrediting remarks about the instruction they had received in Iraq. Amir added that there had never been any discussion, that they just learned facts from books and repeated them at the exam. Overall, it was clear that they did not feel very comfortable talking with me about how the West and colonialism had been taught to them at school. They discredited the teaching strongly, and when I did managed to get them to tell me some things they had been taught, they repeated a few points but made it clear that they themselves did not believe in them.

At the end of the class, I gave them, very briefly, my interpretation of *The Lion in the Sand*, pointing out our different positionality and how interesting it had been for me to hear what they had to say about it. I said that I had focused much more on the negative ways in which Arabs were represented in the text, on passages in which violence and silly, childish behavior were associated with Arabs. I pointed them to paragraphs in which Britain's overall role in the Middle East was presented as a benevolent source of order, criticizing this portrayal. After listening to my interpretation, the students were quiet, until Rana said, with some passion, but also laughingly: "Yes, what you say is also true, but we see these matters differently because we are fed up with focusing on the negative!"

To me, as a field researcher, this episode principally highlighted the way that my interlocutors and Iraqi fellow students contested my own assumptions, attitudes, and projections about them. Regarding myself as a critical thinker, politically supportive of the emancipation of people in the Middle East and critical of (post)colonial and racist stereotyping, my mind was primed to detect demeaning orientalist attitudes. It therefore came as an even greater shock when my Arab friends and students enjoyed and thought highly of a text that, from my perspective, was rife with orientalist condescension. Rather than drawing negative lessons from *The Lion in the Sand*, the students focused on aspects of it that made them feel good and happy and proud to be Arabs. And even more interestingly, the lesson that they considered as emerging from the episode of the rioting schoolboys was the ability of Arabs to distinguish between their anger about the politics of a government and their position toward an individual ruled by this government. The, from my perspective, arrogantly amused tone of the author that I had picked up on as an indication of his patronizing view of silly and irrational Arabs had been lost on them, or of no importance. This latter point was relevant for the analysis of state sovereignty, as it again pointed to local manifestations about how state sovereignty was lived, understood, and felt in the Middle East. The British author and I perceived the discrepancy between the schoolboys' singing of anti-Churchill songs and their helpful attitude toward the British teacher as illogical and surprising because an effective analysis of colonialism should have (from our perspective) understood the British teacher as a representative of British sovereignty, along the lines of the ideal unity of government, territory, and people. Yet from the perspective of the Arab schoolboys and the Iraqi students, this connection was far from obvious, which indicated that in their minds, sovereignty did not stipulate such unity or any form of representative link between government and people.

The other interesting moment of contestation was delivered in the seminar's punchline, in Rana's retort that they were fed up with the negative view of the West that had been spoon-fed to students under Saddam

Hussein. The students had experienced the worst form of intervention and aggression by the United States and the United Kingdom, which in many ways confirmed the anticolonial teaching they had received in Iraq. Yet their resentment against authoritarian and dogmatic teaching received during the Saddam government also ran deep. Not wanting to mimic the opinions that they had perceived as being forced on them during earlier schooling, and indeed expressing embarrassment of having conformed to it, the students interpreted *The Lion in the Sand* in the opposite manner. The students' position thus reflected the different forms of violence that had sadly been visited on them through the various, and particularly aggressive, forms of state-sovereignty enforcement they had experienced. The US-led invasion, based on the most brute form of sovereign violence and hubris, had exposed the students to deadly manifestations of state power, as well as displayed to them the apparent weakness and "badness" of the Iraqi nation, territory, and state. The experience of this violence mobilized resistance to US constructions of Iraq and opposition to the continued presence of US soldiers on Iraqi territory. Yet the oppressive experiences the students had experienced through the Iraqi government previous to the invasion also meant that they felt resistance to the ways in which Iraqi state sovereignty had been forced into their lives, for example, through dogmatic education to which no resistance had been tolerated. Various constructions of sovereignty, in this case extreme and highly visible, shaped the way students' considered their Iraqi identity, their stance toward the US invasion, and their reaction to how the Middle East was represented in different texts.

Turning now to a very different, and perhaps more sobering, incident of contestation and opposition of Iraqis against the migration governance applied to them, the following paragraphs describe a visit to a UNHCR processing center. Every Tuesday at this center, where a number of administrative and bureaucratic procedures concerning UNHCR's Iraq program were undertaken, Iraqis could ask about the status of their resettlement file. One day, a young Iraqi woman and I visited the center together to inquire whether there was any news about her file. Aware that there would be hundreds of other people approaching the center that day, we prepared for a long wait and arrived around 7:30 am, when there were already two to three hundred people standing in front of the center, a relatively makeshift building constructed from plywood and metal containers. As the hours wore on and the heat increased, with no shelter or sitting area provided, some women around us began to become restless. The waiting crowd of perhaps six hundred people was separated into men and women; both groups had a separate entry. Since the early morning, a UNHCR employee, a young Syrian man, had been performing a form of crowd control. At first, he had handed out paper slips with numbers that allocated a place in the queue. As the day wore on, he became more and more aggressive and agitated in his announcements and attempts to convince people without numbers to return home.

The longer we waited and the hotter it became, the more anxious and unhappy the slowly diminishing crowd of women became. We had now been shouted at several times by the UNHCR employee, who would appear about every 45 minutes to let the next set of people ("All numbers below 160 please step forward!") into the building. Several times he had angrily shouted that people without a number should not wait, but go home, that people from areas other than Damascus were not going to be served here, and that there were "NO MORE NUMBERS!" today, and so forth. He looked harassed, even though the crowd was relatively calm. We noticed that the men were being processed faster; despite there having been many more men than women at the beginning of the day, at the end, the last hour perhaps, there were only women left. I wondered whether the men were being processed faster because they were assumed to become aggressive more quickly in protest against the wait and bad treatment.

The sun was getting hotter and more signs of exhaustion appeared in the crowd. One woman was sitting on a single plastic chair with her handbag over her head to shield against the burning sun. Then an old woman in a black abaya, unable to stand the sun any longer, started becoming angry and said loudly to the UNHCR man that this was not appropriate treatment. After the UNHCR guy argued with her and she kept shouting, a Syrian soldier in uniform and carrying a gun, who had already intervened a couple of times when minor scuffles broke out, walked up to the old woman and quite rudely told her to calm down, which she eventually did, still standing in the sun. I was struck by the fact that neither the UNHCR employee, nor the guards, nor the soldier suggested any way to alleviate her pain, or offered to bring her a chair from inside the building, or some water, or any form of assistance. The soldier's appearance sorted things out. A related, memorable instance was a calm discussion between the soldier and a woman in which I just overheard him saying, "You don't have a residence permit?" and saw the woman talking to him in a calming-down, sycophantic manner. The effect of this discussion was that the bystanders, who had been pressing down on the entrance, moved away to avoid the soldier and the discussion.

Unlike the previous episodes, this visit to the UNHCR site described a very visible experience of exclusion and of boundaries being forced into the lives of Iraqis in Syria. It also instructed about the ultimate violence and force that backed up these boundaries, which taught Iraqis that they were sovereignty-less and without a government protector. The attempts by waiting Iraqi women to complain against the treatment handed out to them by UNHCR were noteworthy, as they voiced disagreement with the actual rules of UNHCR's game. In this way they qualitatively differed from attempts to defraud UNHCR (discussed below), which were rather efforts to manipulate the rules in one's favor. Yet the complaints observed during the long wait were perhaps chiefly striking for their weakness. Despite the considerable discomfort of an hours-long wait, standing in the sun without water or shade, hardly any signals were made to the UNHCR clerk that the women had had enough or demanded help.

Throughout its rhetoric, the UNHCR described Iraqi refugees as innocent victims in need of help, and described itself as the agency in charge of delivering compassionate assistance. This rhetoric suggested that the agency was Iraqi refugees' interim protector to ensure that the citizenship rights of sovereignty-less refugees would be met. Yet the treatment experienced while attempting to access a service, in this case resettlement inquiries, which UNHCR had established on its own volition, created more than any other situation that I observed in Syria the impression that Iraqis were not sovereign subjects but nonsovereign persons under the power of whichever agency was interested in governing them. Given this discrepancy, much more protest than the feeble complaints described above could have been expected. The weakness of the protests could clearly be explained by the way in which UNHCR relied on Syrian internal security forces to regulate and quell any visible complaints, as was demonstrated by the intervention of the Syrian soldier. Iraqis knew that any form of vocal complaining could land them in hot water with Syrian authorities, who would not tolerate any form or sign of unrest or social instability and would come down hard on any person involved. The fact that even the complaints of a visibly elderly woman, who raised her voice after hours in the heat, were not treated with compassion but provoked the intervention of a security guard, showed how delicate the situation was. In Syria, elderly persons were generally treated with particular respect, thus the incident was doubly remarkable and showed the reaction when "elderly persons at risk," in UNHCR parlance, strayed from their assigned post of meek victim to a demander of rights. The convergence of UNHCR bureaucracy and Syrian state violence in the disciplining of potentially unruly Iraqis once more showed how the conventional dichotomy of authoritarian and liberal power was blurred in practice, and highlighted the violence that ultimately backed up liberal forms of power when they were put to the test.

These episodes present only a small selection from numerous observations of Iraqi contestation and protests, which remained generally small scale, private, and under the radar. Other minor and major contestations included, for example, the ad-busting of UNHCR's logo, which shows two hands shielding a sexless human figure, by an Iraqi friend. He digitally manipulated the logo so that the two hands opened and left the figure unguarded. Another interlocutor, a gay Iraqi man in his early forties, openly attracted attention through his flamboyant wardrobe and mannerisms, in this way contesting a whole host of dominant notions applied to him as an Iraqi migrant man in Syria. The students at ISP engaged in innumerable acts of smaller and larger protests, whether it concerned deliberately crossing set-in-stone rules when the organization's directors were not looking, or eloquently voicing disagreements with the NGO's principles and baseline assumptions. The broad lesson that could be gleaned from these observations was that migrant governance emerged out of a thick, and dynamic, interaction between actors mobilizing their power to influence each other. This power could lie in expensive bureaucratic structures and assumptions about the other as powerless, or in the ability to manipulate these assumptions and contradict them. Yet it was only from the interaction of people and their different ways of influencing each other's actions that the overall effect of power appeared.

Disobedience

This last section focuses on episodes in which Iraqi migrants applied various forms of trickery and deception to undermine and manipulate the governance applied to them by various actors in Syria. In the United States and Europe, migrants are often negatively stereotyped as fraudsters and cheats who misrepresent their situation to selfishly obtain benefits and residency permits. It is not at all my intention to support this blanket, and often racist, assumption about migrants, which I firmly reject. The following analysis of how deception formed part of power relations related to state sovereignty is not aimed at creating any form of moral judgment over those who consciously deceived. The humanitarian programs aimed at Iraqis also contained, in a less visible way, deceptions and lies about links to vested interests that had little to do with Iraqi welfare. From this perspective, it appeared as a hardly avoidable outcome that the interactions between Iraqis and humanitarian and state actors were riddled with half-truths and misrepresentations.

One early, dark, and rainy evening in January 2010, I was riding a public minibus in central Damascus with one of my Iraqi friends, a young woman called Karima. We were both on our way home from the flat of the NGO Iraqi Student Project (ISP), where I had taught a seminar to a group of Iraqi students that day. As we chatted, squeezed into the backseat of the *serviis*, Karima's mobile rang. She took the mobile from her bag, looked at it, sighed, and obviously did not want to answer. She said: "It's the UN, but they are calling for my aunt, she gave them my number. I don't want to answer them." She explained that her aunt had gone to Baghdad after her three-month residency in Syria had expired, and that she had given

Karima's number to the UNHCR in case they would call. "I don't want to answer because I don't want to lie to them," Karima said. I asked whether the UNHCR were not allowed to know about her aunt's expired residency, but Karima explained that it had to do with another matter.

Her aunt, who had obtained her three-month residency for health reasons, did not want to obtain a residency permit through UNHCR, as she wanted to return to Iraq regularly. Obtaining a permit via the UNHCR protection paper included a stamp into the passport stating that a return to Iraq was not possible, as one was supposedly threatened in Iraq. Karima said: "She has her daughter there [in Baghdad], and also she and her husband worked and now they are retired so they receive a pension, which she wants to collect." Karima added that her aunt did not want to tell the UNHCR that she was in Baghdad because previously, when the aunt had stayed in Syria, she had received money from the UNHCR: "They were old, so they received money," Karima said, adding, "Yes, they were greedy, you don't want to be a relative of people like that, they took everything they could get, even the food, they received food and money from the UN when they were here and then they lived off this money and did not spend their pension, they were here and spent this money on touristy things."[9]

Karima's mobile rang again; this time she answered. I heard her explain that there were two numbers for the person the caller was looking for; that this was Karima's number, which had been provided when the other person did not have a phone. She said that she did not know what was going on with that person and that she did not have a clue. Then she hung up. Karima had been speaking quite fast and slightly grumpily; it was clear to me that she did not enjoy doing this and that she was annoyed with her aunt for putting her into this situation. Nevertheless, she told me very freely about the cheating committed by her aunt (although once we left the *serviis*, it was also clear to me that she did not want the other friends who were near us to hear about it, as we changed the topic).

In the backseat, Karima continued talking about her aunt: "Then one day the UNHCR called and said that my aunt had received resettlement to Sweden." I exclaimed: "Wow, so they got what everyone wants!" and Karima said, "Yes, what everyone wants." I asked why her aunt had been selected, and Karima said that she had no idea and that she also did not understand why they were selected, as her aunt and uncle were old and had very good lives in Baghdad, collecting USD 1,500 in retirement money and living in a big house in a good neighborhood, and that they were safe, as they had had no association with the military or the former government. "They are having the life that we used to have in Baghdad, they used to be our neighbors and they live in a good neighborhood. The money they collect is really good. Other people are in a much worse situation." She explained that her father had been a pilot in the military, and therefore had been in a very bad security situation after the war. (I later learned that her father had in fact disappeared, in all likelihood killed by militants owing to his association with the former government's army.) Karima expressed a lack of understanding that her aunt and uncle were selected despite their age. "He is so old, over seventy. They should send people who can still make something out of their life. Why do they want to start a completely new life in Sweden, with a new language, a new everything? They are old."

This episode summarizes several complex layers of deception, misunderstanding, and disagreement in the relationship between Karima, her aunt, and UNHCR. Its emphasis lies in the aunt's successful manipulation of UNHCR's humanitarian "priority profiles" (which included the category "older person at risk") to her and her husband's benefit. The deception, which presumably involved hiding from UNHCR clerks the facts of her pension and property in Baghdad, and her frequent return trips to the city, not only resulted in cash benefits paid out in Syria, but also to a resettlement ticket to Sweden, which would include additional benefit payments from the Swedish state. More important for our analysis, the aunt's deception resulted in a failure of UNHCR's stated goal to resettle only those refugees with the greatest needs, for whom integration or return was permanently impossible. Not only was return to Iraq an evident option for the aunt, but her state pension and trouble-free travel also powerfully dispelled UNHCR's construction of a refugee as a sovereignty-less person, a person without the protection of a state. Clearly the aunt had a stable, and at least partly positive, relationship with the Iraqi state. Through the aunt's deceit, the effect of UNHCR's intervention was turned into something completely different from what was portrayed in UNHCR's publications; the organization's powerful constructions about Iraqis' "needs" were revealed as mythical, or at least badly as implemented. Further, the image of UNHCR as an all-knowing and fair quasi-sovereign was shattered.

Although Karima disapproved of her aunt's behavior, which she characterized as "greedy," she also criticized the UNHCR's role and selection process that enabled her aunt to magnify her deceit from cash support to receiving resettlement. Echoing the opinions of several observers I encountered during field research, Karima disagreed with UNHCR's focus on vulnerabilities, which selected people with few skills and opportunities for a life abroad. The selection was considered as illogical and unfair, not only resettling people who might in fact be better off remaining in Syria, as they lacked the skills to succeed in a foreign environment, but also depriving those who could indeed make the most of resettlement of a chance to begin a new life abroad. Instead of achieving the image of a compassionate and generous protector, the UNHCR appeared as an illogical, unfair, unpredictable, and random patron-sovereign that was not using available resources in the best possible way.

Karima also drew attention to the potentially fatal effect of UNHCR's political preferences in choosing beneficiaries. Pointing out her aunt's relatively secure situation, Karima compared it with the heightened danger that her father had found himself in, owing to his position as a retired army pilot. Her father's association with the army had not only been the key reason for her family's near-immediate flight to Syria after the invasion in 2003, but had, in all likelihood, also resulted in his murder on the border between Iraq and Syria, where militias maintained blacklists of former officers. As discussed in chapter 4, UNHCR's programs explicitly excluded persons associated with the former regime, who were suspected of having participated in war crimes or crimes against humanity. This essentially political choice was lost on Karima, who as a consequence perceived UNHCR criteria not as focused on the most vulnerable and endangered refugees, but as incomprehensible and strange. Yet the actual, quasi-sovereign right of UNHCR to categorize and select Iraqis, and decide, via resettlement, on their location and citizenship, was not questioned. As did most interlocutors, she accepted UNHCR as a power-that-is without wondering about the organization's legitimacy or raison d'être, indicating a relationship to government and authority not shaped by ideas and expectations of representation, but of unpredictability and beyond influence.

Karima, who had a great sense of humor, was also a good source on the ways in which the students participating in the ISP program sought to undermine or contradict the heavy authority that the ISP's directors attempted to extend over them. The ISP environment was governed by certain rules, which were displayed on posters around the apartment admonishing students to be on time, not hang around outside the entrance, to avoid attention, to listen attentively to fellow students, and so forth. In particular the female director tried to impress certain values and ideas, one of which was her strong dislike of any romantic attachments by the students, which in her view would impede studies and should wait for later. Nevertheless, as the following extracts show, behind the director's backs, crushes and erotic tensions were a constant and popular theme among the "ISP kids." These tensions may not show an obvious link to constructions of state sovereignty. Yet as the power over the Iraqi students that the directors were able to exercise was closely linked to their US citizenship, it was noteworthy to observe how the students sought to undermine this power in even the most minimal way at every opportunity, which allowed them to maintain small spaces of independence from the ISP directors' overwhelming presence. As described in chapter 4, several times the ISP directors expelled students from the program for unclear and minor digressions of the rules, creating fear and insecurity among the rest. Even little misdemeanors, or simple expressions that one might not agree with the directors' prescriptions, were considered risky; a further reason why any mocking or disobedience had to be kept strictly secret. In this sense, the strategy to (secretly) emphasize activities that the directors' strongly disapproved of showed an example of how even the smallest areas of life could become arenas in which applications of power, linked to sovereign constructions, were contested.

One weekend afternoon I had invited a group of friends for a late biryani lunch to the flat I shared with another student. Karima also joined, and at some point we began chatting about ISP. Our conversation turned to a former ISP volunteer called Ian, who had recently traveled back to the United Kingdom. I said that he had told me he was planning a trip to Sweden because that was where his fiancée lived, who, scandalously, was a former ISP student. I said this with a grin, to inform Karima that I knew about this controversial and slightly taboo story. Karima laughed and said that he had told the directors that he was going to the United Kingdom, but that he probably lied and was in fact in Sweden. In the next couple of minutes we filled each other in on how much we knew about the incident, Karima confirming that Ian had said that he had immediately fallen in love with the girl, who was later resettled to Sweden. We both giggled and smiled throughout this conversation, aware that it was a naughty thing that Ian had done, as a romance between a foreign ISP teacher and an ISP student was even worse than a regular romantic attachment an ISP student may have. It was clearly something that the directors were not happy about, especially as only Iraqi students without a chance of getting resettled were supposed to join the program. I also said that I had been told that Ian had converted to Islam, and Karima then added that, ah, maybe that was why he had always asked them things about Islam, like how one prayed and things like this (again smiles and giggles).

Karima then started talking about erotic tensions between the volunteer teachers and ISP students, asking whether I knew who Andrew was—another volunteer, who was considered by the students to be attractive. She said that when he first started teaching, all the girls fancied him: "You know how Shiriin and Rana are, they really liked him—but even I liked him!" It had then come as a huge disappointment when, in the second or third week, he had mentioned that his girlfriend was coming to visit. Karima—for comic effect—sighed dramatically, grimaced, and repeated how all the girls had been disappointed when he said that (indirectly of course pointing out the fantasy that they must have had about themselves becoming his girlfriend). Karima carried on talking about a new female teacher called Seema, saying that she was very attractive and that the boys all thought that she was good looking. The codirector had told the young men in advance: "There is this new teacher, Seema, she is very good looking, but don't look at her like that!" Karima repeated this at least twice, raising her voice in a strict tone to mimic the director, saying that she had repeated, "but don't look at her like that!" I answered that this was a silly move because it would get everyone even more curious and excited about the new teacher, to which Karima replied "Of course!" In fact, she added, after that episode, fellow student Hamud had said that he now was already in love with Seema, even though he had never met her! I then asked whether all the ISP students were single, but didn't get a straight answer out of her: "No, no, they are seeing people. She [the director] always says to us, 'Don't see anyone, don't have a boyfriend, don't get married before finishing your studies,' but no one can do that . . . four years in college . . . how can you. . . ."[10]

These undercurrents, which were kept strictly secret from the ISP directors by talking about them in Arabic and out of class, could be read as small attempts to weaken the overwhelming power that the directors wielded over the students' future. Such expressions of opposition to the directors' vision of how Iraqi students should and could achieve a successful life revealed the power structures inherent in the presumed liberating and selfless NGO program. They showed that rather than fostering an atmosphere of truthful, trusting learning and intellectual growth, the ISP program attempted to shape the participants according to very narrow ideas of what constituted acceptable behavior. Although these observations did not teach immediate insights into questions of sovereignty, they highlighted the intense power relations contained in humanitarian aid projects, and how power was contained in well-intentioned ideas and imaginations.

Employees of humanitarian organizations were aware of the deception attempted by some Iraqis. One afternoon I was having coffee at the house of a Syrian friend who had worked at the IOM for several months, dealing directly with Iraqi resettlement cases. My friend's aunt (here referred to as "GA"), who volunteered at a small Syrian charity that worked with Iraqis, was also present. GA had taken the post of volunteer (which awarded a small stipend) after she was suddenly fired from her previous job in the public sector in retribution against her husband's human rights work (her husband, a human rights lawyer, was at the time of the interview serving a three-year prison sentence). GA started talking about her work at the charity, immediately mentioning that there were a lot of problems and a lot of corruption. She claimed that Iraqis engaged in false and corrupt behavior in order to obtain aid. She described how since UNHCR started providing money to women whose husbands had been killed, married Iraqi women with children moved to Syria with fake death certificates for their husbands in order to claim the aid. While the husband continued working in Iraq, the wife claimed the extra money in Syria. GA's eyes were wide open when talking about this and she was relatively animated. Her outrage about this behavior appeared moderate to me, it was more a description of facts about life rather than an angry rant. "There are lots of problems," she said repeatedly. GA added that once the nuns started providing aid in the Masakin Barza area of Damascus, Iraqis from all over the city start going there to claim aid. Another scam that she described related to aid provided to victims of domestic violence, in which women came and claimed that their husbands abused them, even if this was not the case.[11]

Another perspective on apparent fraudulent behavior was offered by a UNHCR official who, during an interview, highlighted how the organization was highly sensitive to a perceived constant threat of fraud on behalf of Iraqis, and how bureaucratic structures were put in place to minimize this perceived danger of cheating. He explained:

> At the same time, exactly because there is such a high number, we have to ensure that there is enough control measures to exclude possibilities of fraud. Because like I said, exactly because these people are so desperate, there could be a lot of potential fraud attempts. And this ranges from, you know, identity fraud, people coming up with stories that have never happened, people coming up with fake children or family members that have died, which they said made them leave the country, people coming up with a lot of false documents and also attempts to contact various people in UNHCR, in IOM, outside, in government bodies, in

> immigration departments, for example, and offering bribes. And I can relate to that, I can understand where that desire comes from, because for each of these refugees . . . I'm there every day and it's very interesting because it helps you get the vibe of what's the feeling among the community, you will have a lot of people telling you, "I am the most deserving." And you can understand why they are saying that. . . .
>
> Now the way resettlement works here is again one measure to exclude fraud. The resettlement unit is quite big, it's about sixty people and we don't do self-referrals. So we don't select which cases we are going to look at. We get these cases preselected by other units of UNHCR. So we have this first step done by other units, so that offers us a degree of protection. . . .
>
> We have a scheduling team. The scheduling team randomizes the selection of case workers and interpreters for particular cases, which again excludes any possibilities for the interpretation team to decide which case should go, and decide who should deal with that. So that also does not happen. Then the case worker is selected randomly, the interview is conducted, after the interview the case worker recommends to the seniors, not a decision but a recommendation, whether this case should go ahead with resettlement or not. If that recommendation is approved then the case will be sent to our regional hub. The regional hub in Beirut then does another check of the case and then the case is submitted to the resettlement country.[12]

In this account, the Iraqi population does not appear any longer as the downtrodden and traumatized community that was presented in NGO and UN publications and in media reports. Instead, Iraqis are described as a population that is constantly attempting fraud and that has to be kept under strict disciplinary control so as not to undermine the supposed fairness of the systematic delivery of humanitarianism. This extract highlights once again the disciplinary element contained in the aid bureaucracy, and the expectations about the attitudes and behaviors that aid recipients should display. The turn toward increasingly draconian measures to discipline and enforce humanitarian bureaucracy has been documented since the earliest days of humanitarian activity in the Middle East.[13]

Relating these observations to questions of sovereignty, it became clear that Iraqi deception also posed an important dilemma for UNHCR. Iraqis' fraud attempts not only dispelled the fiction of a partnership of solidarity between humanitarians and beneficiaries, but also undermined the idea that Iraqis could become sovereign citizens who understood their relationship to government as one of rights and duties, in which the government was understood as a part of the population via representation. If Iraqis would lie to UNHCR, which was acting as their caretaker sovereign as long as they were left without any other sovereign protector, how could they have the potential to become honest citizens on whichever foreign territory that would eventually offer them a "durable solution"? Iraqi deception undermined a whole host of humanitarian fictions about refugee-hood, on which the humanitarian edifice rested.

In this regard it was interesting to compare the way the Syrian volunteer GA spoke about Iraqi deception with the descriptions given by the UNHCR official. GA spoke about the various scams she had witnessed quite neutrally, but still with a degree of disgust and rejection. She clearly did not consider this behavior particularly surprising, yet judged it as a human failure. Her narrative was unsympathetic to Iraqis, whose image emerged as unpleasant and deceitful, especially as they were, in her view, stealing from nuns and volunteers. The UNHCR manager, on the other hand, immediately offered an explanation of Iraqi behavior that fit into the humanitarian narrative: Iraqis deceived because they were desperate. Going further, and presenting an image of fundamental similarity and solidarity between him and the Iraqi "beneficiaries," he stated that he understood Iraqis' behavior, adding that he would be acting in the same way if he were in their situation. Instead of engaging in moral judgment, the UNHCR management used an apparently neutral technical solution to the rationally understandable but problematic Iraqi deception. Education through leaflets and explanations during appointments, and discipline and bureaucratic control measures, were devised to minimize the opportunities and possibilities that Iraqis might engage in fraud. But evidently, UNHCR also had to keep this aspect of Iraqi behavior under wraps: nowhere in any UNHCR publication on Iraqi refugees was the problem of fraud, lies, and deceit publically discussed, even though it was clearly a major concern that had led to operational restructuring and to mistakes in selection procedures. Manipulation, secrecy, and deceit were thus a significant feature in the daily-life encounters between Iraqis in Syria and humanitarian governance. These moments formed part of the emerging governance and management of Iraqi migration. As Iraqis tried to manipulate and deflect humanitarian governance and power, organizations reacted with bureaucratic changes, further education, or sanctions aimed at making Iraqis conform with humanitarian ideas and rules.

Conclusion

If all people I encountered during fieldwork were difficult to categorize, the Iraqi interlocutors that I sought out were even more so. The group comprised individuals from very different backgrounds, with different lifestyles and wildly different personalities. Considering this diversity, it appeared meaningless to attempt to analyze this group according to standard categories such as "gender" or "wealth"; rather my research soon began to focus on how interlocutors dealt with the condition they all shared, that of being exiled or migrants in Syria. This shared condition placed all interlocutors into the focus of sovereignty-constructing power, which was applied to them by various institutions and organizations. How interlocutors reacted to this power, how they conformed to, contested, and disputed it in the day-to-day was the focus of this chapter. These interactions on the one hand demonstrated the effects of sovereignty-constructing power on intimate aspects of Iraqi lives, but on the other also showed the limits of this power, which appeared whenever Iraqis' words and actions contradicted or undermined it. As the observations and analyses of this chapter showed, such undermining took place in direct and indirect ways. Directly, when Iraqis engaged in behavior and voiced opinions that weakened and criticized fundamental notions or routines demanded from them by state and nonstate agents. Indirectly, when such nonconforming behavior forced ostensibly liberal agents of power to reveal the violence that ultimately backed up their nonviolent techniques of bureaucracy and service provision. Such momentary destruction of the self-image and self-portrayal of humanitarian agents shattered their image as a meek protector of right-less Iraqis, and instead revealed their connection to and application of a certain understanding of statehood in which Iraqis in fact where not holders of sovereign rights, but rather had nonsovereign lives over which these humanitarian agents could claim control.

Iraqis' reactions to the bureaucratic, biopolitical, and violent forms of power focused on their lives were individual rather than organized. They arose mostly out of instinctive frustrations and rejections of daily-life experiences rather than conscious efforts to weaken or change such power. These individualized reactions could be in part explained with the individualized nature of many of the biopolitical techniques of power highlighted in this chapter, which targeted Iraqis very specifically according to their particular situation (demonstrating one of the benefits of such techniques, which, in the absence of collectivity, are much more difficult to reveal as power and are much harder to resist). The absence of organized responses was also connected to the Syrian context, in which any form of social organization was a likely target for government suppression. But beyond these contextual insights, this observation contains important methodological and theoretical implications and emphasizes how power that is diffused through daily life is met with what James Scott perhaps first referred to as "everyday forms of resistance."[14] Although Iraqis' everyday resistance may not have had the potential to overturn orders of rule, this resistance was nevertheless important to understand where the limits of sovereignty constructions lay. The ethnographic approach of this thesis played a key role in making these strategies visible, which may have easily been missed by other research methods focused only on documents or interviews.

Reflecting this importance of ethnography, this chapter's structure and writing style differed from previous chapters in that pride of place was given to extracts from field notes and interviews, which present a variety of interlocutors' perspectives and opinions. By grouping observations according to three themes, conformity, contestation, and deception, arguments were presented about how Iraqis related to humanitarian and state governance, and to the way that state sovereignty was produced by governing institutions.

The first theme, conformity, highlighted a case in which an Iraqi man was informed during the resettlement process that his poor health, due to overweight and smoking, was problematic. Each resettlement case required a sponsor in the United States; if there were no relatives or friends, a case would be assigned to a charity or migrant-support group. Yet no organization was willing to accept persons with potentially expensive health risks, as such costs might have to be covered by the sponsor. In response to the negative result of the health check, the Iraqi man in question began a regime of exercise and stopped smoking, with the result that after one year, he successfully passed the resettlement health check, and his case, which also involved his wife and children, was able to proceed. A second example of how Iraqis conformed with migrant-governance concerned the story of an Iraqi friend hoping to be hired as a waiter, and the requirement to obtain an official residency permit from Syrian state authorities for this job. After not planning on renewing his residency for a few months, the friend decided to renew it immediately in order to be able to work. Both events were characterized by an interesting conversion of disciplinary measures and laissez-faire conditions shaping Iraqi life: both men could have chosen not to be resettled, or not to take a job, yet when opting to do so, a set of controls had to be obliged with. Further, the examples emphasized that local manifestations of state sovereignty could differ in terms of the type of power through which they were maintained. In the case of the man requiring a new permit, the fact that his permit had expired did not register with Syrian state institutions, but was pointed out and enforced by a private businessman.

Contestation, the second theme of the chapter, collected several observations in which Iraqi interlocutors directly contradicted or disputed aspects of how they were governed as migrants in Syria. Specifically, these observations focused on moments in which interlocutors voiced criticisms about ideas or concepts that related to the sovereign ideal or other sovereignty-related constructions. In particular, two discussions during a seminar with a group of Iraqi students were illuminating. When, on one occasion, students were prompted to consider their national identity, very different positions on the question of "being Iraqi" emerged. In particular, one young woman held a minority position by contesting the necessity to identify with one's hereditary nation, in this way disagreeing with one of the most fundamental assumptions of state sovereignty. During a second discussion, the students surprised my own assumptions and projections about them, highlighting that the positionality of researcher and interlocutors might not be the same.

Finally, the third theme, deception, emerged as an important topic in interlocutors' relationship with the UNHCR; frequently interlocutors complained about the way people misrepresented facts during UNHCR interviews, or reported themselves about fraudulent portrayals of heightened suffering that were considered to up one's chances with the agency. The UNHCR in turn had put in place bureaucratic procedures such as randomization and double checks to prevent fraud; in an interview a UNHCR manager spoke at considerable length about these concerns. In another relevant instance, Iraqi students participating in an NGO program secretly contravened the rules and ideas set up by the NGO's directors. While outwardly pretending to agree and live by these rules, behind the directors' backs students frequently engaged in behavior they knew was considered undesirable. These two examples showed ways in which Iraqis manipulated and played with humanitarian forms of governance employed by UNHCR and NGOs. In the case of the UNHCR, deceptive Iraqi agency also undermined the organization's portrayal of Iraqis as meek would-be citizens who were seeking to become responsible and productive subjects. Further, it showed that Iraqis did not concur with, or were not even aware of, these UNHCR constructions, and instead considered the UNHCR as an often unfair and unpredictable patron-sovereign that did not use resources particularly wisely or logically.

This chapter presented only a small selection from a wider pool of observations and quotes in which interlocutors critically or humorously undermined different forms of power applied to them. The overall governance of Iraqi migration to Syria emerged from this interplay of regulation, contestation, and violence in the human encounters at UNHCR centers, Syrian state offices, and NGO projects. Power was located in different locations and resources: in humanitarian bureaucracies and money, in the ability to manipulate or conform, in state repression and control. The interactions in this field of migration management were infused with constructions of state sovereignty, as ideas about migration, territory, and nationhood led to shifting boundaries and exclusions for Iraqis in their lives in Syria. The fusion of the different manifestations of the sovereignty of the Syrian state, the humanitarian sector and Iraqis themselves, ultimately led to the local form of state sovereignty as experienced by Iraqi migrants in Syria at the time of field research.

Conclusion

The revolutionary uprisings that happened across Syria from 2011 onward give new meaning to the Iraqi migration crisis. Quite probably, these uprisings would not have occurred, at least at this time and in this form, without their Tunisian and Egyptian precedents. Still, they would have also not happened if the conditions inside Syria had not been favorable to massive public discontent.

The Syrian revolution spoke to a hunch that I developed during research, but was far from able to prove or even significantly document. This hunch concerned the effect of the growing role that development and humanitarian emergency aid had begun to play in Syrian politics during Bashar al-Asad's second term in office. The increased use of aid as a mechanism to care for the poor belonged to the larger drama about introducing economic liberalism while maintaining an ironclad grip on the political sphere. Development projects for impoverished farmers and humanitarian programs for refugees, I believe, need to be analyzed alongside other elements of liberalization, such as the reduction of subsidies or giving up state monopolies.[1] Restricting such latter innovations purely to the economic sphere, and preventing them from leading to demands for political and social empowerment, is a formidable task.[2] Aid projects, I argue, present an even more difficult challenge to illiberal rule. This is because although development and humanitarianism present the alleviation of poverty as a technical challenge—resolvable via tools such as microloans or teaching business skills—they also transport political ideals of liberal statehood and state-society relations.

This is not an argument about Western imperialism in the guise of NGOs and the UN. Instead, it concerns the position of "illiberal" or "authoritarian" (for want of a better shorthand) states toward an international system fundamentally based on the values of national-liberal statehood and representative politics. Though no state implements these values perfectly, some states are more effective at performing them than others. In Syria, the arrival of international aid NGOs highlighted the tension between Syria's domestic version of statehood and its international version, which was necessarily based on internationally hegemonic standards of nationalism and liberalism. At a point when the contradictions between these two representations of the Syrian state became too dramatically obvious, and domestic conditions moved ever further from even beginning to realize the promises of citizenship and representative government, conditions for revolution were ripe. I argue that the Iraqi refugee crisis catalyzed this development.

Internationally Hegemonic Standards of Statehood

The contentious effects of Bashar al-Asad's economic reform project have been well documented. As only a small business elite captured the resources generated by growing economic liberalization, the appearance of ostentatious wealth in Syria highlighted the simultaneous growth of underserved suburbs and slums. In particular, the rapid reduction in the relative value of public-sector wages led to a pauperization of the middle class, itself not a new phenomenon, but a widely observed effect of, in particular, International Monetary Fund (IMF) and World Bank deregulation programs across the world, to which Syria, incidentally, was never subjected. Bashar al-Asad's attempts to de-statify the economy were voluntary efforts designed to make Syrian industry and trade more dynamic and competitive, and to ensure a stable stream of foreign revenue.[3] This reform showed that the regime did worry about the destabilizing effects of economic crisis and believed that adapting to the demands of globalized, capitalist production was necessary.[4] Clearly, the Syrian government was actively engaged in what has been called "authoritarian upgrading" to manage future regime survival, and was attempting to follow the Chinese path: gradual redistribution of economic assets and decision making from state institutions to private individuals, without loosening political restrictions and keeping the overall reigns firmly in government hands.[5]

But a second aspect of the gradual withdrawal of the state from economic management, namely, the growing mobilization of foreign aid in the fight against poverty, has not been adequately considered in the debate about how changes to Syria's economic model affected the subsequent revolution. Certainly, toward the end of Bashar al-Asad's second term in office, this mobilization was in full swing, as I myself witnessed while researching development projects for the poor in villages around Aleppo in 2005. Under the leadership of Bashar's wife Asma, a range of government-controlled quasi-NGOs had sprung up (referred to as "gongos," government-organized NGOs, or "quangos," quasi-NGOs), which channeled state funds into microcredit schemes and charitable projects for poor villagers. These gongos cooperated with UN agencies such as UNDP and made significant efforts to diversify their funding base, hire international expertise, and woo the international development community. Their management was controlled by regime insiders. For example, in 2005 I interviewed one of the senior managers at the flagship umbrella organization FIRDOS, who was the daughter of Syria's foreign minister. The publications and programs of these gongos expressed precisely the jargon and values of the international aid sector, including references to empowerment, human rights, and active citizenship.[6] This copying of the internationally dominant model of (neo)liberal development aid, which emphasizes individual initiative and entrepreneurship, argues Salam Kawakibi, had the unintended effect that these organizations' programs materially changed state-society relations in Syria. For example, writing about FIRDOS, Kawakibi states: "The assumption that Syria needed to maximize its economic potential by investing in the skills of its rural labour force fit with the duty of the Firdos as a GONGO, and might seem innocent enough. But the idea of challenging ministerial directives in order to follow an alternative path of development autonomously worked out within the local community was rather revolutionary in Syria."[7]

The liberal-economic frameworks of these organizations required from its beneficiaries a kind of behavior toward state institutions that contradicted Syria's patronage politics and centralized decision making, and "pushed the boundaries that more independent organizations could not push, leaving them paradoxically, much better placed to engender what might be described as a 'subversive discourse.'"[8]

Most definitely, Asma al-Asad's gongos prepared the ground for the entry of international emergency NGOs to Syria in the wake of the Iraqi refugee crisis. First, because the gongos' work created the initial acceptance among the political elite for nonstate welfare provision, but also because they introduced to Syria practices that international NGOs required, such as Syrians working alongside international staff, less hierarchical team structures, and availability of bilingual professionals with experience in the modus operandi of the aid world. The arrival of international emergency NGOs strengthened and broadened the introduction of these globally hegemonic standards of aid delivery, which relied on state-society relations and ideas of statehood very much at odds with the day-to-day reality of Syrian politics.

For the argument about the diffusion of internationally hegemonic norms of statehood that I am attempting to make, it was especially relevant that the expansion of emergency NGOs in Syria happened in tandem, and as a result of, the expansion of UNHCR. This is important because UNHCR belongs to the United Nations, of which Syria is a member, and which has a mandate from the international community as a whole. And while other UN agencies, such as UNDP, UNICEF, and UNIFEM had been active alongside UNHCR in Syria for years, their activities were on a far lesser scale than those of UNHCR after Iraqi migration began to receive international attention and funds.

UNHCR's budget comes nearly entirely from the richest OECD members, and the lion's share from the United States. But the agency's claim to international representation mitigates potential accusations of Western infiltration, on which Syria's long-standing hostility against foreign organizations had been based. Somehow, UNHCR acted as a central channel for the international standards of liberal statehood. This "channeling" was carried out through UNHCR's employment of hundreds of staff and volunteers, its provision of funds to international NGOs, through financial and bureaucratic transactions with the government, through elite negotiations between UNHCR's top management and senior government officials, and at international conferences and negotiations. Since 2008, UNHCR has continued a vast expansion across the Middle East and understanding the political effects of this expansion has emerged as an important, still underconsidered aspect of regional dynamics.

The internationalization of Syria's aid sector via the Iraqi refugee crisis multiplied the contradictions between Syrian domestic politics and the internationally dominant standards of good statehood, which the homegrown gongos had introduced. International attention paid to the Iraqi emergency led to numerous workshops, meetings, and conferences, at which Syrian officials held speeches according to the international rhetoric of rights-based protection, citizenship, and what it means to be a refugee. This made the *direct* contrast between the tactics and effects of the two different types of rule much more visible. A growing number of Syrians employed in refugee aid projects, many young and highly educated, were exposed to this tension between Syria's international performance of statehood and its domestic reality, an injury smartened by the insult that the Syrian government reaped international praise for its protection of Iraqis while the oppression and impoverishment of Syrians continued unabated.

This book showed throughout how in numerous ways the construction of Iraqi migration as an international emergency and the arrival of the international aid sector in its wake introduced—ideationally and materially—the values of liberal state-society relations into Syria. The exchange between Syria and international norms of liberalism has been analyzed before, as has the difficulty of "liberalizing" the economy while controlling individual initiative and political aspiration. But always, such analyses, for example in Raymond Hinnebusch's classic and brilliant study of Syrian state-society relations under Hafez al-Asad, *Revolution from Above,* have focused on the business elite and their empowerment via privatization, what Hinnebusch refers to as "Bourgeoisification." This book's topic, the introduction of liberal political rationality via aid, adds a new and qualitatively different step along this path because aid exposed the poor and middle class to its ideas and principles, rather than the business elites.

In Syria, the integration of Iraqis was made much easier by the relative lack of nation-based statehood and the absence of an ethno-national body at the core of the Syrian state. This situation meant that Syria's political system not only differed starkly from the workings of European or North American liberal democracy, where statehood is linked to the necessity to carefully construct a national citizenship based on ethnic, historical, or normative harmony. It also placed Syrian politics at odds with the representative ideal of politics on which much international diplomacy is based, first and foremost the UN system. Most of the United Nations, including the General Assembly, but also its foundational documents, speak the language of national self-determination and will, according to which states are naturally based on a harmonious unity between territory, the people residing on it, and the government that expresses their voice. At least since the founding of the United Nations, this national statehood works as the foundation of political and economic liberalism, in which governments are considered representatives of the national will. This view of statehood has become a normative, hegemonic yardstick against which the legitimacy and correctness of regimes is measured. The Syrian state, like many postcolonial states, arrived late to this twinning of liberalism and nationalism, and, while acquiring its outward appearances, never managed to shape its population in their image.

Thus, measured according to the global yardstick of liberal and national statehood, Syrian statehood was incomplete and contentious. To partake in the international system of diplomacy and UN proceedings, Syrian government officials were required to present Syria *as if* the country's statehood stemmed from popular representation. Such mimicking of international norms was also observable in the context of the Iraqi refugee crisis, as Syrian officials used the language of nationalism in their encounters with UNHCR officials and other international conferences. Here, notwithstanding the contradictory reality occurring in the corridors of Syrian immigration offices and suburban streets in Damascus, Syrian officials spoke of the Syrian nation as a unity that generously welcomed the Iraqi outsiders. Similarly, in exchanges with humanitarian aid organizations, officials echoed the humanitarian language of needs and vulnerabilities of the Iraqi migrant population, despite the clear evidence that Iraqis per se were not more vulnerable than Syrians. This mirroring of hegemonic expectations of how a government *should* order its sovereign realm points to mechanisms through which liberal and national norms of state sovereignty were spread via an international humanitarian emergency, which here emerged as an astonishingly transformative dynamic.

The Authoritarian-Democratic Dichotomy

A second, central finding of this book is that the liberal state-society relations that the aid sector emphasizes do not necessarily spell greater overall freedom, in the sense of lesser restrictions and violence by state institutions, especially for migrants and refugees. Rather, differences in statehood appear to be not about a dichotomy between democratic and authoritarian, and are not measurable along a continuum of democratic participation. Instead differences are about how freedoms are distributed across society. As this book showed throughout, migrants and refugees in Syria were not treated significantly different from Syrian citizens. As long as they maintained the essential red lines of public loyalty to the government, they enjoyed substantial freedoms to reside, work, and thrive, despite the absence of official papers. This was a far cry from the harshly violent regimes of border control and bureaucratic exclusion exercised against migrants and refugees by democratic European and American states. Who was allowed entry onto Syrian territory was not subject to a careful consideration of lifestyle and, once admitted, not subject to numerous restrictions and a laborious, multiyear legalization process. Thus, this book found that whereas the authoritarian Syrian state did not require the ostracizing of migrants, the democratic states of Europe and North America did. Not only did this finding dispel any notion of a clear dichotomy between authoritarian and democracy based on freedom or an absence of violence, but there was also clear evidence that the introduction of liberal state-society relations into Syria via the international aid sector was leading to a growing restriction of Iraqis' freedoms.

Thus, this book's research results lead to a problematization and indeed a rejection in parts of the prominent literature on Syrian and Arab statehood set around the notions of "authoritarianism," "democratization," and "authoritarian learning and upgrading." This literature has constantly analyzed the availability and distribution of freedom in prewar Syria through a perspective heavily shaped by an ontology of liberalism, and thus failed to see where democratic states may actually be more repressive than authoritarian states, and where the latter may actually provide significant degrees of freedom.[9] To understand and be able to overcome this ontology, I argue that a close reading of everyday politics is unavoidable. To understand the contradictory effect of power that Iraqis in Syria experienced via the Syrian state and via international aid, it was absolutely necessary to move beyond measuring variables such as "mass participation" or "elite competition" as ways to understand statehood. Instead, this book used the field of Iraqi migration to analyze in detail how certain kinds of freedom were distributed across Syrian society in what way, and how this distribution could be explained by, and in turn explain, Syrian state-society relations.

Despite the vulnerability of anyone's existence on Syrian territory, Syrian society opened opportunities for Iraqis and was in many ways much more liberal than the systemically restrictive way in which mass migration is handled in European and North American contexts. There, growing and deadly violence against unwanted migrants has become a battleground for human rights activists, who protest against systematic practices such as detaining children, carrying out forced returns, and harsh border enforcement, including outside the physical state territory to prevent migrants from reaching Europe or the United States. Democratic states, which heavily depend on notions of "popular will," "representation," and a "protective" relationship between government and citizenry, are particularly threatened by any large-scale arrival of foreigners, whose exclusion is required to maintain the national fundament of statehood. The laissez-faire treatment of Iraqis by Syria's illiberal regime demonstrated, in reverse, that the violent and harsh exclusion of migrants was not required in the Syrian context, where the state drew its power not from pretending to represent an imagined national community, but from real and pretend loyalty to the president, who embodied the state and nation. Instead of constructing national belonging and citizenship as a guarantor of rights, the ability to reside and integrate into the Syrian body politic depended on whether an individual or community preserved the government's prestige and did not create any unwelcome social disturbances.

This book's analysis of migrant life in Syria draws attention to the question of how "strong" Syria's prewar state actually was, and, indeed, what the strength of a state consists of. Similarly to the lack of control exercised over the daily-life activities of Iraqis, it may be argued that beyond the very obvious sectors of formal politics and education, the Syrian state exercised remarkably little oversight over the civil life of the Syrian population. Compared with the existing and growing sophistication of Western states' ability to use surveillance and data gathering, the Syrian intelligence apparatus, as cruel and insidious as it was and is, appears crude and not particularly skilled. Ironically, the shock experienced by Syrians when interrogators produced files with detailed information about their lives pointed to this, because it spoke about a lack of belief, or awareness, that the state had the capacity to systematically collect personal information. In Western, democratic states, numerous state institutions, ranging from tax agencies to national health services, manage detailed information about their populations in sophisticated databases, which can be summoned at the touch of a button. Also, unlike in Western states, the Syrian governments' strategies of discipline, violence, and propaganda, which were used to establish at least a semblance of loyalty, did not successfully target or change people's private activities and attitudes. Such private activities were *precisely* the target of newly established aid programs for Iraqis, which immediately began to work on transforming such intimate matters as dietary habits (to improve health), family relations (to improve gender equality), or attitudes to conflict management (favoring nonviolent resolution). Here, the internationalizing of the Iraqi emergency truly provided a snapshot of how liberal power works, aiming for a deep transformation of life itself, and of how it differs from sovereign power, which aims for "mere" acquiescence.

A Battle over the Expansion of the Liberal Heartland

Currently, it is an open question whether the war in Syria is ultimately going to make the international community less liberal, or whether instead Syria is going to move towards the liberal heartland. Having established two central arguments, namely, (1) that the humanitarian aid sector introduced ideas and practices of liberal state-society relations into Syria, and that (2) these contained their own forms of oppression and violence, in this last section, I want to develop how these two points speak to Syria's revolution and ongoing war. In summary, I argue here that one important structure that underpins the war in Syria is the global contest between what Mark Duffield has referred to as the "strategic complexes of liberal peace"[10] and nonliberal actors, who are in competition about the forms of authority and regulation they wish to establish. Considered from a global perspective, the Syrian war is also about what form of statehood is permissible and acceptable in today's international system, and about the successful conversion of the world to liberal state-society relations. Economic deregulation, which is the most visible and openly contested aspect of the spread of liberal governance, has inevitably drawn after it conflicts over how to apply the resources gained from privatization and innovation. Donor governments and development economists consider deregulation as one of a range of good governance measures that will eventually result in political liberalization.[11] But among nonliberal actors privatization "can represent an innovative way to further the non-liberal political logic of the complex concerned."[12] This is precisely the process that could be observed in prewar Syria, where the appropriation of the spoils of privatization by corrupt elites served to stabilize an illiberal regime, rather than promote political diversification. Still, as argued above, the particular type of subjecthood required by neoliberal economic production and its characteristics of independence, initiative, innovation, and creativity, was starting to introduce contradictions to the demands of Syrian politics under Bashar al-Asad's rule. Interestingly, this was most evident in the government-led, pro-poor development programs, modeled on currently hegemonic, neoliberal international development jargon. The sudden internationalization of Syria's homegrown aid sector via the Iraqi refugee crisis catalyzed these contradictions between Syrian domestic politics and the promises of global liberalism toward popular uprising.

Since then, the Syrian government's willingness to openly flout more and more previously hegemonic norms of international liberalism has turned the war in Syria into an all-out contest about the power of these norms, and about the need to even pay them lip service.[13] The relentless bombing of civilian infrastructure by the Syrian Army, its attacks on breadlines, schools, and medical facilities, its documented use of mass forced disappearances and torture, and in particular its use of chemical weapons in densely populated residential neighborhoods have not solicited *any* significant response from the international community. The first chemical weapons attack, which killed over one thousand inhabitants of a Damascus suburb, most in their sleep, not only took place *after* the US president had announced that chemical weapons use represented a "red line" for his government to take action, but also directly under the noses of UN weapons' inspectors visiting Syria during the attack. The inspectors were allowed access to the site of the attack only several days after, when it had become clear that Barack Obama's "red line" announcement had turned out to be a red herring: instead of suffering a military response, the Syria government agreed to destroy its chemical weapons arsenal and join the UN chemical weapons ban, in a move that ultimately served to shore up the Syria government's international standing.[14] Thus, the war in Syria has so far forced the international guardians of liberal statehood to confront their own weakness and hypocrisy, and is raising the specter of a growing international acceptance of openly applied state violence against domestic, civilian populations.

The unwillingness of the Syrian government to relinquish power has not just brought the initially slow-burning domestic conflicts in Syria to a head. Bashar al-Asad's clinging to power has brought on an international war, which is revealing both the internal and external boundaries and limits of liberal ideology. The internal limits concern the liberal world's self-understanding as a realm of peace and consensual rule. From the European men and women joining fanatical groups such as the "Islamic"

State (also referred to as ISIS or Daesh), to the increasing use of constant drone surveillance and attack, to the mass drowning of migrants in the Mediterranean, the war is pulling the "liberal" mask off democratic states and bringing into the open a number of issues addressed in this book. The external limits refer to the actual territorial borders of liberal rule. With Russia and Iran to one side, and NATO on the other, these borders currently appear to run straight through Syria, where their definitive line remains contested and unclear.

In an article titled "The Erosion of International Norms in the Syria Conflict," Bente Scheller argues that the war has exposed the hollowness of the "responsibility to protect" concept, and has severely weakened a number of important institutions of international liberalism, including the United Nations, the convention against the use of chemical weapons, and the neutrality of humanitarian aid.[15] The strategies of Russia and Iran have been decisive from the outset, guided by a clear vision to maintain strategic assets, whereas those of the United States and Europe have been piecemeal and inconsistent. Similarly, Russia and Iran have spent significant resources and sent soldiers to their death in Syria, whereas the United States and Europe are not able to mobilize comparably to defend liberalism abroad.

The current war in Syria is the result of a breaking point at which the contradictions between Syria's domestic state-society relations and the expectations of international liberalism and nationalism came to a head. The moment Syria's population vocally demanded a greater say in politics and better representation, and the crucial fear of government repression dissipated, the Syrian government was no longer able to maintain outward appearances "as if" it were governing a liberal nation-state. And instead of correcting the imbalance between projection and reality by adjusting its domestic order to that of national, liberal, representative statehood, it began a war that is doing precisely the opposite.

The humanitarian catastrophe of the Syrian refugee crisis is resulting in a growing involvement of liberal actors in Middle East politics. UNHCR's operations have moved smoothly from handling the Iraqi crisis to delivering aid to Syrian refugees and IDPs. Since 2013, the Syrian government has permitted UNHCR to serve *internally* displaced Syrians, though only in government-controlled areas. NGOs have similarly been forced to choose whether to deliver aid in rebel- or government-held areas: in the few cases in which NGOs attempted to maintain their independence and deliver in both areas, the Syrian government expelled them from the country.[16] Thus, the dynamics described in this book have continuously expanded since the time of research. The most tragic example of this may be Jordan, where the government closed its borders to nearly all Syrian immigration in late 2014 and is in 2015 gradually forcing more and more Syrians into two large camps, which were built using UNHCR/NGO expertise and funds. The second of these camps, Azraq, appears as the culmination of a process in which the most repressive aspects of "liberal" Western migration management coincide with the most violent elements of Jordan's "illiberal" statehood.[17] Azraq is essentially a prison camp in the desert, which is run in increasingly secretive cooperation between humanitarian agencies and Jordanian security forces. Even Lebanon moved to introduce visas for Syrians in 2015, while Turkey's borders have in 2016 closed to Syrians, with increasingly frequent reports of Turkish border guards shooting at Syrians trying to cross the border. Despite these catastrophic development, which I believe are tragically related to the growing humanitarian governance of refugees, the overall social and political tolerance of the large-scale arrival of Syrian refugees in Middle Eastern states has remained far in excess of what is considered normal in Europe.[18]

So should the overall conclusion be that, in fact, the war in Syria is resulting in a "convergence of governance" between authoritarian and democratic regimes?[19] Francesco Cavatorta's argument about a mutual move toward a "middle ground of depoliticization" has proved mistaken owing to his misinterpretation of disenchantment with the status quo as an indicator for depoliticization. But his idea of a "convergence" nevertheless is a rich one when read in conjunction with the literature on authoritarian learning, which has emerged invigorated since the successful counter-revolutions in several Arab states.[20] The war in Syria may indeed be considered as a highly dynamic instance of international "mutual learning."[21] In particular the war's "emergency complex" has become a mechanism "for the globalisation of economic, political and scientific relations" and an "axis of social reordering," around which several powerful transformations to state-society relations are occurring both in the domestic and international spheres.[22] This does not mean that the Syrian domino is eventually going to fall in liberalism's unstoppable march, nor that Europe will soon be ruled by Asad-style regimes. But what current developments in the Middle East's new humanitarian sector point out is that the export of liberalism to the region may not result in greater political participation, mass inclusion, elite competition, or polyarchy, but rather new forms of population management and technical capacities for states to surveil and control, which ultimately empower governments to be more effectively oppressive than before. In the reverse direction, more atrocities carried out by Syria's government with more and more confidence that no significant international response will follow may empower democratic governments to consider even lip service to liberal values as unnecessary.

What Became of Iraqi Refugees in Syria?

The Syrian war spelled an end to the safe haven that Iraqis found in the country. Most were forced to migrate further or to return to an unstable and dangerous Iraq. But when in 2013 conflict escalated in Iraq's northeast, thousands of Iraqis again crossed into war-torn Syria. Today, Syrians and Iraqis alike are being chased around from one pocket of temporary "peace" to the next. Tens of thousands are camping in brutal conditions outside border crossings, which have been mercilessly closed to them—be it on the borders of the United Kingdom, Jordan, or Turkey. UNHCR's 2015 planning figures, based on estimates, guess that around 100,000 Iraqi refugees remain in Syria in January 2015, of which around 20,000 receive some form of service from the agency. This, of course, is still a substantial number, especially if one considers that no European country outside Sweden ever agreed to receive an even remotely similar number of Iraqi refugees. UNHCR's enormous resettlement program for Iraqis, which probably resettled around 50,000 Iraqis between 2007 and 2010, has ground to a halt. In addition to resettlement, many thousands of Iraqis found other ways of further migration, including through work visas, student visas, family reunification, asylum claims, and illegality. Compared with the enormous estimates of around 2 million Iraqis displaced to Syria in 2010, the overall arrivals in wealthy states remained relatively low: for example, in Germany, the number of registered Iraqi citizens rose by 20,000 between 2000 and 2009, from around 50,000 to around 70,000. Sweden, which received the greatest number of Iraqi refugees, took in around 70,000 Iraqis, which raised Sweden's overall Iraqi population from around 50,000 to around 120,000.

Regarding my group of research participants, among those I am still in touch with or know about, all the above-mentioned forms of onward or return migration are found. None that I know of remain in Syria. Those who have returned to Iraq live either in Baghdad or in Erbil, capital of Iraq's booming Kurdish region. In Erbil, which has seen an enormous influx of Syrian refugees, Iraqis might well bump into old acquaintances from Damascus who have decided that northern Iraq today offers a better place than Syria. The roles of refugee and citizen, if they were ever distinct, have been reversed. Despite the growing use of humanitarian categorizations, and increasingly tight border regimes, the Middle East's "authoritarian" governments and societies still demonstrate a significant willingness to integrate migrants, despite their own difficult political and economic environments. This willingness, based perhaps on a more intuitive and merciful understanding that flight may happen to all of us sometime, should give food for thought about what an alternative to Fortress Europe or Fortress America could look like.

Notes / Bibliography / Index

Notes

Introduction

1. Mark Duffield, *Global Governance and the New Wars: The Merging of Development and Security* (London: Zed Books, 2001), 13.

2. Faisal al-Miqdad, "Iraqi Refugees in Syria," *Forced Migration Review*, Special Issue (June 2007): 19–21.

3. Bente Scheller, *The Wisdom of Syria's Waiting Game* (London: Hurst, 2013).

4. Giorgio Agamben, *Homo Sacer: Sovereign Power and Bare Life* (Stanford, CA: Stanford Univ. Press, 1998).

1. The Politics of Iraqi Migration to Syria

1. Patricia Weiss Fagen, *Iraqi Refugees: Seeking Stability in Syria and Jordan* (Washington, DC: Georgetown Univ. Press, 2007).

2. Timothy Mitchell, *Rule of Experts: Egypt, Techno-Politics, Modernity* (Berkeley: Univ. of California Press, 2002); Timothy Mitchell, "The Limits of the State: Beyond Statist Approaches and Their Critics," *The American Political Science Review* 85, no. 1 (1991): 77–96; Lisa Wedeen, *Ambiguities of Domination: Politics, Rhetoric, and Symbols in Contemporary Syria* (Chicago, IL: Univ. of Chicago Press, 1999); Salwa Ismail, *Political Life in Cairo's New Quarters: Encountering the Everyday State* (Minneapolis: Univ. of Minnesota Press, 2006).

3. Hanna Batatu, "Some Observations on the Social Roots of Syria's Ruling, Military Group and the Causes for Its Dominance," *Middle East Journal* 35, no. 3 (1981): 331–44. Volker Perthes, *The Political Economy of Syria under Asad* (New York: I. B. Tauris, 1995).

4. Kheder Khaddour and Kevin Mazur, "The Struggle for Syria's Regions," *Middle East Research and Information Project* MER 43, no. 269 (2013).

5. The term "liberal" here and throughout the book refers to states that have laws to limit the government's power to intrude into individuals' lives. Liberal states draw their legitimacy from a claim to represent the popular will of a nation. The term "illiberal" is used as a similarly clumsy shorthand to describe a state in which the government's power to suddenly intrude into individual life is unfettered, and in which national citizenship and

representation are not foundational for government legitimacy. As I point out throughout this book and argue in the conclusion, the distinction between these two types of states lies not so much in the absolute difference of freedom and oppression, but rather to whom freedom and oppression is allocated. I use "authoritarian" and "illiberal" as interchangeable terms.

6. Daniel Neep, *Occupying Syria under the French Mandate* (Cambridge: Cambridge Univ. Press, 2012).

7. Raymond Hinnebusch and Tina Zintl, eds., *Syria from Reform to Revolt*, vol. 1, *Political Economy and International Relations* (Syracuse, NY: Syracuse Univ. Press, 2015).

8. Steven Heydemann, *Authoritarianism in Syria: Institutions and Social Conflict, 1946–1970* (Ithaca, NY: Cornell Univ. Press, 1999); Oliver Schlumberger, *Debating Arab Authoritarianism Dynamics and Durability in Nondemocratic Regimes* (Stanford, CA: Stanford Univ. Press, 2007); Perthes, *Political Economy of Syria under Asad*; Raymond Hinnebusch, *Syria: Revolution from Above* (London: Routledge, 2001).

9. The phrase "politics of as if" was coined by Lisa Wedeen in her classic account of politics under Hafiz al-Asad, *Ambiguities of Domination*. For a more recent analysis of the politics of national cohesion under Bashar al-Asad, see Salwa Ismail, "Urban Subalterns in the Arab Revolutions: Cairo and Damascus in Comparative Perspective," *Comparative Studies in Society and History* 55, no. 4 (2013): 865–94.

10. For example, a staff member of the European Commission in Damascus recounted a meeting with IMF officials in 2009 who lacked any knowledge or evidence about the economic effect of Iraqi immigration and did not have the means to obtain any data on this question.

11. The UNHCR budget in 2009 alone amounted to around USD 130 million; further bilateral donations from the EU and individual donor states were received.

12. Ashraf al-Khalidi, Sophia Hoffmann, and Victor Tanner, *Iraqi Refugees in the Syrian Arab Republic: A Field-Based Snapshot* (Washington, DC: The Brookings Institution, 2007).

13. See Reinoud Leenders, "Iraqi Refugees in Syria: Causing a Spillover of the Iraqi Conflict?" *Third World Quarterly* 29, no. 8 (2008): 1563–84; Reinoud Leenders, "Refugee Warriors or War Refugees? Iraqi Refugees' Predicament in Syria, Jordan and Lebanon," *Mediterranean Politics* 14, no. 3 (2009): 343–63; Joseph Sassoon, *The Iraqi Refugees: The New Crisis in the Middle-East* (London: IB Tauris 2008); Erlend Paasche, "Iraqi Refugees in a Damascus Suburb: Carriers of Sectarian Conflict?" *International Journal of Contemporary Iraqi Studies* 5, no. 2 (2011): 247–62.

14. Bassam Haddad, *Business Networks in Syria: The Political Economy of Authoritarian Resilience* (Stanford, CA: Stanford Univ. Press 2012).

15. Geraldine Chatelard, "What Visibility Conceals: Re-Embedding Refugee Migration from Iraq," in *Dispossession and Displacement: Forced Migration in the Middle East and Africa*, ed. Dawn Chatty (London: British Academy, 2009).

16. Polly Pallister-Wilkins, "Interrogating the Mediterranean 'Migration Crisis,'" *Mediterranean Politics* 21, no. 2 (2016): 311–15, doi:10.1080/13629395.2016.1145826.

17. Laura Ruiz de Elvira and Tina Zintl, *Civil Society and the State in Syria: The Outsourcing of Social Responsibility* (Boulder, CO: Lynne Rienner, 2012).

18. Ismail, *Political Life in Cairo's New Quarters*; Jörg Michael Dostal and Anja Zorob, *Syria and the Euro-Mediterranean Relationship* (Boulder, CO: Lynne Rienner, 2008).

19. See, for example, the open criticism by the former head of Syria's economic planning commission Tayssir Raddawi against Deputy Prime Minister Abdullah Dardari; Raddawi was subsequently fired from his position by presidential decree. Syria Comment Blog, October 20, 2009.

20. See, for example, UNHCR Syria, "UNHCR Syria Update Autumn 2010" (Damascus: UNHCR Syria, 2010); Jeff Crisp et al., *Surviving in the City: A Review of UNHCR's Operations for Iraqi Refugees in Urban Areas of Jordan, Lebanon and Syria* (Geneva: UNHCR Policy Development and Evaluation Service, 2009).

21. Expert on Iraqi migration, interview with the author, October 29, 2009.

22. Crisp et al., *Surviving in the City*; UNHCR official, interview with the author, January 21, 2010.

23. Timothy Mitchell, "The Limits of the State: Beyond Statist Approaches and Their Critics," *The American Political Science Review* 85, no. 1 (1991): 77.

24. Ilana Feldman, *Governing Gaza: Bureaucracy, Authority, and the Work of Rule, 1917–1967* (Durham, NC: Duke Univ. Press, 2008), 10–15.

25. Perthes, *Political Economy of Syria under Asad*; Bente Scheller, *The Wisdom of Syria's Waiting Game: Foreign Policy under the Assads* (London: Hurst, 2013); Raymond Hinnebusch, Marwan Kabalan, Bassma Kodmani, and David Lesch, *Syrian Foreign Police and the United States from Bush to Obama* (Boulder, CO: Lynne Rienner, 2010); Radwan Ziadeh, *Power and Policy in Syria: Intelligence Services, Foreign Relations and Democracy in the Modern Middle East* (London: I. B. Tauris, 2012); Patrick Seale, *Asad: The Struggle for the Middle East* (Oakland: Univ. of California Press, 1990).

2. The Syrian State and Iraqi Migration

1. This ambiguity has been captured in many studies of twentieth-century Syrian politics, most carefully perhaps in Lisa Wedeen's classic *Ambiguities of Domination*.

2. Website of the Syrian Bureau of Statistics: http://www.cbssyr.org/.

3. Philip S. Khoury, "Syrian Urban Politics in Transition: The Quarters of Damascus during the French Mandate," *International Journal of Middle East Studies* 16, no. 4 (1984): 507–40.

4. The newer phenomenon of expensive gated-community suburban developments, which are fully designed and planned, are somewhat exceptional to this observation (see, for example, the newly developed luxury flats in the Kafer Sousseh area). Nevertheless, even these developments sometimes also display signs of incompleteness and rough building.

5. Observations by the author in Damascus in 2009 and 2010.

6. Wedeen, *Ambiguities of Domination.*

7. Laleh Khalili, "Grass-Roots Commemorations: Remembering the Land in the Camps of Lebanon," *Journal of Palestine Studies* 34, no. 1 (2004): 6–22; Laleh Khalili, *Heroes and Martyrs of Palestine: The Politics of National Commemoration* (Cambridge: Cambridge Univ. Press, 2007); Hadia Hakim, *Palestinian Identity-Formation in Yarmouk: Constructing National Identity through the Development of Space* (Irvine: Univ. of California Irvine School of Social Sciences, 2009).

8. Tahir Zaman, "Lessons Learned: Palestinian Refugees from Baghdad to Damascus," *International Journal of Contemporary Iraqi Studies* 5, no. 2 (2011): 263–76.

9. It is unclear when this policy began. In 2007, conversations with Iraqis who had then lived in Syria for several years never brought up this topic, and preexisting Iraqi business in Damascus confirmed that during earlier times, Iraqis could access the Syrian employment market legally.

10. Ali Ali and Kamel Dorai, *Under the Radar, but Not Invisible: Iraqi Activity in Syria's Informal Economic Sector* (Damascus: UNHCR Syria, 2010), 8.

11. Aihwa Ong, *Neoliberalism as Exception: Mutations in Citizenship and Sovereignty* (Durham, NC: Duke Univ. Press, 2006), 99.

12. Gianluca Parolin, *Citizenship in the Arab World* (Amsterdam: Amsterdam Univ. Press, 2009); Batatu, "Some Observations."

13. Beverly Levine, "On Obtaining Your Residence Permit (*iqama*) and Extending Visas," Syrian Studies Association, http://www.ou.edu/ssa/p-learn/Iqama.htm.

14. Iraqi Couple, interview with the author, February 20, 2010.

15. This excludes the paying of bribes to local police or other security officers, which was frequently done for various reasons; although Iraqis (as Syrians) complained about the soliciting of bribes, this was not considered intimidating or threatening.

16. Author, conversation with Iraqi woman, Damascus, November 3, 2009.

17. Faisal al-Miqdad, "Iraqi Refugees in Syria," *Forced Migration Review*, Special Issue (June 2007): 19–21; The Syrian Arab Republic Ministry of Foreign Affairs, "Paper Presented by the Government of Syrian Arab Republic to the International Conference on Addressing the Humanitarian Needs of the Refugees and Internally Displaced Persons inside Iraq and in the Neighbouring Countries," unpublished report, 2007.

18. For some of these negative portrayals of Syria, see Barry Rubin, *The Truth about Syria* (Basingstoke, England: Palgrave Macmillan, 2007); David Schenker, *Syria's Role in Regional Destabilization: An American View* (Jerusalem: Jerusalem Center for Public Affairs, 2007).

19. Syrian Arab Republic Ministry of Foreign Affairs, "Paper Presented by the Government of Syrian Arab Republic to the International Conference."

20. Mark Duffield, "Social Reconstruction and the Radicalization of Development: Aid as a Relation of Global Liberal Governance," *Development and Change* 33 (2002): 1049–71.

21. UNHCR, *Country Operations Plan 2007 Syrian Arab Republic* (Geneva: UNHCR, 2007).

22. Carole Laleve (UNHCR Press Officer), e-mail communication with the author, February 2008, 2011.

23. UNHCR Syria, *UNHCR Syria Update Summer 2010* (Damascus: UNHCR Syria, 2010).

24. UNHCR Syria employee, conversation with author, November 23, 2009; UNHCR Syria manager, interview with author, October 26, 2009; Employee at European Commission Syria, conversation with author, October 9, 2009.

25. Observations by author in Damascus, 2010.

26. Stephen Starr, "Syrian Civil Society Empowerment 2010: New Directions for Syrian Society," *Forward Magazine Syria*, no. 37 (March 3, 2010). Asma al-Asad, "Inaugural Speech to the First International Development Conference of Syria 2010," www.presidentassad.net.

27. Ismail, *Political Life in Cairo's New Quarters*; Dostal and Zorob, *Syria and the Euro-Mediterranean Relationship*; Mitchell, *Rule of Experts*.

28. See, for example, the open criticism by the former head of Syria's economic planning commission Tayssir Raddawi against Deputy Prime Minister Abdullah Dardari. Raddawi was subsequently fired from his position by presidential decree. Syria Comment Blog, October 30, 2009.

29. UNHCR Syria, UNHCR Syria Update Autumn 2010; Katherine Kraft, "Two Changing Spheres: NGOs and Iraqis in Syria" (Brea, CA: Middle East Fellowship, 2008).

30. Employee at International Medical Corps Damascus, interview with author, October 19, 2009.

31. Jordanian researcher, conversation with author, October 30, 2009.

32. Various employees at international NGOs in Damascus, conversations with author, 2009 and 2010.

33. Barry Hindess, "Neo-Liberal Citizenship," *Citizenship Studies* 6, no. 2 (2002): 127–43.

34. The two American NGOs present, International Rescue Committee and International Medical Corps, both focused on relatively technical, emergency relief programs that did not contain elements of human rights or democracy promotion.

35. Mark Duffield, "Development, Territories, and People: Consolidating the External Sovereign Frontier," *Alternatives* 32, no. 2 (2007): 225–46; Hindess, "Neo-Liberal Citizenship."

36. See Alan George, *Syria: Neither Bread nor Freedom* (London: Zed Books, 2003); David Lesch, *The New Lion of Damascus: Bashar al-Asad and Modern Syria* (New Haven, CT: Yale Univ. Press, 2005).

37. Claudie Fioroni, "'Société civile' et évolution de l'autoritarisme en Syrie: Le cas du Syria Trust for Development," Master's thesis, The Graduate Institute Geneva, 2010.

3. UNHCR and Iraqi Migration

1. UN General Assembly, *Convention Relating to the Status of Refugees*, United Nations, Treaty Series 189 (July 28, 1951), 137.

2. Gil Loescher, "The UNHCR and World Politics: State Interests vs. Institutional Autonomy," *International Migration Review* 35, no. 1 (2001): 33–56. Michael Barnett, "Humanitarianism with a Sovereign Face: UNHCR in the Global Undertow," *International Migration Review* 35, no. 1 (2001): 244–77.

3. Dimitris Papadopoulos and Vassilis Tsianos, "How to Do Sovereignty without People: The Subjectless Condition of Postliberal Power," *boundary 2* 34, no. 1 (2007): doi:10.1215/01903659-2006-030. Michael Barnett, "Sovereignty, Nationalism, and Regional Order in the Arab State System," in *State Sovereignty as Social Construct*, ed. Thomas Biersteker and Cynthia Weber (Cambridge: Cambridge Univ. Press, 1996), 148–89; Kalpana Rahita Seshadri, "When Home Is a Camp Global Sovereignty: Biopolitic and Internally Displaced Persons," *Social Text* 26, no. 1 94 (2008): 29–58.

4. UNHCR, "UNHCR Resettlement Handbook" (Geneva: UNHCR, 2004); UNHCR, "UNHCR Projected Global Resettlement Needs 2011" (Geneva: UNHCR, July 2010).

5. IRIN News, "Starving to Survive: Iraqi Refugees Resort to Desperate Measures," Dubai, January 2, 2008.

6. The word "beneficiaries" is placed in quotation marks because it is a specific, much-criticized term frequently used in the aid world. The term is criticized, for example, because it reduces the victims of humanitarian disasters to recipients of handouts, negating their agency and political role, and implies that aid will necessarily have "beneficial" effects, although, in some cases, as has been shown, it has created more harm than good.

7. Michael Barnett, "UNHCR and the Ethics of Repatriation," *Forced Migration Review*, no. 10 (2001): 31–34; Stephen Hopgood, *Keepers of the Flame: Understanding Amnesty International* (Ithaca, NY: Cornell Univ. Press, 2006); Mark Duffield, Joanna Macrae, and Devon Curtis, "Politics and Humanitarian Aid," *Disasters* 25, no. 4 (2001): 269–372; Alan J. Kuperman, "The Moral Hazard of Humanitarian Intervention: Lessons from the Balkans," *International Studies Quarterly* 52, no. 1 (2008): 49–80.

8. Crisp et al., *Surviving in the City*; UNHCR, "Audit Report UNHCR Iraq Situation in Syria" (Geneva: UNHCR, April 2009).

9. Volunteer at UNHCR Syria, conversation with author, November 1, 2009.

10. Head of UNHCR Syria Community Services Program, interview with author, October 26, 2009.

11. Crisp et al., *Surviving in the City*.

12. UNHCR, "UNHCR Syria Update April 2008" (Damascus: UNHCR Syria, April 2008); UNHCR, "A Round Up of 2008"(Damascus: UNHCR Syria, 2009); UNHCR, "UNHCR Syria Update Autumn 2009" (Damascus: UNHCR Syria, 2009); UNHCR, "UNHCR Syria Update Summer 2010"; "UNHCR Syria Update Autumn 2010."

13. UNHCR Status Determination Officer, conversation with author, October 4, 2009.

14. UNHCR Syria, "UNHCR Syria Update Summer 2010"; "UNHCR Syria Update Autumn 2010."

15. Crisp et al., *Surviving in the City*. From the perspective of UNHCR this appears to be an issue of state sovereignty in which governments, reluctant to deal with the political implications of integrating a group of outsiders, make use of state privileges to refuse international refugee rights. However, in the Syria context, this view contains a serious misunderstanding about how the Syrian state practices its sovereignty with regard to *all* people living on its territory. In Syria, approved legislation carries only weak power, whereas a mix of wary laissez-faire politics, unreliable tolerance, state patronage, and violence are governance techniques on which the production of sovereignty relies. In this sense, Iraqis were in fact integrated into the order of sovereignty in Syria, though this order does not correspond to that version of sovereignty contained in the standards of UNHCR.

16. UNHCR, "UNHCR Policy on Refugee Protection and Solutions in Urban Areas" (Geneva: UNHCR, 2009).

17. Manager of UNHCR Syria Resettlement Unit, interview with author, January 21, 2010.

18. UNHCR Syria, "A Round Up of 2008"; UNHCR, "Audit Report UNHCR Iraq Situation in Syria"; UNHCR Syria, "UNHCR Syria Update Summer 2010."

19. United Nations Office for the Coordination of Humanitarian Affairs (OCHA), "Regional Response Plan for Iraqi Refugees" (New York: United Nations, 2010).

20. UNHCR Syria Protection Document, as seen by author in Damascus in 2010.

21. OCHA, "Regional Response Plan for Iraqi Refugees."

22. At the time of research, the participating resettlement countries were Australia, Belgium, Canada, Denmark, Finland, France, Germany, Ireland, the Netherlands, Luxembourg, Norway, New Zealand, Portugal, Sweden, Switzerland, the United Kingdom, and the United States.

23. UNHCR, "UNHCR Projected Global Resettlement Needs 2011."

24. Manager of UNHCR Syria Resettlement Unit, interview with author. European Resettlement Network, "Norway," http://www.resettlement.eu/country/norway (accessed May 12, 2016).

25. Statute of the Office of the United Nation High Commissioner for Refugees (UNHCR), "Statutes," http://www.unhcr.org/3b66c39e1.html; United Nations, *Convention Relating to the Status of Refugees*.

26. Emma Haddad, *The Refugee in International Society: Between Sovereigns* (Cambridge: Cambridge Univ. Press, 2008).

27. Mohamed K. Dorai, "Le renouveau de la question de l'asile au Proche-Orient: L'exemple des refugies Irakiens en Syrie," paper presented at the conference Migrants Craints et Espoirs, Le Monde Diplomatique Carrefour de la Pensee, Le Mans, March 14–16, 2008.

28. Manager of UNHCR resettlement unit, interview with author; Crisp et al., *Surviving in the City*.

29. Iraqi woman, interview with author, March 16, 2010; Iraqi man, interview with author, January 17, 2010; Iraqi man, interview with author, February 20, 2010.

30. Iraqi UNHCR volunteer, interview with author, November 1, 2009.

31. UNHCR, "Frequently Asked Questions about Resettlement," 2010, http://www.unhcr.org/pages/4a16b1676.html (retrieved November 29, 2010). With regard to the Iraqis in Syria, UNHCR considered that integration was not possible owing to the temporary residency permits issued to Iraqis and the official work prohibition placed on them, and voluntary return was not advocated because of the continuing lack of security in Iraq.

32. UNHCR Working Group on Resettlement, "Resettlement of Iraqi Refugees, Notes," Geneva, March 12, 2007.

33. Ibid., 4–5.

34. It is highly interesting and relevant to observe that the refugee convention's inclusion of persecution due to one's political opinion has been included in these categories only in relation to persons who have shown their alliance with actors related to the invasion of Iraq. Thus, former Ba'thists fleeing Iraq for fear of persecution are not mentioned in the criteria and would in fact be considered "exclusion cases" by UNHCR owing to their unacceptable political beliefs and actions in the past.

35. Author, field notes, Damascus, February 4, 2010.

36. Interview with Iraqi man, February 20, 2010.

37. Interview with Iraqi woman, March 16, 2010; Interview with Iraqi woman, February 24, 2010.

38. It should be noted that I do not wish to argue that UNHCR's perspective on Iraqis in Damascus was fundamentally false. Iraqi life in Damascus contained all those aspects referred to by UNHCR, just as it contained those stressed by my observations. However, by weeding out those elements that did not correspond to UNHCR's ideas about sovereignty, UN programs continuously emphasized only those elements that did, and in this way was able to produce Iraqis' location in Syria as an unambiguous correspondence with the sovereign ideal.

39. George, *Syria*; Wedeen, *Ambiguities of Domination*. I myself as a research student working without a permit was very aware of this technique, which in the case of conducting research worked in reverse: by generally not providing research permits, but also generally tolerating social research in (never defined) uncontroversial areas, the Syrian government never committed either way yet always allowed for the possibility of arrest and deportation.

40. Author, field notes, Damascus, January 15, 2010.

41. Author, field notes, Damascus, March 23, 2010; Author, field notes, Damascus, February 25, 2010.

42. Author, field notes, Damascus, November 5, 2009.

43. Author, field notes, Damascus, January 23, 2010.

44. An important caveat to this statement: State affiliation did impact on protection in the sense that if a person held citizenship in a country that is likely to intervene on his or her behalf in case of rights violations or arrest, Syrian state agents would be much more cautious. So whereas Iraqis (for example) could not turn to their embassy to seek protection, EU citizens could, and were therefore much less exposed to harassment or arrest.

45. During research I met one woman who had returned after being resettled from Amman to the United States: she was unable to secure a means of survival after her six months of support ran out. Other informants told me about a handful of other cases, as did UNHCR interviewees. A number of press reports appeared in US papers on the issue; however, statistics on this issue do not appear to exist.

46. Author, field notes, Damascus, October 9, 2009.

47. The situation of displaced Iraqis inside Iraq was much worse in this regard.

48. Chatelard, "What Visibility Conceals."

49. UNHCR also managed and helped non-Iraqi refugees in Damascus, and has done so for years (mainly Somalis and Afghanis); however, non-Iraqis had been completely swamped and made invisible by the focus on Iraqis.

50. An interesting exception was a report about UNHCR's Syria programs by UNHCR's internal audit committee. Technical and neutral in tone, it queries procedures and the management of UNHCR's relationship with local partners, with no mention of vulnerabilities and the usually encountered tone of compassion and kindness.

51. UNHCR, "Country Operations Plan 2007 Syrian Arab Republic"; "UNHCR Global Appeal 2010–2011 Syrian Arab Republic"; UNHCR Syria, "UNHCR Syria Update Autumn 2009"; IRIN News, "Starving to Survive."

52. Omar Dewachi, "'Between Iraq and a Hard Place': Urban Governance and Transnational Laboratories of Intervention of Displaced Iraqis in Syria, Jordan, and Lebanon," 2010.

53. Ibid.

54. In fact, as will be discussed further below, UNHCR rhetoric constantly stressed the Syrian government's generosity in hosting the Iraqis, despite the supposed strain it placed on Syria's public finances, and rather than, for example, pressing the government to do more, such as allowing Iraqis to work.

55. UNHCR, "Press Release: Syrian Women's Union and UNHCR Inaugurate Centre to Empower Refugee Women," Damascus, November 25, 2009; Observations and recordings on the day of the opening of the center.

56. UNHCR Syria, "UNHCR Syria Update Summer 2010."

57. UNHCR, "Audit Report UNHCR Iraq Situation in Syria." This report mentions several poorly set up financial processes that would have easily allowed persons to siphon off money for personal gain, which highlights a further twist to the UNHCR-Syria relationship.

58. In this sense, it was instructive to observe what an important role the Palestinians from Iraq, some of whom were forced to reside in desperate conditions for several years in

tents in the desert between the Iraqi and Syrian borders, played in UNHCR programs. Fully dependent on UNHCR aid, these several thousand families always featured prominently in UNHCR publications and rhetoric.

59. These were just some of the accolades heaped on the Syrian government by UNHCR representatives speaking at the launch of the agency's regional response plan 2010 in January 2010.

4. International NGOs and Iraqi Migration

1. Dewachi, "'Between Iraq and a Hard Place.'"

2. Emma Haddad, "The Refugee: The Individual between Sovereigns," *Global Society* 17, no. 3 (2003): 297–322.

3. In 2009, fourteen INGOs had received government permission to operate: Première Urgence (France), the Danish Refugee Council (Denmark), International Rescue Committee (USA), Enfants du Monde (France), Secours Islamique France (France), Turkish Blue Crescent (Turkey), Help (Germany), L'Institut Européen de Coopération et de Développement (IECD, France), International Medical Corps (IMC, UK), Terres des Hommes (Italy, Switzerland), Ricerca e Cooperazione (Italy), Médecins du Monde (France), Action against Hunger (ACF, Spain), and Italian Institute for University Cooperation (ICU, Italy). Source: UNHCR Syria, "UNHCR Syria Update Autumn 2009."

4. Duffield, "Development, Territories, and People."

5. Chatelard. "What Visibility Conceals."

6. UNHCR, "UNHCR Signs Landmark Accord in Syria with International INGO," UNHCR Press Release, May 8, 2008.

7. UNHCR Syria, "UNHCR Syria Update Autumn 2009."

8. Kraft, "Two Changing Spheres."

9. Weiss Fagen, *Iraqi Refugees;* Salome Philmann and Nathalie Stiennon, *10,000 Refugees from Iraq: A Report on Joint Resettlement in the European Union* (Brussels: International Catholic Migration Commission and International Rescue Committee, May 2010); IRC, *A Tough Road Home.*

10. Dewachi, "'Between Iraq and a Hard Place,'" 3.

11. Interlocutors with INGO experience in Syria reported on an existing ban on US-based INGOs that was stated in Syrian government documents, so it remains unclear why IRC was allowed to register.

12. Two employees at the International Rescue Committee, interview with the author, October 19, 2009.

13. Ibid.

14. IRC, *A Tough Road Home;* IRC, *Five Years Later, A Hidden Crisis* (New York: IRC, March 2008); IRC, "IRC Press Release: International Rescue Committee Set to Begin Aid Programmes for Iraqi Refugees in Syria (Damascus: IRC, September 2, 2008).

15. IRC, *A Tough Road Home,* 13.

16. Danish Refugee Council, "Humanitarian Needs," http://www.drc.dk/relief-work/where-we-work/middle-east/syria/ (accessed 2010). The website has been updated and the quoted text is no longer available online. Danish Refugee Council, "Quarterly Report (Syria) October–December 2010" (Damascus: DRC, 2011); DRC, "Quarterly Report (Syria) July–September 2010" (Damascus, Syria: DRC, 2010).

17. Terres des Hommes Switzerland, "Regional Assistance to Iraqi Refugees," http://www.tdh.ch/en/countries/syria---jordan (accessed 2010). The website has been updated and the quoted text is no longer available online.

18. Two employees at the International Rescue Committee, interview with the author, October 19, 2009. Incidentally, follow-up e-mails to the interview were never answered.

19. Mary Kaldor, *Global Civil Society: An Answer to War* (Cambridge: Polity, 2003).

20. This is not to say that no public sphere existed in Syria. As argued in other chapters, the laissez-faire element in Syrian rule, which was focused on certain red lines of political behavior, frequently resulted in less state intrusion into areas of life heavily controlled in liberal societies. The experience of Iraqi migrants is one such example. The key point here is that the construction of the Syrian public sphere was created through different forms of governance than those assumed in liberal theorizing.

21. Enza di Iorio and Martine Zeuthen, *The Benefits of Engaging and Building Trust with a Reluctant Government: The Experience of Community Center for Iraqis in Syria* (Washington, DC: Middle East Institute 2011), 5.

22. UNHCR, "Audit Report UNHCR Iraq Situation in Syria."

23. In 2007 I visited a soup kitchen and shelter run by two churches. At both sites, volunteers reported an increase in attendance of Iraqi visitors (i.e., these were preexisting projects aimed at all poor people). Although the volunteers were certainly aware of who was an Iraqi, they emphasized their openness to anyone in need and did not keep tabs on Syrian and Iraqi visitors.

24. Author, interview with program manager at Terres des Hommes, Damascus, November 10, 2009.

25. IRC, "FY 2010 Financial Statement" (New York: IRC, 2011); Danish Refugee Council, "Annual Report 2009" (Copenhagen: DRC, 2010).

26. UNHCR, "UNHCR Global Appeal 2011 (update) Syrian Arab Republic" (Geneva: UNHCR, 2010); UNHCR, "UNHCR Global Appeal 2010–2011 Syrian Arab Republic" (Geneva: UNHCR, 2009).

27. Author, interview with diplomat, Damascus, October 10, 2010.

28. Kim D. Reimann, "A View from the Top: International Politics, Norms and the Worldwide Growth of INGOs," *International Studies Quarterly* 50, no. 1 (2006): 45–68; Matthew Bolton and Alex Jeffrey, "The Politics of INGO Registration in International Protectorates: The Cases of Bosnia and Iraq," *Disasters* 32, no. 4 (2008): 586–608; Ishan Ashutosh and Alison Mountz, "Migration Management for the Benefit of Whom? Interrogating the Work of the International Organization for Migration," *Citizenship Studies* 15, no. 1 (2011): 21–38.

29. ISP's website: www.iraqistudentproject.org.

30. Author, field notes, Damascus, January 16, 2010.

31. Author, field notes, Damascus, February 8, 2010.

32. Author, conversation with Iraqi woman, Damascus, January 2010.

33. Author, observations in Damascus, January 18, 2010.

34. Author, field notes, Damascus, October 22, 2009.

35. David Campbell, *Writing Security—United States Foreign Policy and the Politics of Identity* (Manchester, England: Manchester Univ. Press, 1992). Mark B. Salter, *Barbarians and Civilization in International Relations* (London: Pluto Press, 2002).

36. In 2011, Native without a Nation had collected around USD 2,800, according to its website.

37. All texts taken from Native without a Nation's website: http://nativewithouta nation.blogspot.com/.

5. Western Donor States in Syria

1. Ashutosh and Mountz, "Migration Management for the Benefit of Whom?"

2. Unlike the situation today, illegal onward migration played only a small role during the Iraqi migration crisis, and the highly frequented, dangerous maritime route across the Mediterranean was not discussed as an option by Iraqis. The use of this dangerous route (as of this writing), which is enabled by Libya, highlights the importance of the changed political situation in that country, but, more important, also shows the tragic effect of the much more restricted options of legal migration available to Syrians today.

3. Mohammed K. Dorai, "Iraqis in Exile: Migratory Networks as a Coping Strategy," *International Journal of Contemporary Iraqi Studies* 5, no. 2 (2011): 215–30.

4. Geraldine Chatelard, "The Politics of Population Movements in Contemporary Iraq: A Research Agenda," in *Writing the History of Iraq: Historiographical and Political Challenge*, ed. Ricardo Bocco, Jordi Tejet, and Peter Sluglett (London: World Scientific Publishers/Imperial College Press, 2011); Geraldine Chatelard, Oroub El-Abed, and Kate Washington, "Protection, Mobility and Livelihood Challenges of Displaced Iraqis in Urban Settings in Jordan" (Geneva: ICMC, 2009).

5. Author, interview with Iraqi man, Damascus, January 17, 2010.

6. Mark B. Salter, "The Global Visa Regime and the Political Technologies of the International Self: Borders, Bodies, Biopolitics," *Alternatives: Global, Local, Political* 31, no. 2 (2006): 167–89.

7. All quotes taken from IOM, "Information Sheet" (New York: IOM, 2008).

8. Ashutosh and Mountz, "Migration Management for the Benefit of Whom?"

9. Yassin Musharbash, "Irak-Flüchtlinge wollen keinen Christenbonus," *Der Spiegel* online, May 23, 2008, http://www.spiegel.de/politik/ausland/schaeubles-hilfsangebot-irak -fluechtlinge-wollen-keinen-christen-bonus-a-554838.html (accessed March 15, 2016).

10. For funding figures broken down according to donor state, see OCHA, "Regional Response Plan for Iraqi Refugees."

11. Frauke Riller, "On the Resettlement Expectations of Iraqi Refugees in Lebanon, Jordan and Syria" (Geneva: UNHCR and ICMC, 2009).

12. Lisa Wedeen, "Seeing Like a Citizen, Acting Like a State: Exemplary Events in Unified Yemen," *Comparative Studies in Society and History* 45, no. 4 (2003): 680–713.

13. Mark Duffield, "Governing the Borderlands: Decoding the Power of Aid," *Disasters* 25, no. 4 (2001): 308–20.

14. UNHCR Syria, "UNHCR Syria Update Summer 2010."

15. German Interior Ministry, "41.332 Asylantraege im Jahr 2010," press release, January 17, 2011.

16. Andrea Kothen, "Irakflüchtlinge: Zweierlei Mass, allerlei Gesetze" (Frankfurt, Germany: Pro Asyl, May 11, 2009).

17. Michel Foucault, Mauro Bertani, and Alessandro Fontana, *"Society Must Be Defended": Lectures at the Collège de France, 1975–76* (London: Allen Lane, 2003).

18. Author, interview with Iraqi family, Damascus, February 2010.

19. Wendy Brown uses the term "Janus faced" to describe sovereignty's paradoxes. Wendy Brown, *Walled States, Waning Sovereignty* (New York: Zone Books, 2010).

20. Rejection letters simply contained several boxes with statements such as "not credible," of which one or several were ticked. Appealing these decisions was practically impossible.

21. Amnesty International Germany, "EU muss irakische Flüchtlinge aufnehmen und Nachbarstaaten des Irak unterstützen," press release, April 16, 2007.

22. Pro Asyl, "BVerwG: Widerruf der Anerkennung irakischer Flüchtlinge," press release, February 25, 2011.

23. German Federal Government (Bundesregierung), "Antwort der Bundesregierung auf die kleine Anfrage der Abgeordneten Ulla Jelpe, Jan Korte, und der Fraktion DIE LINKE," *Bundesanzeiger*, August 18, 2006.

24. Reinhard Grindel MP, "Rede zu irakischen Flüchtlingen im Bundestag," speech, December 13, 2007, https://www.cducsu.de/themen/auslaender/durchfuehrung-der-widerrufsverfahren-fuer-irakische-asylberechtigte-durch-das-bundesamt-fuer-migration-und-fluechtlinge-ist.

25. The key criticism that leftwing German parties made of the revocations was that they were invented as work-creating measures at overstaffed immigration authorities to hide the overstaffing and general mismanagement.

26. Finn Stepputat, "Violence, Sovereignty, and Citizenship in Postcolonial Peru," in *Sovereign Bodies: Citizens, Migrants, and States in the Postcolonial World*, ed. Thomas Blom Hansen (Princeton, NJ: Princeton Univ. Press, 2005), 61–81.

27. "120 Iraqi Refugees Resettled in Germany," *Syria Today*, April 2009, www.syria-today.com. [The magazine and website are now defunct.]

28. UNHCR, "Resettlement to Germany of Iraqi Refugees in Syria Gets Under Way," press release, March 19, 2009, http://www.unhcr.org/49c273aa2.html.

29. "Erste Irak-Fluechtlinge in Hannover gelandet," *Focus*, March 19, 2009, www.focus.de/politik/deutschland/konflikte-erste-irak-fluechtlinge-in-hannover-gelandet_aid_381892.html.

30. Ibid.

31. Musharbash, "Irak-Flüchtlinge wollen keinen Christenbonus."

32. Daniel C. Martin, "Annual Flow Report Refugees and Asylees: 2010" (Washington, DC: US Department of Homeland Security, May 2011). UNHCR Syria, "UNHCR Syria Update Summer 2010."

33. Riller, "On the Resettlement Expectations."

34. Author, interview with Iraqi man, Damascus, January 17, 2010.

35. Author, interview with Iraqi woman, Damascus, January 2010.

36. Author, interview with Iraqi man, Damascus, January 17, 2010.

37. Chatelard, "What Visibility Conceals."

38. J. Mowbray, "Visa Denial Puts Heroic Iraqi Translator in the Crosshairs," Fox News, April 3, 2009, http://www.foxnews.com/story/2009/04/03/visa-denial-puts-heroic-iraqi-translator-in-crosshairs.html; Paul Tait, "Iraqi Translators Struggle for Safety and a Visa," *Reuters*, August 24, 2007, http://www.reuters.com/article/us-iraq-translators-idUSL2353098020070824.

39. James Agnew, "The Territorial Trap: The Geographical Assumptions of International Relations Theory," *Review of International Political Economy* 1 (1994): 53–80.

40. Chansonette Hall, et al., "Perfect Allies? The Case of Iraq and Al Qaeda," *International Studies Perspectives* 8, no. 3 (2007): 272–86; Anthony H. Cordesman, "Four Wars and Counting . . . : Enduring Conflict and the Need for a New Approach to US Strategy and Force Planning," *The RUSI Journal* 149, no. 1 (2004): 24–30.

41. Ghazi-Walid Falah, Colin Flint, and Virginie Mamadouh, "Just War and Extraterritoriality: The Popular Geopolitics of the United States' War on Iraq as Reflected in Newspapers of the Arab World," *Annals of the Association of American Geographers* 96, no. 1 (2006): 142–64.

42. Author, field notes, Damascus, January 15, 2010.

43. UNHCR, "Contributions to UNHCR for Budget Year 2010" (Geneva: UNHCR, 2011).

44. OCHA, "Regional Response Plan for Iraqi Refugees."

45. George Russell, "U.N. Refugee Agency Budget Explodes as U.S. Foots Much of the Bill," Fox News, November 5, 2009, http://www.foxnews.com/world/2009/11/05/refugee-agency-budget-explodes-foots.html.

6. Iraqis in Syria

1. Geraldine Chatelard, *Mobility Opportunities and Strategies for Iraqi Refugees in Syria and Jordan* (Geneva: ICMC 2009); Chatelard, "What Visibility Conceals"; Sassoon, *Iraqi Refugees.*

2. For more information about the resettlement procedure, please refer to chapters 4 and 5.

3. Author, field notes, Damascus, March 17, 2010.

4. Didier Bigo, "Security and Immigration: Toward a Critique of the Governmentality of Unease," *Alternatives* 27, no. 1 (2000): 63–92; Robert Latham, "Social Sovereignty," *Theory Culture Society* 17, no. 4 (2000): 1–18.

5. Michel Foucault, *"Security, Territory, Population": Lectures at the Collège de France, 1977–76* (Basingstoke, England: Palgrave Macmillan, 2007.

6. Ibid.

7. Nikolas Rose and Peter Miller, "Political Power beyond the State: Problematics of Government," *The British Journal of Sociology* 43, no. 2 (1992): 173–205.

8. A rude expression translating roughly to "Fuck the Iqama!"

9. Author, field notes, Damascus, January 19, 2010.

10. Author, field notes, Damascus, January 23, 2010.

11. Author, field notes, Damascus, October 9, 2009.

12. UNHCR official, interview with the author, January 21, 2010.

13. Ilana Feldman, "The Quaker Way: Ethical Labor and Humanitarian Relief," *American Ethnologist* 34, no. 4 (2007): 689–705.

14. James Scott, *Weapons of the Weak: Everyday Forms of Peasant Resistance* (New Haven, CT: Yale Univ. Press, 1985).

Conclusion

1. Salwa Ismail, "Authoritarian Government, Neoliberalism and Everyday Civilities in Egypt," *Third World Quarterly* 32, no. 5 (2012): 845–62.

2. Samir Seifan, "The Road to Economic Reform in Syria," *Syria Studies* 2 (2010): 1–79.

3. Dostal and Zorob, *Syria and the Euro-Mediterranean Relationship.*

4. Haddad, *Business Networks in Syria.*

5. Steven Heydemann and Reinoud Leenders. "Authoritarian Learning and Authoritarian Resilience: Regime Responses to the 'Arab Awakening,'" *Globalizations* 8, no. 5 (2011): 647–53. Andre Bank and Miriam Edel, "Authoritarian Regime Learning: Comparative Insights from the Arab Uprisings" (Hamburg: GIGA, 2015). Francesco Cavatorta, "The Convergence of Governance: Upgrading Authoritarianism in the Arab World and Downgrading Democracy Elsewhere?" *Middle East Critique* 19, no. 3 (2010): 217–32.

6. Salam Kawakibi, "What Might Have Been: A Decade of Civil Activism in Syria," openDemocracy, March 11, 2013, https://www.opendemocracy.net/salam-kawakibi/what-might-have-been-decade-of-civil-activism-in-syria (accessed March 15, 2016).

7. Ibid.

8. Ibid.

9. Lisa Anderson, "Searching Where the Light Shines: Studying Democracy in the Middle East," *Annual Review of Political Science* 9 (2006): 189–214.

10. Mark Duffield, *Global Governance and the New Wars: The Merging of Development and Security* (London: Zed Books, 2001).

11. Giacomo Luciani, "Linking Economic and Political Reform in the Middle East: The Role of the Bourgeoisie," in *Debating Arab Authoritarianism Dynamics and Durability in Nondemocratic Regimes* (Stanford, CA: Stanford Univ. Press, 2007).

12. Duffield, *Global Governance*, 16.

13. Bente Scheller, "Die Erosion der Internationalen Normen im Syrien-Konflikt" (Berlin: German Ministry of Defense, 2014).

14. Ibid.

15. Ibid.

16. Martin Chulov and Emma Beals, "Aid Group Mercy Corps Forced to Close Damascus Operations," *The Guardian*, April 23, 2014, http://www.theguardian.com/world/2014/may/23/aid-group-mercy-corps-forced-to-close-damascus-operations-syria (accessed March 16, 2016).

17. Sophia Hoffmann, "Wen Schützen Flüchtlingslager? Care and Control im Jordanischen Lager Azraq," *Peripherie* 35, nos. 138–39 (2015): 281–302.

18. Patrick Wintour, "UK Agrees to Take Up to 500 of the Most Traumatised Syrian Refugees," *The Guardian*, January 29, 2014, http://www.theguardian.com/world/2014/jan/28/syria-refugees-uk-agrees-up-to-500 (accessed March 15, 2016).

19. Cavatorta, "Convergence of Governance."

20. Bank and Edel, "Authoritarian Regime Learning"; Heydemann and Leenders, "Authoritarian Learning and Authoritarian Resilience."

21. Darius Rejali, *Torture and Democracy* (Princeton, NJ: Princeton Univ. Press, 2009).

22. Duffield, *Global Governance*.

Bibliography

Adamson, Fiona B., and Madeleine Demetriou. "Remapping the Boundaries of `State' and `National Identity': Incorporating Diasporas into IR Theorizing." *European Journal of International Relations* 13 (2007): 489–526.

Agamben, Giorgio. *Homo Sacer: Sovereign Power and Bare Life*. Stanford, CA: Stanford Univ. Press, 1998.

Agier, Michel. *Managing the Undesirables: Refugee Camps and Humanitarian Government*. Cambridge: Polity Press, 2010.

Agnew, James. "The Territorial Trap: The Geographical Assumptions of International Relations Theory." *Review of International Political Economy* 1, no. 1 (1994): 53–80.

Ali, Ali, and Kamel Dorai. *Under the Radar, but Not Invisible: Iraqi Activity in Syria's Informal Economic Sector*. Damascus: UNHCR, Syria 2010.

Anderson, Lisa. "Searching Where the Light Shines: Studying Democracy in the Middle East." *Annual Review of Political Science* 9 (2006): 189–214.

Appadurai, Arjun. "Sovereignty without Territoriality: Notes for a Postnational Geography." In *The Anthropology of Space and Place*, edited by Setha Low and Denise Lawrence-Zuniga, 337–47. Oxford: Blackwell, 2003.

Ashutosh, Ishan, and Alison Mountz. "Migration Management for the Benefit of Whom? Interrogating the Work of the International Organization for Migration." *Citizenship Studies* 15, no. 1 (2011): 21–38.

Baitenmann, Helga. "NGOs and the Afghan War: The Politicisation of Humanitarian Aid." *Third World Quarterly* 12, no. 1 (1990): 62–85.

Bank, Andre, and Miriam Edel. "Authoritarian Regime Learning: Comparative Insights from the Arab Uprisings." Hamburg: GIGA, 2015.

Barnett, Michael. *Empire of Humanity: A History of Humanitarianism*. Ithaca, NY: Cornell Univ. Press, 2011.

———. "Humanitarianism with a Sovereign Face: UNHCR in the Global Undertow." *International Migration Review* 35, no. 1 (2001): 244–77.

———. "Sovereignty, Nationalism, and Regional Order in the Arab State System." In *State Sovereignty as Social Construct*, edited by Thomas Biersteker and Cynthia Weber, 148–89. Cambridge: Cambridge Univ. Press, 1996.

———. "UNHCR and the Ethics of Repatriation." *Forced Migration Review*, no. 10 (2001): 31–34.

Barnett, Michael, and Raymond Duval. *Power in Global Governance*. Cambridge: Cambridge Univ. Press, 2005.

Bartelson, Jens. *A Genealogy of Sovereignty*. New York: Cambridge Univ. Press, 1995.

Batatu, Hanna. *The Egyptian, Syrian and Iraqi Revolutions: Some Observations on Their Underlying Causes and Social Character*. Washington, DC: Georgetown Univ. Press, 1984.

———. "Some Observations on the Social Roots of Syria's Ruling Military Group and the Causes for Its Dominance." *Middle East Journal* 35, no. 3 (1981): 331–44.

Bigo, Didier. "Security and Immigration: Toward a Critique of the Governmentality of Unease." *Alternatives* 27, no. 1 (2000): 63–92.

Binder, Martin. "Humanitarian Crises and the International Politics of Selectivity." *Human Rights Review* 10, no. 3 (2009): 327–48.

Bolton, Matthew, and Alex Jeffrey. "The Politics of INGO Registration in International Protectorates: The Cases of Bosnia and Iraq." *Disasters* 32, no. 4 (2008): 63–92.

Brown, Wendy. *Walled States, Waning Sovereignty*. New York: Zone Books, 2010.

Campbell, David. *Writing Security—United States Foreign Policy and the Politics of Identity*. Manchester, England: Manchester Univ. Press. 1992.

Cavatorta, Francesco. "The Convergence of Governance: Upgrading Authoritarianism in the Arab World and Downgrading Democracy Elsewhere?" *Middle East Critique* 19, no. 3 (2010): 217–32.

Chalfin, Brenda. *Neoliberal Frontiers: An Ehtnography of Sovereignty in West Africa*. Chicago, IL: Univ. of Chicago Press, 2010.

———. "Sovereigns and Citizens in Close Encounter: Airport Anthropology and Customs Regimes in Neoliberal Ghana." *American Ethnologist* 35 (2008): 519–38.

Chatelard, Geraldine. *Mobility Opportunities and Strategies for Iraqi Refugees in Syria and Jordan*. Geneva: ICMC, 2009.

———. "The Politics of Population Movements in Contemporary Iraq: A Research Agenda." In *Writing the History of Iraq: Historiographical and Political Challenge*, edited by Ricardo Bocco, Jordi Tejet, and Peter Sluglett, 359–78. London: World Scientific Publishers/Imperial College Press, 2011.

———. "What Visibility Conceals: Re-Embedding Refugee Migration from Iraq." In *Dispossession and Displacement: Forced Migration in the Middle East and Africa*, edited by Dawn Chatty, 17–44. London: British Academy, 2009.

Chatelard, Geraldine, Oroub El-Abed, and Kate Washington. *Protection, Mobility and Livelihood Challenges of Displaced Iraqis in Urban Settings in Jordan*. Geneva: ICMC, 2009.

Cordesman, Anthony H. "Four Wars and Counting . . . : Enduring Conflict and the Need for a New Approach to US Strategy and Force Planning." *The RUSI Journal* 149, no. 1 (2004): 24–30.

Crisp, Jeff, et al. *Surviving in the City: A Review of UNHCR's Operations for Iraqi Refugees in Urban Areas of Jordan, Lebanon and Syria*. Geneva: UNHCR Policy Development and Evaluation Service, 2009.

Danish Refugee Council. "Annual Report 2009." Copenhagen: DRC, 2010.

———. "Quarterly Report Syria July–September 2010." Copenhagen: DRC, 2010.

———. "Quarterly Report Syria October–December 2010." Copenhagen: DRC, 2011.

Darius, Rejali. *Torture and Democracy*. Princeton, NJ: Princeton Univ. Press, 2009.

Della Ratta, Donatella. "Dramas of the Authoritarian State." *Middle East Report Online*, February 2011. http://www.merip.org/mero/interventions/dramas-authoritarian-state.

Denham, Mark E., and Mark Owen Lombardi. *Perspectives on Third-World Sovereignty: The Postmodern Paradox*. International Political Economy Series. Basingstoke, England: Macmillan, 1996.

Devadason, Ranji. "Humanitarians without Borders: Mobility and Wellbeing in UNHCR." New Issues in Refugee Research. UNHCR, 2012.

Dewachi, Omar. "'Between Iraq and a Hard Place': Urban Governance and Transnational Laboratories of Intervention of Displaced Iraqis in Syria, Jordan, and Lebanon." Unpublished paper, 2010.

Di Iorio, Enza, and Martine Zeuthen. *The Benefits of Engaging and Building Trust with a Reluctant Government: The Experience of Community Center for Iraqis in Syria*. Washington, DC: Middle East Institute, 2011.

Donini, Antonio. "The Far Side: The Meta Functions of Humanitarianism in a Globalised World." *Disasters* 34 (2010): 220–37.

Donini, Antonio, Larry Minear, and Peter Walker. "The Future of Humanitarian Action: Mapping the Implications of Iraq and Other Recent Crises." *Disasters* 28 (2004): 190–204.

Dorai, Mohamed K. "Iraqis in Exile: Migratory Networks as a Coping Strategy." *International Journal of Contemporary Iraqi Studies* 5, no. 2 (2011): 215–30.

———. "Le renouveau de la question de l'asile au Proche-Orient: L'exemple des refugies Irakiens en Syrie." Paper presented at the conference Migrants Craints et Espoirs, Le Monde Diplomatique Carrefour de la Pensee, Le Mans, March 14–16, 2008.

Dostal, Jörg Michael, and Anja Zorob. *Syria and the Euro-Mediterranean Relationship.* Boulder, CO: Lynne Rienner, 2008.

Doty, Roxanne Lynn. "States of Exception on the Mexico–U.S. Border: Security, 'Decisions,' and Civilian Border Patrols." *International Political Sociology* 1 (2007): 113–37.

Duffield, Mark. "Development, Territories, and People: Consolidating the External Sovereign Frontier." *Alternatives* 32, no. 2 (2007): 225–46.

———. *Global Governance and the New Wars: The Merging of Development and Security.* London: Zed Books, 2001.

———. "Governing the Borderlands: Decoding the Power of Aid." *Disasters* 25, no. 4 (2001): 308–20.

———. "Social Reconstruction and the Radicalization of Development: Aid as a Relation of Global Liberal Governance." *Development and Change* 33 (2002): 1049–71.

Duffield, Mark, Joanna Macrae, and Devon Curtis. "Politics and Humanitarian Aid." *Disasters* 25, no. 4 (2001): 269–372.

Duffield, Mark, and John Prendergast. "Sovereignty and Intervention after the Cold War." *Middle East Report* 24 (1994): 9–15.

Eckert, Amy E. "Peoples and Persons: Moral Standing, Power, and the Equality of States." *International Studies Quarterly* 50 (2006): 841–60.

Elvira, Laura Ruiz de, and Tina Zintl. *Civil Society and the State in Syria: The Outsourcing of Social Responsibility.* Boulder, CO: Lynne Rienner, 2012.

Fafo. "Iraqis in Jordan 2007: Their Number and Characteristics." Amman: Fafo, 2007.

Falah, Ghazi-Walid, Colin Flint, and Virginie Mamadouh. "Just War and Extraterritoriality: The Popular Geopolitics of the United States' War on Iraq as Reflected in Newspapers of the Arab World." *Annals of the Association of American Geographers* 96, no. 1 (2006): 142–64.

Feldman, Ilana. *Governing Gaza: Bureaucracy, Authority, and the Work of Rule, 1917–1967.* Durham, NC: Duke Univ. Press, 2008.

———. "The Quaker Way: Ethical Labor and Humanitarian Relief." *American Ethnologist* 34, no. 1 (2007): 689–705.

Ferguson, James, and Akhil Gupta. "Spatializing States: Toward an Ethnography of Neoliberal Governmentality." *American Ethnologist* 29 (2002): 981–1002.

Fioroni, Claudie. "'Société civile' et évolution de l'autoritarisme en Syrie: Le cas du Syria Trust for Development." Master's thesis, The Graduate Institute Geneva, 2010.

Foucault, Michel. *"Security, Territory, Population": Lectures at the Collège de France, 1977–76*. London: Allen Lane, 2003.

Foucault, Michel, Mauro Bertani, and Alessandro Fontana. *"Society Must Be Defended": Lectures at the Collège de France, 1975–76*. London: Allen Lane, 2003.

Foucault, Michel, James D. Faubion, and Robert Hurley. *Power: Essential Works of Foucault, 1954–1984*. New York: New Press, 2000.

George, Alan. Syria: *Neither Bread nor Freedom*. London: Zed Books, 2003.

Gramsci, Antonio, Geoffrey N. Smith, and Quintin Hoare. *Selections from the Prison Notebooks of Antonio Gramsci*. Lincolnwood: International Publishers, 1971.

Grindel, Reinhard, MP. "Rede zu irakischen Flüchtlingen im Bundestag." Speech, December 13, 2007.

Haddad, Bassam. *Business Networks in Syria: The Political Economy of Authoritarian Resilience*. Stanford, CA: Stanford Univ. Press 2012.

Haddad, Emma. "The Refugee: The Individual between Sovereigns." *Global Society* 17, no. 3 (2003): 297–322.

———. *The Refugee in International Society: Between Sovereigns*. Cambridge: Cambridge Univ. Press, 2008.

Hakim, Hadia. *Palestinian Identity-Formation in Yarmouk: Constructing National Identity through the Development of Space*. Irvine: Univ. of California Irvine School of Social Sciences, 2009.

Hall, Chansonette, et al. "Perfect Allies? The Case of Iraq and Al Qaeda." *International Studies Perspectives* 8, no. 3 (2007): 272–86.

Hansen, Thomas Blom, ed. *Sovereign Bodies: Citizens, Migrants, and States in the Postcolonial World*. Princeton NJ: Princeton Univ. Press, 2005.

Heydemann, Steven. *Authoritarianism in Syria: Institutions and Social Conflict, 1946–1970*. Ithaca, NY: Cornell Univ. Press, 1999.

Heydemann, Steven, and Reinoud Leenders. "Authoritarian Learning and Authoritarian Resilience: Regime Responses to the 'Arab Awakening.'" *Globalizations* 8, no. 5 (2011): 647–53.

Hilhorst, Dorothea, and Bram J. Jansen. "Humanitarian Space as Arena: A Perspective on the Everyday Politics of Aid." *Development and Change* 41 (2010): 1117–39.

Hindess, Barry. "Neo-Liberal Citizenship." *Citizenship Studies* 6 (2002): 127–43.

Hinnebusch, Raymond. *Syria: Revolution from Above*. London: Routledge, 2001.

Hinnebusch, Raymond, Marwan Kabalan, Bassma Kodmani, and David Lesch. *Syrian Foreign Police and the United States from Bush to Obama*. Boulder, CO: Lynne Rienner, 2010.

Hinnebusch, Raymond, and Tina Zintl, eds. *Syria from Reform to Revolt*, vol. 1, *Political Economy and International Relations*. Syracuse, NY: Syracuse Univ. Press, 2015.

Hoffmann, Sophia. "Wen Schützen Flüchtlingslager? Care and Control im Jordanischen Lager Azraq." *Peripherie*, 35, nos. 138–39 (2015): 281–302.

Hopgood, Stephen. *Keepers of the Flame: Understanding Amnesty International*. Ithaca, NY: Cornell Univ. Press, 2006.

Huisman, Kimberly. "'Does This Mean You're Not Going to Come Visit Me Anymore?': An Inquiry into an Ethics of Reciprocity and Positionality in Feminist Ethnographic Research." *Sociological Inquiry* 78 (2008): 372–96.

Hyndman, Jennifer. *Managing Displacement: Refugees and the Politics of Humanitarianism*. Minneapolis: Univ. of Minnesota Press, 2000.

International Crisis Group. "Failed Responsibility: Iraqi Refugees in Syria, Jordan and Lebanon." Brussels, Belgium: Crisis Group, 2008.

International Rescue Committee. *Five Years Later: A Hidden Crisis*. New York: IRC, March 2008.

———. "FY 2010 Financial Statement." New York: IRC, 2011.

———. *A Tough Road Home: Uprooted Iraqis in Jordan, Syria, and Iraq*. New York: IRC, 2010.

IOM. "Information Sheet." New York: IOM, 2008.

Ismail, Salwa. "Authoritarian Government, Neoliberalism, and Everyday Civilities in Egypt." *Third World Quarterly* 32, no. 5 (2012): 845–62.

———. *Political Life in Cairo's New Quarters: Encountering the Everyday State*. Minneapolis: Univ. of Minnesota Press, 2006.

———. "Urban Subalterns in the Arab Revolutions: Cairo and Damascus in Comparative Perspective." *Comparative Studies in Society and History* 55, no. 4 (2013): 865–94.

Jennings, Ronald C. "Sovereignty and Political Modernity: A Genealogy of Agamben's Critique of Sovereignty." *Anthropological Theory* 11 (March 1, 2011): 23–61.

Kahn, Paul W. *Political Theology: Four New Chapters on the Concept of Sovereignty.* New York: Columbia Univ. Press, 2011.

Kaldor, Mary. *Global Civil Society: An Answer to War.* Cambridge: Polity, 2003.

Kalmo, Hent, and Quentin Skinner. *Sovereignty in Fragments: The Past, Present and Future of a Contested Concept.* Cambridge: Cambridge Univ. Press, 2011.

Kawakibi, Salam. "La migration irreguliere en Syrie: Les refugies Irakiens comme cas d'etude." Analytical and Synthetic Notes. Florence: EUI, 2008.

———. "What Might Have Been: A Decade of Civil Activism in Syria." *openDemocracy,* March 11, 2013.

Khaddour, Kheder, and Keven Mazur. "The Struggle for Syria's Regions." *Middle East Research and Information Project* MER 43, no. 269 (2013). http://www.merip.org/mer/mer269/struggle-syrias-regions.

Khalidi, Ashraf al-, Sophia Hoffmann, and Victor Tanner. *Iraqi Refugees in the Syrian Arab Republic: A Field-Based Snapshot.* Washington, DC: The Brookings Institute, 2007.

Khalili, Laleh. "Grass-Roots Commemorations: Remembering the Land in the Camps of Lebanon." *Journal of Palestine Studies* 34, no. 1 (2004): 6–22.

———. *Heroes and Martyrs of Palestine: The Politics of National Commemoration.* Cambridge: Cambridge Univ. Press, 2007.

Khoury, Philip S. "Syrian Urban Politics in Transition: The Quarters of Damascus during the French Mandate." *International Journal of Middle East Studies* 16, no. 4 (1984): 507–40.

Koser, Khalid. "Refugees, Transnationalism and the State." *Journal of Ethnic and Migration Studies* 33 (2007): 233–54.

Kraft, Katherine. "Two Changing Spheres: NGOs and Iraqis in Syria." Brea, CA: Middle East Fellowship, 2008.

Krasner, Stephen D. *Sovereignty: Organized Hypocrisy.* Princeton, NJ: Princeton University Press, 1999.

Kuperman, Alan J. "The Moral Hazard of Humanitarian Intervention: Lessons from the Balkans." *International Studies Quarterly* 52, no. 1 (2008): 49–80.

Landgren, Karin. "The Future of Refugee Protection: Four Challenges." *Journal of Refugee Studies* 11 (January 1, 1998): 416–32.

Latham, Robert. "Social Sovereignty." *Theory Culture Society* 17, no. 4 (2000): 1–18.

Leenders, Reinoud. "Iraqi Refugees in Syria: Causing a Spillover of the Iraqi Conflict?" *Third World Quarterly* 29, no. 8 (2008): 1563–84.

———. "Refugee Warriors or War Refugees? Iraqi Refugees' Predicament in Syria, Jordan and Lebanon." *Mediterranean Politics* 14, no. 3 (2009): 343–63.

Lefevre, Raphael. *The Ashes of Hama*. London: Hurst, 2013.

Lesch, David. *The New Lion of Damascus: Bashar al-Asad and Modern Syria*. New Haven, CT: Yale Univ. Press, 2005.

Loescher, Gil. "The UNHCR and World Politics: State Interests vs. Institutional Autonomy." *International Migration Review* 35, no. 1 (2001): 33–56.

Luciani, Giacomo. "Linking Economic and Political Reform in the Middle East: The Role of the Bourgeoisie." In *Debating Arab Authoritarianism Dynamics and Durability in Nondemocratic Regimes*. Stanford, CA: Stanford Univ. Press, 2007.

Lukes, Steven. *Power: A Radical View*. London: Macmillan, 1974.

Malkki, Liisa H. *Purity and Exile: Violence, Memory and National Cosmology among Hutu Refugees in Tanzania*. Chicago, IL: Univ. of Chicago Press, 1995.

Mamadouh, Virginie. "Just War and Extraterritoriality: The Popular Geopolitics of the United States' War on Iraq as Reflected in Newspapers of the Arab World." *Annals of the Association of American Geographers* 96, no. 1 (2006): 142–64.

Marcus, George E. "Ethnography in/of the World System: The Emergence of Multi-Sited Ethnography." *Annual Review of Anthropology* 24 (1995): 95–117.

Martin, Daniel C. "Annual Flow Report Refugees and Asylees: 2010." Washington, DC: US Department of Homeland Security, May 2011.

Mitchell, Timothy. "The Limits of the State: Beyond Statist Approaches and Their Critics." *The American Political Science Review* 85, no. 1 (1991): 77–96.

———. *Rule of Experts: Egypt, Techno-Politics, Modernity*. Berkeley: Univ. of California Press, 2002.

Moulin, Carolina, and Peter Nyers. "'We Live in a Country of UNHCR'—Refugee Protests and Global Political Society." *International Political Sociology* 1 (2007): 356–72.

Mountz, Alison. "Where Asylum-Seekers Wait: Feminist Counter-Topographies of Sites between States." *Gender, Place & Culture: A Journal of Feminist Geography* 18, no. 3 (2011): 381–99.

Neep, Daniel. *Occupying Syria under the French Mandate*. Cambridge: Cambridge Univ. Press, 2012.

Olwan, Mohamed Y. "Iraqi Refugees in Jordan: Legal Perspective." CARIM Analytic and Synthetic Notes 2009. Florence: EUI, 2009.

———. "Iraqi Refugees in Neighbouring Countries: A New Forced Protracted Displacement in the Region." Research Reports. Florence: EUI, 2009.

Ong, Aihwa. *Neoliberalism as Exception: Mutations in Citizenship and Sovereignty*. Durham, NC: Duke University Press, 2006.

Paasche, Erlend. "Iraqi Refugees in a Damascus Suburb: Carriers of Sectarian Conflict?" *International Journal of Contemporary Iraqi Studies* 5, no. 2 (2011): 247–62.

Pallister-Wilkins, Polly. "Interrogating the Mediterranean 'Migration Crisis.'" *Mediterranean Politics* (2016): 311–15. doi:10.1080/13629395.2016.1145826.

Papadopouloa, Dimitris, and Vassilis Tsianos. "How to Do Sovereignty without People: The Subjectless Condition of Postliberal Power." *boundary 2* 34, no. 1 (2007). doi:10.1215/01903659-2006-030.

Parolin, Gianluca. *Citizenship in the Arab World*. Amsterdam: Amsterdam Univ. Press, 2009.

Perthes, Volker. *The Political Economy of Syria under Asad*. New York: I. B. Tauris, 1995.

Philmann, Salome, and Nathalie Stiennon. *10,000 Refugees from Iraq: A Report on Joint Resettlement in the European Union*. Brussels: International Catholic Migration Commission and International Rescue Committee, 2010.

Pierret, Thomas. *Religion and State in Syria*. Cambridge: Cambridge Univ. Press, 2013.

Pierret, Thomas, and Kjetil Selvik. "Limits of Authoritarian Upgrading in Syria: Private Welfare, Islamic Charities and the Rise of the Zayd Movement." *International Journal of Middle East Studies* 41 (2009): 595–614.

Rain, David. "Damascus: A Geographical Field Note." *Geographical Review* 99 (2009): 94–104.

Reimann, Kim D. "A View from the Top: International Politics, Norms and the Worldwide Growth of INGOs." *International Studies Quarterly* 50, no. 1 (2006): 45–68.

Rejali, Darius. *Torture and Democracy*. Princeton, NJ: Princeton Univ. Press, 2009.

Riller, Frauke. "On the Resettlement Expectations of Iraqi Refugees in Lebanon, Jordan and Syria." Geneva: UNHCR and ICMC, 2009.

Romano, David. "Whose House Is This Anyway? IDP and Refugee Return in Post-Saddam Iraq." *Journal of Refugee Studies* 18 (December 2005): 430–53.

Rose, Nikolas, and Peter Miller. "Political Power beyond the State: Problematics of Government." *The British Journal of Sociology* 43, no. 2 (1992): 173–205.

Rubin, Barry. *The Truth about Syria*. Basingstoke, England: Palgrave Macmillan, 2007.

Salter, Mark B. *Barbarians and Civilization in International Relations*. London: Pluto Press, 2002.

———. "The Global Visa Regime and the Political Technologies of the International Self: Borders, Bodies, Biopolitics." *Alternatives: Global, Local, Political* 31, no. 2 (2006): 167–89.

Sassoon, Joseph. *The Iraqi Refugees: The New Crisis in the Middle-East.* London: I. B. Tauris, 2008.

Scheller, Bente. "Die Erosion der Internationalen Normen im Syrien-Konflikt." Berlin: German Ministry of Defense, 2014.

———. *The Wisdom of Syria's Waiting Game: Foreign Policy under the Assads.* London: Hurst, 2013.

Schenker, David. *Syria's Role in Regional Destabilization: An American View.* Jerusalem: Jerusalem Center for Public Affairs, 2007.

Schlumberger, Oliver. *Debating Arab Authoritarianism Dynamics and Durability in Nondemocratic Regimes.* Stanford, CA: Stanford Univ. Press, 2007.

———. "Opening Old Bottles in Search of New Wine: On Nondemocratic Legitimacy in the Middle East." *Middle East Critique* 19, no. 3 (2010): 233–50.

Schmitt, Carl. *Political Theology: Four Chapters on the Concept of Sovereignty.* Studies in Contemporary German Social Thought. Cambridge, MA: MIT Press, 1985.

Scott, James. *Weapons of the Weak: Everyday Forms of Peasant Resistance.* New Haven, CT: Yale Univ. Press, 1985.

Seale, Patrick. *Asad: The Struggle for the Middle East.* Oakland: Univ. of California Press, 1990.

Seifan, Samir. "The Road to Economic Reform in Syria." *Syria Studies* 2 (2010): 1–79.

Sending, Ole Jacob, and Iver B. Neumann. "Governance to Governmentality: Analyzing NGOs, States, and Power." *International Studies Quarterly* 50 (2006): 651–72.

Seshadri, Kalpana Rahita. "When Home Is a Camp Global Sovereignty: Biopolitic and Internally Displaced Persons." *Social Text* 26, no. 1 (2008): 29–58.

Slim, Hugo. *Essays in Humanitarian Action.* Oxford, England: Oxford Institute of Ethics, Law and Armed Conflict, 2012.

Soguk, Nevgaz, and Geoffrey Whitehall. "Wandering Grounds: Transversality, Identity, Territoriality and Movement." *Millennium Journal of International Studies* 28 (1999): 675–98.

Söndergaard, Hans Peter, Solvig Ekblad, and Töres Theorell. "Self-Reported Life Event Patterns and Their Relation to Health among Recently Resettled Iraqi and Kurdish Refugees in Sweden." *The Journal of Nervous and Mental Disease* 189 (2001): 838–45.

Starr, Stephen. "Syrian Civil Society Empowerment 2010: New Directions for Syrian Society." *Forward Magazine Syria*, no. 37 (March 3, 2010).

Stepputat, Finn. "Violence, Sovereignty, and Citizenship in Postcolonial Peru." In Hansen, *Sovereign Bodies*, 61–81.

Tascon, Sonia Magdalena. "Refugees and Asylum-Seekers in Australia: Border-Crossers of the Postcolonial Imaginary." *Australian Journal of Human Rights* 8 (2002): 125–39.

Thompson, E. *Colonial Citizens: Republican Rights, Paternal Privilege, and Gender in French Syria and Lebanon*. The History and Society of the Modern Middle East. New York: Columbia Univ. Press, 2000.

Tripp, Charles. *A History of Iraq*. 3rd ed. Cambridge: Cambridge Univ. Press, 2007.

Troeller, Gary G. "Refugees in Contemporary International Relations: Reconciling State and Individual Sovereignty." New Issues in Refugee Research. Geneva: UNHCR, 2003.

Turner, Simon. "Suspended Spaces—Contesting Sovereignties in a Refugee Camp." In Hansen, *Sovereign Bodies*, 312–32.

UN General Assembly. *Convention Relating to the Status of Refugees*. United Nations, Treaty Series 189, July 28, 1951.

UNHCR. "Audit Report UNHCR Iraq Situation in Syria." Geneva: UNHCR, 2009.

———. "Contributions to UNHCR for Budget Year 2010." Geneva: UNHCR, 2011.

———. "Country Operations Plan 2007, Syrian Arab Republic." Geneva: UNHCR, 2007.

———. "Frequently Asked Questions about Resettlement." 2010. http://www.unhcr.org/pages/4a16b1676.html. Accessed November 29, 2010.

———. "Resettlement Handbook." Geneva: UNHCR, 2004.

———. "Statutes." 1951. http://www.unhcr.org/3b66c39e1.html.

———. "UNHCR Global Appeal 2010–2011 Syrian Arab Republic." Geneva: UNHCR, 2009.

———. "UNHCR Global Appeal 2011 Update Syrian Arab Republic." Geneva: UNHCR, 2010.

———. "UNHCR Policy on Refugee Protection and Solutions in Urban Areas." Geneva: UNHCR, 2009.

———. "UNHCR Projected Global Resettlement Needs 2011." Geneva: UNHCR, 2010.

———. "UNHCR Syria Update April 2008." Quarterly Update. Damascus: UNHCR Syria, 2008.

UNHCR Syria. "A Round Up of 2008." Damascus: UNHCR Syria, 2009.

———. "UNHCR Syria Update Autumn 2009." Quarterly Update. Damascus: UNHCR Syria, 2009.

———. "UNHCR Syria Update Autumn 2010." Quarterly Update. Damascus: UNHCR Syria, 2010.

———. "UNHCR Syria Update Summer 2010." Quarterly Update. Damascus: UNHCR Syria, 2010.

UNHCR Working Group on Resettlement. "Resettlement of Iraqi Refugees, Notes." Geneva, March 12, 2007.

United Nations Office for the Coordination of Humanitarian Affairs (OCHA). "Regional Response Plan for Iraqi Refugees." New York: United Nations, 2010.

Weber, Cynthia. "Reconsidering Statehood: Examining the Sovereignty/Intervention Boundary." *Review of International Studies* 18 (1992): 199–216.

Wedeen, Lisa. *Ambiguities of Domination: Politics, Rhetoric, and Symbols in Contemporary Syria*. Chicago, IL: Univ. of Chicago Press, 1999.

———. "Seeing Like a Citizen, Acting Like a State: Exemplary Events in Unified Yemen." *Comparative Studies in Society and History* 45, no. 4 (2003): 680–713.

Weir, Lorna. "Sovereignty, Governance and the Political: The Problematic of Foucault." *Thesis Eleven* 94 (2008): 49–71.

Weiss Fagan, Patricia. *Iraqi Refugees: Seeking Stability in Syria and Jordan*. Washington, DC: Georgetown Univ. Press, 2007.

Weizman, Eyal. *The Least of All Possible Evils: Humanitarian Violence from Arendt to Gaza*. London: Verso, 2012.

Wendt, Alexander, and Raymond Duvall. "Sovereignty and the UFO." *Political Theory* 36 (2008): 607–33.

Zaiotti, Ruben. "Dealing with Non-Palestinian Refugees in the Middle East: Policies and Practices in an Uncertain Environment." *International Journal of Refugee Law* 18 (2006): 333–53.

Zaman, Tahir. "Lessons Learned: Palestinian Refugees from Baghdad to Damascus." *International Journal of Contemporary Iraqi Studies* 5, no. 2 (2011): 263–76.

Ziadeh, Radwan. *Power and Policy in Syria: Intelligence Services, Foreign Relations and Democracy in the Modern Middle East*. London: I. B. Tauris, 2012.

Index

Sophia Hoffmann is a political science scholar focused on the international relations of the Middle East. Her primary research areas are forced migration, international humanitarian aid, citizenship, and statehood. She took her PhD at the School of African and Oriental Studies, London, after completing degrees at the London School of Economics and the University of Sussex. Currently she holds a postdoctoral fellowship at the University of Bremen, Germany, where she is researching the security management of humanitarian aid agencies. From 2017, Hoffmann will be carrying out a five-year research project at the Zentrum Moderner Orient, Berlin, looking at the international relations between German and Arab secret service agencies in the past fifty years. She regularly provides her expertise as a consultant to think tanks, government institutions, and the media in the United Kingdom and Germany.